HUMAN RIGHTS IN EDUCATION

Donald Vandenberg

Philosophical Library
New York

I would like to thank
Maxine Greene and Jonas Soltis
for the space and solitude
to complete this book
at Teachers College

Quotations appearing opposite from: Howard Langer, *Human
Rights; A Documentary on the United Nations Declaration of
Human Rights; Featuring an Interview with Mrs. Eleanor Roosevelt*
(Folkway Records); Martin Luther King, Jr., *The Trumpet of Con-
science* (New York: Harper & Row, 1967), p. 17.

Library of Congress Cataloging in Publication Data

Vandenberg, Donald.
   Human rights in education.

   1.   Education—Aims and objectives.   2. Education—
Philosophy.   3. Civil rights.   I. Title.
   LB41.V29   1983   370.11   83-22079
   ISBN 0-8022-2431-8

One of the bases of peace in the world is the recognition of human rights and freedoms.

Eleanor Roosevelt

The storm will not abate until a just distribution of the fruits of the earth enables people everywhere to live in dignity and human decency.

Martin Luther King, Jr.

Table of Contents

Chapter Nine   DEMOCRACY IN EDUCATION

Chapter Ten   FRATERNITY IN EDUCATION AS A HUMAN RIGHT

Chapter Eleven   EDUCATION FOR DEMOCRACY

Chapter Twelve   NEUTRALITY IN EDUCATION AS A HUMAN RIGHT

Chapter One

EDUCATION AND TECHNOLOGICAL CONSCIOUSNESS

> The power concealed in modern technology determines the relation of man to that which exists. It rules the whole earth.
>
> Heidegger[1]

The effect of technology on human existence has been lamented by innumerable doom-sayers, beginning with Huxley's *Brave New World* and Orwell's *1984*. The glories of technology have also been cheered wildly in the pages of science fiction. The birth of the "test-tube babies" and actual success in genetic engineering indicate that the brave new world may be close at hand. It is time to consider the significance of the technologizing of the planet for education.

I. The Question of Technological Consciousness

The advance of technology in society has affected education in at least four ways. Three are relatively insignificant in their effect on human existence except when they manifest or accelerate the growth of technological consciousness. The first is the use of technology in education, including not only audio-visual aids, instructional technology, and computer-assisted instruction but also behavior modification techniques, cybernetic models of the human mind, and other

---

[1] Martin Heidegger, "Memorial Address," *Discourse on Thinking*, tr. by John M. Anderson and E. Hans Freund (New York: Harper & Row, 1966), p. 50.

11

ways to "process" students instead of teaching them. The second is the renewed emphasis upon subjects in the curriculum essential to the use of technology in industry, such as mathematics, physics, and chemistry, and the introduction of new subjects related to the technologizing of the world, such as computer science, plastics, and ecology. The third is the way these pedagogic and curricular changes select and educate technological, bureaucratic, and professional elites. If this uses the school to serve some groups rather than others, it raises the question of justice, but if it promotes the development of a technocracy, it constitutes a far more serious dehumanization of political matters without due process of law.

The fourth impact is the effect of technology on the lives of individual people through the development of distinctly modern personality structures. This is the basic question of technology in the educational development of the human being. Has technology so thoroughly altered society that its influences on schooling in the ways specified have been accompanied by a more pervasive and fundamental development of a technological consciousness?

The technological consciousness, or "mind-set," structures one's attitude toward everything encountered, limiting access to things in the world and other people to their aspects of usefulness to oneself. As advanced technology comes to prevail in the transition of technocracy, so does technological consciousness. In the context of the saying regarding the change in the very structure of human existence, Heidegger claimed that the technical relation of man to the world developed only in the seventeenth century and only in Europe, but since then has encompassed the whole planet. Western mathematics and natural science are at the core of the university curriculum in every country in the world. Their intellectual perspectives are no longer Western. The issue is the fulfillment of human needs through the technologizing of the earth and the way in which technology has come to govern the planet through education. When technocratic governance promotes the maximum fulfillment of human needs through the efficient organization of the power latent in technology, it has highly desirable characteristics.

On the other hand, if the development of a purely technological consciousness in advanced industrial societies alters the very structure of existence, and if this change is justified by an ideology deeply at the heart of Western civilization, it also establishes the parameters of education, which then prepares the way for the unacknowledged transition to technocracy. It may be that the profound change in the relation of people to things is not in and of itself dehumanizing, for it may be as human as other modes of consciousness. The threat of dehumanization through excessive technologization, however, indicates it is desirable to balance the encroachments of technology and retain the basic elements of humanity through education.

It is not enough to emphasize subjects in the humanities, or to have a course in the humanities in the tertiary schooling of technicians, engineers, and future technocrats. This is good, but it humanizes the technocrats, not the technocracy. It shows, however, that a humanizing influence can be introduced into schools without creating a counter-cultural, anti-technological, anti-intellectual orientation.

The question concerns the education of everyone, not only the technological and managerial elites but also the people who in democratic societies ought to control such elites. It concerns the young people of varying ability being prepared to live in a society that is becoming increasingly technological and dehumanized, not by the technology itself but by its underlying ideology and the way it affects school programs and the development of technological consciousness.

That the industrial revolution requires a new set of educational ideas was proclaimed by John Dewey at the end of the nineteenth century. He held that the old ones were appropriate for a different clientele, with aims unlike those allowed by an industrial society. His thought had antecedents, for the industrial revolution of the seventeenth and eighteenth centuries had been followed by the reorientation of educational ideas generated by the theories of Rousseau, Froebel, and Pestalozzi. Dewey's own theory professed to formulate a program to enable everyone to acquire the intellectual and moral habits needed to cope with the difficulties inherent in an industrialized society. At the heart of his theory, however, was a technological model of mind. The use of his problem-solving pedagogy promotes the development of technological consciousness. The view of knowledge and mind embedded in his major educational book is even called "instrumentalism," i.e., one perceives things only in terms of their uses, ideas are merely tools to solve problems, and the mind functions only as a tool to control the environment.[2] Dewey took Darwin too seriously when he reduced human characteristics to those of the biological organism, for this committed him to the view of man as a tool-using animal that lay ideologically beneath his explicitly formulated ideas and dominated his thinking.[3] It would be wrong to conclude that Dewey was too much a part of the industrial revolution to maintain perspective and evaluate it adequately. This is true, but his theory was more strongly affected by his nostalgia for his Vermont boyhood, and his recommendations for active occupations in the classroom were based on an understanding of labor as a kind of craftsmanship that had already been superseded by the factory system.

Since the Second World War, moreover, changes in the material culture have occurred so rapidly there is now reason to believe they constitute a second industrial revolution.[4] It is manifested in the obvious things, i.e., the use of nuclear energy, the automation of industry based on computer technology, the emergence of worldwide mass culture through the use of communications satellites and jet flight, and so on. Dewey's point of departure can be accepted if it is updated to mean that existing educational ideas, including his, were for the most part formulated before this second industrial revolution and therefore suitable for a clientele with aims different from those allowed by the post-industrialized society.

The question, then, is whether the "second industrial revolution" has created a society in need of new educational ideas. Existing educational ideologies are no longer appropriate, furthermore, because of their rhetorical distortion by the mass media. Even without the intentional manipulation of educational ideology, the mass media articulate and create the cultural ideology, which affects education. The borderline between the mass media and the curriculum disappears with the technologizing of society, for the mass media

---

[2] John Dewey, *Democracy and Education* (New York: Macmillan, 1916).

[3] Donald Vandenberg, "Education or Experience?" *Educational Theory* 30 (1980): 235-251.

[4] Alvin Toffler, *The Third Wave* (London: Pan Books, 1981).

produce curriculum materials they then promote, and educational controversies are conducted in the media before being studied in teacher training institutions. The status of any of this "knowledge" can be questioned. Is it all ideology? Are the educational ideas prevalent in society what they seem to be? Are they guided by the student's best interest or by someone's personal "hobby horse"? Are they guided by the public interest? When are they guided by private interests that are carefully shielded from public view?

An adequate idea of the kind of education that is in the student's best interest, or in the public interest, is required to answer these questions.

They require the formulation of a theory of education that does not support private interests as a criterion of judgment. Neo-Marxists claim this cannot and will not be formulated, for people with economic and political power will control the technological structures, including the mass media, to serve their own interests by dominating the cultural ideology. They also intimate that anyone who seeks to make his ideas dominant seeks power, not truth. The rhetoric of the populist demagogue is a case in point.

Be that as it may, it is extremely difficult to be objective about the kind of education that would serve the best interest of the student or the public because one's beliefs about education are strongly affected by one's personal experience in school and by one's social class. Then one's ideas serve personal and/or social functions rather than truth. They are ideological in the pejorative sense. On the one hand, personal experience is all anyone has to think with, regardless of how well it is refined. No one can repudiate his or her own education, for it even makes its own repudiation possible. If one transcends one's social class conditioning, furthermore, the resulting classlessness will bear a very strong resemblance to the objectivity of judgment highly valued by upper-middle-class professional people.

A set of ideas that specifies the educational program appropriate for an advanced industrial society is clearly needed. To distinguish it from the ideas about education that become distorted through their use as slogans, rhetoric, and propaganda in the mass media that should be called educational ideology to indicate their psychological, social, and political functions, it should be as rational as currently acceptable modes of theory development allow and deserve the name of educational theory.[5]

II. The Meaning of "Science and Technology"

An ideological critique can remove the non-rational elements from an educational ideology. A critique of the way educational ideologies function in advanced industrial societies can also be made, but it requires the context of social theory. For example, in the last chapter of *Toward a Rational Society* Jurgen Habermas argued that science and technology embody a particular form of rationality that involves the exploitation and domination of nature. Their use by managerial and professional elites to dominate nature in the production of goods develops a form of rationality that is basically a kind of domination that also comes to structure their relation to the underclass. This domination goes unnoticed because of the societal prestige of science and technology. Because science and technology lend a false appearance of rationality, objectivity, and rightness to the domination of the underclass through the use of so-called expert knowledge, they serve hegemonic functions. Habermas explicitly denied direct collusion between science and technology when he said, "The modern sciences produce knowledge which through its *form* (and not through the subjective intentions of scientists) is technically exploitable knowledge, although the possible applications generally are realized afterwards."[6] This exploitability is attributed to all sciences, although Habermas submitted evidence only in physics and presented no credentials authorizing him to speak of all the sciences. The word "produce," moreover, is an economic term, which projects Habermas's own technological consciousness on to science. Knowledge is ordinarily said to be discovered, not produced. Later on, he referred to the reciprocating scientization of technology: "With the advent of large-scale industrial research, science, technology, and industrial

---

[5] For this distinction, see George Eastman, "The Ideologizing of Theories of Education: John Dewey's Education Theory, A Case in Point." *Educational Theory* 17 (1967): 103-119.

[6] Jurgen Habermas, *Toward a Rational Society*, tr. by Jeremy Shapiro (London: Heineman, 1971), p. 99. Emphasis his.

utilization were fused into a system."[7] Although scientific research occurs in industry and universities and the results merge through publication in learned journals, Habermas reified the word "science," thereby also committing the fallacy of composition. It is fallacious to generalize from the fact that some scientists have gone into industry and some industrial research is done at universities to all of science, and it is not evidence that scientists have surrendered their autonomous judgment or that they make managerial decisions in industry. The interrelatedness of some science with some industry is not a "fusion" of all of science with the whole of industry.

On the other hand, Habermas is correct to indicate that where this fusion does occur, it results in the technocratic consciousness, i.e., the attitude that science and government should be allies, that scientific-technical progress is self-legitimating, and that the reason for doing science is to produce usable results, rather than engage in the disinterested pursuit of the truth about a particular phenomenon. He is correct to claim that science and technology are ideologies. He may also have been correct to claim that the "technocratic consciousness" permeates all advanced industrial societies, both in capitalism and "bureaucratic socialism."[8] It is basically a belief that all human or social problems are technical problems that can be solved by scientific-technical means. As such, it occurs only after the breakdown of bourgeois ideology, for it is not structured by the latter's moral language or moral code. For example, the technocratic consciousness considers an unwanted pregnancy a scientific-technical matter and refers to "terminating it" rather than mutilating oneself, and to the "fetus" instead of the baby, in a loss of the moral consciousness of the act of infanticide.

Substantiation of Habermas's point is found in the ordinary language expression, "science and technology," for when these are spoken together, it does indeed indicate a conflation of the two concepts within the cultural ideology. The conflation seems rampant. Habermas based his claim on Marcuse, who in turn acknowledged his debt to Heidegger on the point already cited.[9] As early as 1935,

---

[7] Ibid., p. 104.

[8] Ibid., p. 117.

[9] Ibid., p. 85.

however, Heidegger also said, "From a metaphysical point of view, Russia and America are the same; the same dreary technological frenzy, the same unrestricted organization of the average man."[10] If the technologizing of life is similar in both nations regardless of their differing economic systems, it is unhelpful to infer that the fusion of "science and technology" serves hegemonic purposes to maintain a Marxist ideology, for such an inference is an oversimplification of reality that is not interested in social justice. It is an ideology, but justice can be served only by truth.

To accept an ideological standpoint as Habermas's, furthermore, discourages a more fundamental analysis of the foundation of technological consciousness. It is correct to regard all advanced industrial societies as similar regardless of different political, economic, and social systems, even from the viewpoint of Marx's dialectical materialism. The analysis that bourgeois Marxists like Habermas give to the "ruling class" in capitalist society has its parallel in the analysis given to the "ruling class" in Russia by an authentic participant in the revolution of 1917, Milovan Djilas. In *The New Class* he showed that during the period between Lenin and Stalin, the Communist Party in Russia consolidated its power into a bureaucratic, authoritarian, elitist new class.[11] This bureaucracy made it possible for Stalin to make Hitler look like an amateur. Similarly, in *The Intellectuals on the Road to Class Power* Konrad and Szelenyi told the history of Hungary and then expanded their thesis to fit all Communist countries. They claim that the revolution led by Lenin was not a proletarian revolution. Like other socialist revolutions, it was conducted by the bourgeois intellectual class to gain power for themselves as a class. What Lenin took to Russia was not the socialist revolution. It was the industrial revolution.[12]

It is therefore necessary to go beyond a pseudo-sociological cri-

---

[10] Martin Heidegger, *An Introduction to Metaphysics*, tr. by Ralph Mannheim (New York: Doubleday, 1961), p. 31.

[11] Milovan Djilas, *The New Class* (New York: Praeger, 1959), pp. 40-42.

[12] George Konrad and Ivan Szelenyi, *Intellectuals on the Road to Class Power*, tr. by A. Arato and R.E. Allin (New York: Harcourt Brace Jovanovich, 1979).

tique to understand the meaning of "science and technology" as the ideology of technological consciousness in any society. It is necessary to consider the characteristics of knowledge itself as Alvin Toffler has done to extract the "superideology" lying beneath the ideologies of capitalism and socialism, behind science and technology, constituting the worldview of people in nations that have undergone the industrial revolution.

Toffler claims that the industrial revolution has changed the experience of time, space, things, and causes since the seventeenth and eighteenth centuries. Days, months, and years are natural, cyclical units of time, but the factory system requires that time be measured in terms of hours and weeks, which are linear, non-repeating, quantifiable, and standardized. This linearization of time makes synchronization possible, but it also makes possible the concepts of progress and evolution and the sciences of biology, sociology, history, archeology, geophysics, and astronomy and astrophysics.[13] Space also becomes linearized and objectified. Precise units of length, a sense of architectural space, and detailed maps are developed, making physics possible as the study of matter in motion.[14] On the level of everyday experience, things themselves become perceived as things in space, i.e., as discrete entities, and attention is given to the smallest things, atoms, as constituents of all other things. People become perceived as distinct things, as individuals who can be separated from society, with which they enter into a "social contract."[15] The things of the world are distinguished from each other in terms of the separate sciences, and within biology, for example, Darwin isolated his attention to the genera and species of living things that led him to the theory of biological evolution. Finally, it becomes assumed that events occur according to regular patterns and that these laws can be figured out, predicted, and used to control things. This makes possible the development of technology in the rational pursuit of the satisfaction of needs.[16] The view that science is the prediction and

---

[13] Toffler, *The Third Wave*, pp. 115-117.
[14] Ibid., p. 121.
[15] Ibid., pp. 122-123.
[16] Ibid., pp. 125-126.

control of events is therefore a fusion of science and technology that was present from the beginning of the industrial revolution. It would be easy to substantiate Toffler's thesis by showing elements of the "superideology" to be present in the theories of the philosophers of the seventeenth and eighteenth centuries: Bacon (knowledge is power), Descartes (simple ideas, extension), Berkeley (perceived things), Leibniz (isolated things), Hume (causation as a habit of mind), Kant (things in space and time), and so forth.

It is not germane to argue that the concepts Toffler refers to originated with the Greeks and are inherent in Western metaphysics as such, for his claim concerns the general cultural ideology after the Renaissance and industrial revolution, when the ordinary, everyday consciousness of time, space, things, and causes gradually became restructured. He also claims these were being restructured again in the "second industrial revolution" occurring since World War II, but reference to his futurism is unnecessary to understand the way the "superideology" was involved in the vast, historically great change in the everyday, commonsense consciousness that has eventuated in the ubiquitous presence of the technological consciousness in industrialized nations, capitalist and socialist alike.

The concept of the "superideology" can help retain objectivity, or at least neutrality, toward the prevalence of technological consciousness. Insofar as similar concepts of time, space, things, and causes underlie both science and technology, there is a basis for their cognitive interplay, if not fusion, within the consciousness of anyone involved in both. It is then unnecessary to appeal to social forces to explain the "fusion," which is wholly explicable on cognitive grounds. It is difficult to see the harm in this "fusion," providing it does not necessarily exclude the pursuit of knowledge for the sake of truth and the presence of moral consciousness. After all, it is because of this "superideology" that it is no longer possible to believe in demons, witchcraft, Satan, heaven or hell, or that there are gods in everything, or to trust in magic, sorcery, shamanism, or witch doctors. The shift from a magical consciousness to a technological consciousness is a major improvement in the epistemic characteristics of civilization. Its cognitive and practical values ought not be forgotten when indicating its shortcomings.

By itself, however, the technological consciousness is not a moral consciousness. Habermas is correct, although his critique is insufficiently trenchant. The technological consciousness is not an esthetic, religious, or political consciousness either. In any case, if the knowledge of the sciences is fused with technology and helps the "new class" dominate the underclass, it is not the fault of the knowledge. The deficiency of the technological consciousness is not due to what it possesses but what it lacks, i.e., moral, esthetic, religious, and political awareness.

Knowledge that is technically exploitable is not simply "bourgeois ideology," nor is the state of knowledge in a society determined by the state of its industrialization. To the contrary, only if the knowledge is true knowledge about the real world can it make technology possible. Only if it is not ideological in any significant sense can it be of use to industry, and only then can it develop technological consciousness. Its validity as knowledge, however, cannot prevent it, either under the conditions of capitalism or socialism, from technologizing consciousness.

This attempt to transcend ideology has referred to the concept of the "superideology" to bring its elements into explicit consciousness and show the shortcomings of a Marxist interpretation of the ideology of "science and technology." It utilized the work of a freelance intellectual historian rather than professional philosophers of science because the latter are ideological in the pejorative sense. Their science-talk reifies the word "science" as if there were an objective referent for the abstract noun. There is none, so the science-talk selects one of the sciences, focuses upon some of its characteristics, reifies them, and calls them the features of science in a gross oversimplification that commits the fallacy of composition, i.e., that reasons from the part to the whole, from one of the sciences to science in general.

The ideology inherent in philosophy of science shows in the common choice to select physics as the paradigm science, for it supplies the most useful knowledge from a technological viewpoint. This was Dewey's error. Although his model is inadequate for the physical sciences, which are vastly more conceptual and theoretical than he granted, he nevertheless applied the model of the natural sciences everywhere, running roughshod over the characteristics of the phenomena in all other domains. The logic of the move is to use some of the features of the selected science, experimentation for Dewey, as norms, or criteria of good research, to prescribe methodology to the other sciences even though one has no competency in them. This is exceedingly presumptuous. It is totally lacking in cognitive warrant. If someone in education follows Dewey's procedure by making proposals for pedagogy or curriculum based on a theory of knowledge or philosophy of science, the result is ideology in the pejorative sense.

Everything changes if one begins with the scientific observation that there is no such thing as science. There are all sorts of things called "science" that merely bear family resemblances to each other, to use Wittgenstein's phrase. There are physical sciences, earth sciences, space sciences, life sciences, medical and health sciences, agricultural and veterinary sciences, social sciences, behavioral sciences, linguistic and hermeneutical sciences, logical and mathematical sciences, and so on, as any university calendar will indicate. It is impossible to say scientifically which one of them is most scientific. More importantly, no philosopher of science as such is qualified to ascertain the nature and validity of knowledge in any of the special sciences. The requisite is advanced study that establishes one as a basic theorist in a particular domain.

Someone who attempts to discuss the nature of knowledge in general or the canons of inquiry for a domain of knowledge in which he has not established his authority by a superior mastery of its content is an ideologist, if not a charlatan. An individual philosopher of science is not necessarily blameworthy. Dewey is a good example because he has been a main spokesperson for science in the curriculum even though there is no such thing as science. He was formulating his experimental logic in the first quarter of the century when the various revolutions in the basic concepts of the special sciences were creating new ideas about the nature of knowledge. His training in the traditions of Western philosophy encouraged him to formulate a general theory of knowledge even when the changes in the disciplines that stimulated him made it impossible. The analysis fits all philosophy of science applied to the school curriculum. There are only the many sciences, the basic theorists of which find it a full-time occupation to formulate the methodology appropriate to the disciplined study of their domain-specific phenomena.

The point merely draws the logical conclusion of historical developments. In classical antiquity the name "philosophy" was given to the love of learning in all branches of knowledge. As empirical science has specialized the study of things in one area after another, there has been less and less for philosophy to study in a purely rational, a priori undertaking. This principle of the attrition of philosophy was accepted in Dewey's experimentalism, Russell's empiricism, Wittgenstein's and Ayer's positivism, and Marx's dialectical materialism. It is easy to assume that one area remains, i.e., philosophy of science, particularly if it is reduced to logic and restricted to an examination of the sentences of published scientific writings. These sentences, however, are meaningless when divorced from the phenomena they are about, and expertise in the domain is necessary to discuss the relation of the theoretical knowledge in the sentences to the phenomena. One philosopher of science made an utterly honest admission when he said that the "logic" and "method" of a scientific "explanation" is field-dependent, for this means that the criteria of good logic are field-dependent and domain-specific.[17] This leaves nothing for philosophy but value theory, esthetics, ethics, and political philosophy, which would have sufficed for Socrates.

It would appear that philosophy of science ought to be taken over by people qualified in the various domains who could attest to the validity of the logic of discovery specific to a domain, i.e., by the basic theorists within each of the special sciences. Anything more general is necessarily an ideology in the pejorative sense. It is thus merely an extension of the historical abandonment of philosophy to claim there is no such thing as science in general about which there can be a philosophy. Instead, there are a great variety of sciences, better known as the university disciplines, each with its own methodologies for the discovery of knowledge about the phenomena in its distinct region of the world.

This critique of the philosophy of science establishes that it is

---

[17] Stephen Toulmin, *The Uses of Argument* (Cambridge: Cambridge University Press, 1958), pp. 234, 250, 255.

necessarily ideological because it reifies science or preferred aspects of science without an adequate grasp of the whole process of the disciplined discovery of knowledge in a given domain. No one can be expert within a domain and also expert in science in general at the same time. One reflects either upon the methodology of a particular discipline or upon the ideology of science. The critique is unlike that of the counter-culture, however, for it is directed against philosophers of science in order to transcend their ideologies of knowledge that foster the societal mystique concerning "science and technology." It does not attack any of the special sciences.

The point is merely that the prestige of science in advanced industrial societies has given status to philosophy of science, which in turn gives ideological support to science, and, through the fusion of science and technology, to the technological consciousness. The use of science to dominate and exploit the underclass needs the support of an ideology of science that science does not need.

III. Theoretical Knowledge and Education

The ideological critique of the philosophy of science is made from a position of Socratic ignorance. We do not know what science is. To find out what it is, one should not go to a philosophy department. One should ask a scientist, for it all depends upon the things done by researchers in the various special sciences. It is an empirical question unless one is planning to conduct research. Then the concern is for a domain-specific methodology.

The critique does not concern the sciences themselves except to protect them from the ideologists of science. The implication is that the only knowledge that is appropriate for the school curriculum is that which has been validated by a group of qualified investigators or practitioners. It includes the knowledge of the special sciences considered as university disciplines, but it also includes the knowledge of the arts, crafts, trades, sports, and professions. Each of these has a group of critical experts to attest to the knowledge within the domain, and each has objectivity in the sense of intersubjectively valid truth. The aspect of the knowledge of the arts, crafts, trades, sports, and professions for which classroom instruction is necessary, furthermore, is their theory, i.e., their theoretical knowledge.

This claim transcends ideology because it is reached by default, i.e., by rejection on principle of all theories of knowledge and science because they are ideological and would contribute to the development of technological consciousness rather than the diffusion of knowledge itself. It is not a skeptical view that questions the existence of knowledge. To the contrary, it even resorts to a "sociology of good knowledge" to claim that the knowledge that belongs in the school curriculum is the theoretical components of the knowledge contained in the arts, crafts, trades, sports, professions, and disciplines.

It transcends ideology in several ways. It describes much of the content actually included in the school curriculum already. It allows further determination of the nature of knowledge to be made by properly qualified people. It does not claim that knowledge of the disciplines (i.e., the sciences) is superior to that of the arts, crafts, trades, sports, or professions, as Plato and elitists say. Nor does it claim superiority for the knowledge of the arts, crafts, trades, sports and professions, as Dewey and egalitarians say. Nor does it attack the former as anti-intellectual educationists do, nor the latter as anti-democratic academicians do.

Any implied hierarchy does not come from an ideology of knowledge but from the increasing technologization of work. If it is erroneous to refer to it as a second industrial revolution, there has nevertheless been a phenomenal extension of earlier industrialization since 1945 that requires one to regard developed nations as advanced industrial societies. The increased complexity of work and expansion of technology has not placed a greater valuation on the arts, crafts, and trades but on the theoretical knowledge of the professions and academic disciplines acquired in tertiary schooling. The rapid expansion of tertiary schooling since World War II can be understood through Daniel Bell's thesis regarding the post-industrial society.[18] Pre-industrial societies are based on primary industries, i.e., agriculture, fishing, forestry, and mining. Things are extracted from nature in labor-intensive processes. Industrial societies are more greatly based on secondary industries, i.e., manufacturing. Things are made

---

[18] The following summary is based on Daniel Bell, *The Cultural Contradictions of Capitalism* (New York: Basic Books, 1976), pp. 198-199.

in a capital-intensive process, and the main resource is energy (coal, oil). The struggle is not with nature but with fabricated nature. Bell's thesis is that by 1970 the United States had shifted to a post-industrial society because sixty-five percent of its workers were employed in tertiary industries, i.e., the service industries. People are serviced in knowledge-intensive processes, and the main resource is information and theoretical knowledge. Work is not extracting or making things but processing people.

According to Bell, when the majority of working people in a society are no longer employed in primary or secondary industries, it is a post-industrial society. European countries and Australia had between forty and fifty percent of their workers in tertiary industries in 1973, according to Bell's figures, whereas the United States had about two-thirds in the tertiary sector. This vast transformation in the occupational structure upsets orthodox Marxism, for "the concept 'post-industrial society' emphasizes the centrality of theoretical knowledge as the axis around which the new technology, economic growth, and the stratification of society will be organized."[19] Bell said all three of these things depended upon theoretical knowledge: new technology, economic growth, and social stratification. The implication is that, "In capitalist society the axial institution has been private property and in the post-industrial society it is the centrality of theoretical knowledge."[20] The predominance of the service industries, which rest almost wholly upon the theoretical knowledge of the professional person, means that the criterion for social class membership shifts away from capital, income, property, and inheritance toward professional competency, knowledge, and personal achievement in education. Although the culture is anti-science, anti-technology, and anti-bureaucratic insofar as the "counterculture" is the culture, industry is science-based; and engineers, managerial elites, and scientists come into their own, forming what Bell, not unlike Djilas, called the "new class." If Bell is correct, the "new class" is the progressive element because of its use of new theoretical knowl-

---

[19] Daniel Bell, *The Coming of the Post-Industrial Society* (New York: Basic Books, 1974), p. 112.

[20] Ibid., p. 115.

edge. Because this class is not dominant due to its ownership of the means of production, and because the social, economic, political, and cultural systems develop independently of each other, there is "no specific determinism between a 'base' and a 'super-structure.' "[21] This means the dominant ideology is not determined by the forces of production, nor by the "ruling class." Instead, there is "the rise of a new class which may or may not be struggling to establish a corporate cohesiveness as a ruling class in society."[22]

This makes it easy to see why the social structure in socialist countries has become so similar to that of the free world. In either case the knowledge of the "new class" of professional and managerial elites is essential to maintain the existence of the advanced industrialization, and this is why the principal problem in the post-industrial society becomes national policy regarding science and education. Both kinds of systems have transformed their educational systems to insure that graduates of tertiary schools have the knowledge and skills needed to maintain their economies.

The need of advanced industrial societies for technological and professional elites makes it pointless to criticize the schools for "reproducing" the social structure. The secondary schools are going to have prestigious academic tracks to channel the most academically able students into tertiary schools and the "new class" in all advanced industrial societies. They simply are going to have them. What the schools can do to insure justice regarding social stratification, furthermore, has to occur through the pedagogic interface. The individual teacher, confronting individual students from various social classes, is ethically bound to non-discrimination. She or he cannot discourage youth from professional homes from preparing for tertiary schools and is unlikely to be able to encourage students from working-class homes to prepare for them unless the home supports upward mobility. The teacher's task is neither to encourage nor discourage university attendance but to teach without discrimination the knowledge and skills that make it possible. The teacher has no special obligation or mission to encourage so-called upward mobility

---

21 Ibid., p. 119.
22 Ibid.

among children from working-class homes. It is not the teacher's concern to worry whether some students will eventually be in the "new class" and others not. He or she cannot be responsible for this, only for teaching knowledge and skills effectively. Because everything that happens in schools flows through the pedagogic interface, the schools cannot be held responsible for things that teachers cannot be. They are not responsible if the social structure of a society is "reproduced" through them.

If university graduates are coming to form a new class on the basis of the knowledge of the disciplines and professions, then the "ruling class" is coming to be the educated class. If the ideas about education of these educated classes are becoming the dominant educational ideas, it means that the educated classes are forming educational policy and selecting curriculum emphases. The desirable alternative is not obvious. University experts in the study of education have no expertise that enables their recommendations on curriculum matters to be superior to those of the educated classes, and society faces a major disaster when the ideas of uneducated people become the dominant ideas about education.

On the other hand, the sociologists of education who have called attention to the school's function in reproducing patterns of social stratification are at least half right. If they are scientists, and not ideologists, they cannot say such reproduction is bad, and if the maintenance of the "new class" is essential to the continued existence of technological society, it is to that extent good. This, however, is merely a utilitarian justification. It is a means-end technological justification, concerned with extrinsic purposes of schooling in an advanced industrial society, rather than with the epistemic characteristics of knowledge. The technological consciousness is transcended with the additional recognition that theoretical instruction is the essence of schooling.

To find fault with the school's function in preparing students for tertiary schools is an outcome of an assumption of a macrocosmic view that considers schools in general. The macrocosmic viewpoint as such, however, is ideological. Schools in general do not exist. The macrocosmic fallacy is escaped by realizing that whatever schools do occurs in the pedagogic interface. It is therefore theoretically necessary and correct to eschew the sociological point of view and to assume the parameters of the perspective of the individual practitioner in the pedagogic interface.

The macrocosmic view involves a view of the whole society as a framework within which the entire school curriculum is putatively surveyed, designed, structured, and prescribed to accomplish objectives presumed to be related to the public good. The view of the whole, however, is not possible. By the time the data about the relevant factors is gathered and processed to enable inferences about the whole society to be drawn, things have changed. Because no one in real life goes around planning entire curriculums, furthermore, the macrocosmic views can only result in fantasies that function ideologically and force one into the technological, totalitarian trap. The macrocosmic urge has to be defeated to transcend ideology.

IV. Human Dignity and Education

Primary schools have to prepare students for secondary schools, which have to prepare students for tertiary schools, which have to prepare students for advanced industrial society, or modern civilization collapses. Once this structure is accepted as given, which it is, it also becomes obvious that an attempt to find a solution to the question of the educational development of the technological consciousness in the cognitive domain will become macrocosmic, ideological, totalitarian, and non-functional.

The parameters for a possible solution are the horizons of the pedagogic relation given to the individual teacher within a given curriculum. A comparison with medical practice is illuminating. Doctors have no macrocosmic view of the healthy society about which they become ideological, apocalyptic, and totalitarian, although through countless face-to-face, ad hoc consultations in which the client is always free to reject the advice given, they do a great deal to elevate and maintain the standard of health in a community. Similarly, the educational response to the technologizing of the planet should occur in the pedagogical situations of individual teachers encountering individual students. If some teachers make some difference in the lives of some students, it is enough. It is all there is. The educational reality is individual teachers working with individual pupils in unique classrooms.

It follows that the parameters for a solution are largely in the non-cognitive aspects of pedagogy, in the so-called hidden curriculum. The overt curriculum, the knowledge and skills comprising the cognitive domain, can be taken for granted, relatively speaking, and the solution sought in the domain absent in societies dominated by the ideological fusion of science and technology, i.e., in the moral domain.

The claim that the amorality of the technological consciousness is the result of acquiring a certain kind of knowledge might seem to be anti-intellectual. That knowledge is all right if supplemented by moral, esthetic, political, and perhaps religious awareness. The problem is not that there is no body of moral knowledge available for students to learn as part of the curriculum. The problem is that the study of education has coalesced with the technology of education to interpret pedagogy itself technologically. Increased teaching effectiveness has occurred at the expense of lack of attention to the educative development of moral sensibility.

To avoid resurrecting values from an earlier period already brushed aside as irrelevant to the technological consciousness, the historical situation should be kept in mind. Heidegger's 1935 statement about technological frenzies strangely omitted the frenzy in his own country, but Nazi Germany is usually cited with Stalinist Russia as manifesting the technological consciousness gone mad. This is especially significant because it occurred in the advanced stages of the first industrial revolution, and the Holocaust resulted in the formulation of the Universal Declaration of Human Rights, adopted by the United Nations in 1948. Its Preamble begins, "Whereas recognition of the inherent dignity..." and the first article claims, "All human beings are born free and equal in dignity and rights."

The combination of bureaucracy and technology that has come to be called "technocracy" could not have resulted in the ruthlessness with which national goals in Germany and Russia were pursued at the expense of the lives of millions of people had there been a clear consciousness of human dignity.

The main moral principle embodied in the movement for civil

rights and human rights since the Second World War, furthermore, has been that of human dignity.

The principle seemed so important to Manfred Stanley that he claimed that the conscientious concern for the dignity of other people is the "conscience" that belongs to the technological consciousness. A concern for human dignity is the difference between legitimate uses of technology and technicism. Stanley seems to have overstated the situation when he asserted that social problems have accumulated to the point of crisis and that the choice was between two basically opposing justifications of the social order, the ethics of survival or the ethics of human dignity.[23] This exaggerates, for the only choice is to survive with as much dignity as possible, but it let Stanley make his argument for the concept of dignity:

> In approaching this problem it is well to recall that strong cases can be made by those who deny the dignity of humanity or who consider the whole question meaningless.... Dignity-talk, however indirectly, deals with the limits that can be set upon the technological manipulation of humanity.... Hence, if dignity-talk is considered unintelligible to the modern intellect, then it must follow that there are no theoretical limits to the social legitimation of technicism.[24]

The principle of human dignity is said to underlie the teachings of Jesus, but a careful reading of *Exodus* shows it to be three thousand years old. On the other hand, the recognition of its fundamental importance in secular, political spheres occurred only since World War II. It is a very abstract principle that even the great rationalist Kant had difficulty formulating. It may be that dignity-talk is less intelligible to the intellect than to the heart. With the technologizing of the planet, however, it is possible to become aware of human dignity as if for the first time and to articulate the insight in a theory of human rights.

---

[23] Manfred Stanley, *The Technological Conscience: Survival and Dignity in an Age of Expertise* (New York: The Free Press, 1978), p. 53.

[24] Ibid., p. 59.

For example, Stanley seems quite successful claiming there are two things essential to human dignity: "The truly terminal crisis of human dignity would be a total loss of pretheoretical confidence in the efficacy of both human cognition for comprehending a world and human agency for acting upon it."[25] That is, if we lose our belief in knowledge and moral responsibility we lose our humanity. The belief that we can know things in the world and be responsible for our actions is foundational to our being human, i.e., to our human dignity.

The ancient claim of Plato and Aristotle that rationality is the specific human dignity has been difficult to maintain after Marx, Darwin, Nietzsche, and Freud upset the particular ideologies of rationality that had emerged through the ages. Their ideological critiques, however, were mistaken for the rejection of reason itself. Stanley's statement requires acceptance of rationality as such but not any particular definition of it. No definition of reason is necessary to accept the fact that experts in the various disciplines know something about things in the world and that people qualified in the arts, crafts, trades, sports, and professions know what they are doing. These are minimal claims about the efficacy of human reason in defense of human dignity.

The claim of moral agency goes back to the most ancient of law codes, at least four thousand years to the Code of Hammurabi. The enforcement of laws presupposes liability, i.e., moral responsibility. The claim that adults should be held liable for the violation of statute laws is a minimal claim about moral responsibility for one's actions in defense of human dignity.

According to Stanley the two claims coincide because the characteristic of the human being that is constitutive of human dignity is moral significance.[26] People respect each other and treat each other with dignity because they have a sense of each other's dignity, i.e., a sense of each other's moral significance, of each other as a moral being. This enabled him to say, "The assertion of human dignity, then, is the constitutive act of moral consciousness. It is the entrance

---

[25] Ibid., p. 69.

[26] Ibid., p. 63.

ticket to the community of formal moral discourse. To assert dignity is both to acknowledge the factuality of human creative agency and to accept responsibility for its use."[27]

The appropriate response to the threat of technicism inherent in the technologization of the planet therefore lies in the aspects of schooling concerned with human dignity and basic human rights. Classrooms and schools can be conducted with an appropriate sense of the pupils' moral significance to augment their sense of their own dignity. The more students become aware of their own moral significance, the less likely are they to develop a technological consciousness and the more they will be able to transcend technicism.

Such an education for human dignity requires a theory of human rights in education.

Conclusion

Dewey said that the philosopher of education should formulate the educational program needed to develop the intellectual and moral characteristics necessary to cope with current social life. In a technicist culture it is first necessary to show that there are indeed intellectual and moral characteristics possessed by human beings.

It is also necessary to avoid an ideology, partisan viewpoint, and any macrocosmic view that exceeds existing knowledge, for these aggravate matters by inducing skepticism about the validity of the knowledge in the arts, crafts, trades, sports, professions, and disciplines, and this skepticism is an affront to the experts in these domains and contrary to human dignity. Because the knowledge in the arts, crafts, trades, sports, professions, and disciplines belongs in the school curriculum, it determines the intellectual characteristics the school should develop. This is maintained non-ideologically, as is the claim that there are fundamental moral characteristics the school should develop.

When the school is doing its best within the cognitive domain established by its own advanced scholars, generally found within tertiary institutions of learning, and when its classrooms are conducted with the freedom and responsibility appropriate to the dignity

---

[27] Ibid., p. 70.

of human learning, it is developing the intellectual and moral traits that enhance its integrity as an institution of learning. These are also the traits most appropriate for a social life that embodies human dignity at its very core.

The ideological and technological aspects of advanced industrial societies can re-awaken a sense of the extreme importance of developing personal confidence in the capacity to know things and to engage in responsible conduct.

No special theory of knowledge, ideology, or program is needed to develop intellectual or moral traits other than those indigenous to good schooling when expressed in terms of human rights. The methodology needed to formulate the theory of human rights intrinsic to the institution of learning, however, needs to be carefully considered.

Chapter Two

METHODOLOGY AND MORAL PRINCIPLES

It is not easy to lay down in a law precisely what is consistent with the dignity of a free man and what is not, and the point will have to be determined by those who have won distinction for their aversion to the latter and devotion to the former.

Plato[1]

The man in the icy water of the Chesapeake Bay who handed the lifesaver to the other people to let them be rescued by the helicopter at the cost of his own life manifested human dignity. The woman at a scholarly conference who began with an apology for not following previous patterns of "male" humor because she could not think of a joke to open with, at least not a clean one, manifested human dignity. The black woman who refused to move to the rear of the bus in Montgomery and thereby initiated the civil rights movement showed human dignity. When Benjamin Franklin wore homespun to the Palace of Versailles, he exemplified human dignity.

I. The Question of Methodology

The examples show that the knowledge of values that enables one to act with dignity is acquired through living. Although it is unlikely that the concept of dignity was in mind during the incidents, other

---

[1] Plato, *Laws*, tr. by Trevor Saunders (Middlesex: Penguin Books, 1975), 919.

moral principles may have obligated them to do the right thing in spite of adversity and unpopularity. How did they know what was right? What knowledge of value enabled them to do the right thing?

The three major theories of knowledge of value and right are that we are simply aware of value, or that we know value by reasoning things through, or that an empirical generalization is needed. Presentations of these theories of intuitionism, rationalism, and empiricism, respectively, are often ideologically distorted in haste to disprove two of them, but this merely reveals ignorance of primary sources and the issues. Each theory is formulated to call attention to features of knowing value overlooked by the other theories. Intuitionism is about personal experience in coming to value something, as, for example, when one has been the beneficiary of an act of friendship, promise-keeping, or truth-telling although it involved personal sacrifice by the other person to remain a friend, keep a promise, or tell the truth. Without this personal appreciation in the realization of value, one does not know what he is talking about. Experiential insights into value remain on the perceptual level as the feelings or intuitions of moral sensibility, however, unless they are conceptualized, discussed, and disciplined by reasoning processes, and this is what rationalism is about. These reasoning processes should consider whether the value is in harmony with the aggregate of the conditions of human existence and the facts of the world, among other things, and this is what empiricism and naturalism in value theory is about. Aspects of all three theories need to be accepted to have adequate knowledge of value.

Knowledge of value is therefore like any other knowledge. It requires both perceptual and conceptual consciousness of something in the world. It requires an awareness of something of value, and this awareness has both perceptual and conceptual components. Not all value is moral value. There is also esthetic value and epistemic value. In addition to moral rectitude, there is beauty and truth. Just as knowledge in art and science requires both perceptual and conceptual consciousness of things, so does ethics require the conceptualization of perceptual awareness of interhuman phenomena in the moral domain in order to have knowledge. Moral conduct may not require conceptual deliberation before action, but knowledge about that moral conduct as it is conceptualized in the university discipline devoted to the study of value and morals depends upon some kind of commitment to, and practice of, rationalism in ethics, for the philosopher as philosopher is committed to be as reasonable as possible.

For the most part, however, it has not been obvious to many twentieth century philosophers that they can be very reasonable about substantive questions of value. Perhaps this skepticism is related to the ideologies of science and technology that do not want the question of value raised. The question of an education for human dignity in a technological society, however, does not call for a direct investigation into value nor an attempt to contribute to the discipline called "ethics." It requires an investigation into the ethical dimensions of educational questions and educational phenomena in an attempt to contribute to the disciplined study of education.

If one shares with philosophy the professional commitment to be as reasonable as possible, it is important to note that a Harvard psychologist has accumulated empirical data to prove that some people are in fact eminently reasonable about questions of moral value. They do in fact employ cognitive processes of a very high order of excellence, utilizing universally valid moral principles at a very high level of abstraction. Someone who wanted to be as reasonable as possible about moral problems should therefore try to think about them at the Kohlbergian stage six level, i.e., in terms of universal moral principles and human rights. To be as reasonable as possible about the ethical dimensions of educational problems similarly involves thinking about them in terms of moral principles of universal validity at a "stage six" level. To resolve educational questions, the human rights ethics involved in such reasoning is required. The point is not which theory of value or morals is most defensible when considered from a philosophical or existential point of view, for this important question belongs to another discipline. The quest is for a method to use in the discipline of education to conduct theoretical research into educational questions about human dignity.

The proposal to adopt so-called sixth stage reasoning for heuristic purposes assumes nothing about Kohlberg's theory of human development. It assumes only that he has identified various kinds of thinking about so-called moral dilemmas and correctly arranged them in an order of increasingly complex logic. It does not assume people develop this way, which is for psychologists to determine, nor that these are the only kinds of thinking about morals, nor that thinking about conceptualized dilemmas is like thinking about existential moral choices, nor that more complex cognitive processes facilitate actual moral choices. It assumes only that the cognitive processes Kohlberg placed at the highest level are indeed the most reasonable ones.

A brief exposition of the stages will show why sixth stage reasoning is necessary for theoretical purposes in the study of education. Delinquents, criminals, psychopaths, and degenerates reason at the lowest level. They can obey rules or laws, but the only reasons cogent to them are related to the immediate threat of power and punishment. The cogent reasons given at stage two are self-regarding and relate to self-gratification. At the third stage the reasons for following the rules are concerned with social approval and maintenance of a good self-image. At these stages the reasoning is always concerned with extrinsic factors.

Only at stage four is the technological consciousness transcended and the rules or laws perceived as intrinsically right without regard for ulterior motives. Because the rightness becomes perceived as rightness, and as an externally given obligation, only at this stage, it is the first stage of moral thinking worthy of the name. In the first three stages rightness is defined in terms of something else in the "consequentialist fallacy," but in the fourth stage the obligation to do what is right because it is right involves distinctly moral reasoning. That is, it involves deontological ethics, based on the intuitive recognition of the rightness, or justice, of a rule or law. Stage five reasoning can put the rules or laws back into context and understand them as matters of agreement designed to promote the common good. This utilitarianism is transcended in the sixth stage, where the defense of rules and laws by moral principles makes them right for everyone, regardless of what might be decided by the majority on occasion. Thus sixth stage reasoning is structured by universally valid reasons, i.e., by obligations that each person has to every other person specified in terms of moral principles or human rights.

The only thing assumed by the proposal to reason about the ethical aspects of educational quesions at a Kohlbergian stage six level, then, is something about the relative appropriateness of thinking about them at stages four, five, or six. It assumes that the intuitionism of stage four reasoning and the empiricism and naturalism of stage five reasoning are not so good for theoretical purposes as the rationalism of stage six reasoning, although they should be fully subsumed within such rationalism. This is why the most fundamental thought about education occurs in the context of moral principles and human rights, and why the justification of the principles and rights is less important than their use in some very difficult decisions involving education for moral agency and human dignity.

II. The Use of Moral Principles

Doubt about the existence of moral principles and rights frequently is due to a lack of awareness of their appropriate use in reasoning and their roots in human dignity. A study in ethics would try to demonstrate the validity of some principles, but it suffices here to attend to some legitimate uses. These are more complicated than it may seem. For example, some people seem to think they are refuting the principle against murdering people by citing self-defense as a satisfactory excuse for killing someone. It can be, but it does not refute the absolute validity of the principle. First of all, it must be noted that it falls within the jurisdiction of courts of law, not philosophical debate, to decide if a particular killing in self-defense was justified. If it was, it is not legally defined as murder. This is not a matter of semantics, for killing in self-defense is the exception that proves the rule. It proves that the right to live is an absolute, non-negotiable human right, and that one is entitled to defend this right at all costs, including, if need be, the expense of an assailant's life. This context is so highly defined it demonstrates the principle is completely valid and essentially without exception, for the assailant forfeits his own right to live when he fails to recognize the obligation that flows from the right of others to live. The "exception" tests the rule, and the rule passes the test because the act that appears to be an exception is actually a defense of the rule. Thus a principle has only to be generally applicable to be universally valid.

Perhaps the point can be seen more readily in the context of the principle of truth-telling. One can maintain with Kant that one is always morally obligated to tell the truth. When in doubt, it is always right to tell the truth. In Kant's explication, it is not necessarily wrong to tell a lie. He argued against lying on prudential or benevolent grounds, but he did not say it was wrong to lie for these reasons, only that then one incurred responsibility for the consequences. When one speaks the truth on principle, one does the right thing and, for Kant, is relieved of responsibility for consequences. On the other hand, someone can be said to believe in the principle even if she or he does not always tell the truth. Judging how much integrity someone has is a different matter, but someone can be said to believe in the principle if they sometimes tell the truth when inclined not to do so.

In the abstract it can be claimed that truth-telling is a universally valid principle, and unexceptional, because a morally sensitive person of great integrity and superb fluency can speak truthfully on all occasions without deceit, but this does not mean that ordinary people do not believe in the principle merely because they do not always speak the truth. Intellectual acknowledgement of the rightness of the principle is not the same thing as moral motivation, moral courage, emotional stability, or personal integrity. Ascribing belief in it is a matter of degree, for failure to abide by a principle one believes in is not always hypocrisy.

A somewhat different point can be shown through promise-keeping. The usual casuistry discusses promises that become difficult to keep because of changing circumstances, emergencies, conflicting duties, etc. The principle, however, means that one should not make a promise he or she does not intend to keep. To say that one should always keep one's promises actually implies that it is never right to make a deceitful promise. If one makes no deceitful promises, the issue of whether one ought to keep all of his promises does not arise.

This brings out a very significant feature of all moral principles. The acceptance of promise-keeping as universally valid does not decide which kinds of promises should be made or whether one should make few or many promises. Life is not necessarily full of promise-making. Similarly, acceptance of the principle of truth-telling as absolutely binding upon oneself does not determine what one should talk about or how much one should say. It means that if one accepts the principle, one acknowledges an obligation to one's listeners to speak without deception when one speaks, i.e., whenever one does in fact speak. Moral principles are formal, without substantive content of their own. They cannot determine what one ought to do.

An aspect of their use that can be disillusioning if not understood is the distinction between the first-person and third-person use. A person can be said to believe in moral principles if she or he uses them to govern his own conduct. One actually speaks truthfully on some occasions when inclined not to, one keeps some promises that have become burdensome, etc. This is very different from believing them as articles of a creed or using them as criteria of judgment of other people's action or to make statements like, "Everybody lies," and, "Not many people in today's society keep their word." These are descriptive, sociological statements subject to empirical testing. Even if they are true they have no bearing on the validity of the principles. At best, they mean that no one fulfills his or her obligations to others, not that there are no such obligations.

The distinction can be illustrated with the principle of equal educational opportunity. Its legitimate use as a moral principle occurs during the allocation of funds, the establishment of programs, and the administration of existing programs, i.e., in first-person decisions involving the distribution of resources and access to programs. To use it in the third person to make moral judgments of the schools by measuring outcomes as various sociologists, historians, and so-called radical critics have done is wholly fallacious. It is analogous to using the principle of truth-telling to assert that everyone lies. If equal opportunity is a valid principle for the regulation of the allocation of resources, etc., it does not follow that it is a valid criterion to judge the justice in a school system. The schools are not shown to be unjust, nor the principle a myth, by outcomes that are patently unjust. To the contrary, they can appear to be unjust only if one accepts the principle. Its acceptance, furthermore, decides nothing except to oblige one to stop discrimination. It does not say what kind of resources, programs, materials, etc., ought to be provided to whom, nor what kinds of disadvantage ought to be compensated to establish equal opportunity and equity in education. It requires fairness in whatever is distributed educationally, but it does not define education, effective resources, or fairness.

Principles, in other words, are not rules like "Keep off the grass" that specify exactly what to do. They apply to all situations and therefore are not specified for the particular case. This means they do not eliminate the necessity for moral choices, nor do they make it impossible to err.

It is possible, furthermore, to act in accordance with a principle without having it in mind. Someone who grew up in a home where truth was told might speak the truth consistently without thinking about it at all. Similarly, one can distribute things fairly without having the concept of justice in mind. In fact, it is the person who does not have to remember the principle on every occasion who can be said to act on principle.

Finally, there are at least three different kinds of moral principles, social, personal, and procedural, as shown in the following list. Many philosophers of morals would expect to find most of them invoked in a serious study:

1. Freedom,
2. Equality,
3. Brotherly and sisterly love,
4. Consideration of interest.

5. Truth-telling,
6. Promise-keeping,
7. Debt-paying,
8. Not hurting people,
9. Correcting wrongs,
10. Reducing suffering (benevolence),
11. Respect for persons,
12. Human dignity,
13. Fulfilling obligations (duty).

14. Having good, public reasons for acts affecting others,
15. Discussing these reasons,
16. Impartial objectivity when considering these reasons.

The first group containing the democratic ideals of liberty, equality, and fraternity plus the principle of utility are emphasized by philosophers of morals who take their orientation from social and political philosophy to establish a social ethics. This volume will accordingly focus largely on these principles, omitting separate consideration of the principle of utility because attention to one's own interest structures consciousness technologically in the pursuit of non-moral goals and prohibits the growth of moral consciousness. The professional person's ethical commitment to the client's best interest is subsumed within the obligations due to the client's rights, i.e., within the concern for human dignity and human rights in education. Otherwise the first set will receive the major focus through the investigation of the questions of freedom in education, equality in education, fraternity in education, and democracy in education to show their basis in human dignity and human rights.

The second group of principles are emphasized by philosophers of morals who take their orientation from the conduct of the individual person to establish a personal ethics. This volume will not be directly concerned with the educational questions arising from these principles as it would were it primarily concerned with moral education, although several are involved in the search for resolutions to the questions of freedom, equality, and fraternity in education. The first half of the second set concerns moral conduct, but the principles in the second half refer to moral attitudes. It could be argued that not hurting people is not so much a principle as the reason for morality and similarly that maintaining human dignity, fulfilling obligations, and doing one's duty are not separate principles. They are specified because some philosophers of morals, e.g., Dewey, do not mention them at all.

The third group of principles are criteria of moral reasoning and are not needed unless a rationalistic ethics can be justified. People can be moral and act with rectitude without being able to engage in rational deliberation about moral matters. Giving reasons is supposed to help gain objectivity, as when a smoker gives advice to others not to smoke because of his correct knowledge of the matter. Acceptance of this set of procedural principles presses one toward the Kohlbergian stage six in moral reasoning, and they are necessarily involved at this stage.

Kohlberg's list of sixth stage principles was not drawn up from his knowledge of the history of ethics but from his own questionnaire data. He said that the following were invariably associated with sixth stage reasoning:

1. Justice,
2. Reciprocity and equality of human rights,
3. Respect for the dignity of human beings as individual persons,
4. The sacredness of human life represented in individuals,
5. Impersonality and universality of judgment,
6. Benevolence, the welfare of others.[2]

The conspicuous absence of freedom and love may be due to the particular dilemmas Kohlberg used to gather "data," to sampling error, or to the conduct of research in contrived situations. At any rate, justice, reciprocity, and respect were the only principles Kohlberg would accept at stage six, and he tried to reduce these to justice.[3] His search for the formal principles embedded in the cognitive processes of mature moral reasoning required the elimination of principles that were not content-free. On the other hand, Kant thought truth-telling, promise-keeping, and correcting previous wrongs could be proven universally valid on formal grounds alone. It is more likely that all moral principles and human rights are content-free.

A specification of moral principles to establish the general moral context for questions of human rights in education would be incomplete without explicit attention to the values inherent in the Judeo-Christian tradition. Their theological context makes it difficult to abstract them in a publicly defensible, objective manner. Perhaps

---

[2] Lawrence Kohlberg, "The Child as a Moral Philosopher," *Psychology Today* (September, 1968); reprinted in *Moral Education*, ed. by B.I. Chazan and J.F. Soltis (New York: Teachers College Press, 1973), pp. 131-143.

[3] Lawrence Kohlberg, "Stages of Moral Development as a Basis for Moral Education," *Moral Education: Interdisciplinary Approaches*, ed. by C. Beck, B.S. Crittenden, and E.V. Sullivan (Toronto: University of Toronto Press, 1971), pp. 62-66.

something can be learned from the Ten Commandments if the first four theological principles are omitted:

5. Honor your father and your mother,
6. You shall not kill,
7. You shall not commit adultery,
8. You shall not steal,
9. You shall not bear false witness against your neighbor,
10. You shall not covet your neighbor's house;
    you shall not covet your neighbor's wife,
    or his man servant, or his maid servant,
    or anything else that is your neighbor's.[4]

These can be subsumed within the previous list. Truth-telling stands behind the ninth commandment, as does not hurting others, which also lies behind the injunction against murder. Stealing seems to violate a law rather than a principle, but in any case the point is included in respect for persons. One does not take things from a respected person without asking permission. The rule against adultery can be subsumed within the principle of promise-keeping, for the marriage vow includes the promise to forswear all others. The rule against envy can also be subsumed within the principle about respect for persons.

On the one hand, these so-called commandments appear to be a set of moral rules formulated by Moses that are not as general as the principles already stated. They are like Kohlbergian stage four statements that can be expressed more abstractly and universally in so-called sixth stage reasoning. From this perspective it is easy to see how Jesus was able to claim there were only two commandments, one theological, the other to replace the six quoted commandments.[5] If one loved one's neighbor as oneself, he would neither kill him, lie about him, nor steal his things or spouse. This suggests that love is a sixth stage principle.

On the other hand, Buber said the sixth through ninth command-

---

4 *Exodus*, ch. 20. Revised Standard Version.
5 *Matthew*, ch. 22: 39-40.

ments concern the protection of life, marriage, property, and social honor, which are "basic goods and basic rights of personal existence."[6] Moses seems to have written the first formulation of human rights.

III. Ultimate Values and Human Dignity

The attempts by Kohlberg and Jesus to reduce everything to an ultimate value represents a moral and theoretical necessity. Moral choices often require a unique juxtaposition of several principles and force a decision between principles. One has to decide which is most relevant to the specific situation. For example, granting extra funds for compensatory education takes money away from other uses and thus depends on believing that equal opportunity is more important than the freedom of other children to compete on existing grounds. Similarly, opponents of busing to achieve racial balance in schools believe freedom to attend the school of one's choice is more important than the effort to establish equal conditions of learning. That is, two equally rational people can disagree about what should be done in a specific situation, even when both are reasoning at "stage six." They cannot both be right. There is something wrong, too, when one looks around for principles to support a preconceived choice rather than examining the principles to discover one's obligations. This unsatisfactory state of affairs leads moral philosophers to seek the most basic principle. If they can be arranged in a hierarchy, the problem of choosing between principles is resolved, for one merely decides things in terms of the more fundamental principle.

For example, when Jesus reduced the last six commandments to one, he found the ultimate principle at the core of his ethics. The reduction is reported in the fifth chapter of Matthew's account. About killing, he said not to be angry at all with another person. About adultery, he said one ought not even look lustfully at a person of the other gender. About false oaths, he said not to make any oaths at all. About stealing he said to give someone who wants your coat, your cloak, too. He implied that the conduct literally required by the

---

6 Martin Buber, *The Writings of Martin Buber*, ed. by Will Herberg (New York: Meridian Books, 1956), p. 195.

commandments is overt behavior, but what matters is the subjective intention. So he said that if one had the right subjective intention, i.e., if he loved his neighbor, all the things required by the laws of Moses would follow.

If one is formulating an argument for the justification of moral principles, it is theoretically convenient and parsimonious if the justification of the first principle facilitates the justification of the other principles. After one justifies loving one's neighbor as oneself, for example, it is easy to justify rules about lying, stealing, killing, etc. Loving one's neighbors involves an emotional structure of affection for them, but respect for persons also includes a structural awareness of their existence tinged with admiration and awe. This in turn is founded upon a sense of their personal dignity. Kant's idea of a good will was a retreat to moral motivation as such, for it made a first principle out of wanting to do the right thing, or duty.

There are at least three other candidates for the ultimate principle in philosophy of education. Peters' argument for the necessity for principles is based on equality, which therefore seems to be his first if not ultimate principle.[7] The second option is Dewey's idea, "The only ultimate value which can be set up is just the process of living itself."[8] His lifetime penchant for attacking absolutes and ultimates did not prevent him from declaring his own ultimate value without argument, and it is in fact crucial to his answers to questions of freedom in education, democracy in the classroom, etc. The third principle is utility, i.e., the greatest happiness of the greatest number, but when one adds the necessary "excluding no one" it leaves utilitarianism and becomes a eudaemonism based on universal rights like Jefferson's "unalienable right to life, liberty, and the pursuit of happiness." Then an act is right if it promotes happiness, but the principle becomes a criterion of value when it is decided that something has value in proportion to the happiness it produces, including life itself. This leads to a value judgment that a life without happiness is meaningless and not worth living. This is not true. One's life is valuable even if one is not happy.

---

[7] R.S. Peters, *Ethics and Education* (London: Allen & Unwin, 1966), pp. 120-126.

[8] *Democracy and Education*, p. 281.

This criticism can also be made of the love principle. It is not true that an action is right if it is motivated by love. Some people do great harm to others by acting on love. To redefine love to save the principle is intellectually dishonest. Acceptance of the principle, moreover, can also lead to a judgment that a life without love is meaningless and not worth living. This is not true. Paul was wrong. One's life is valuable even without love.

If a person's life is valuable even without love or happiness, it is because the very process of living is more fundamental than "happy living" or "loving living," and Dewey's claim is superior. Living itself is so valuable it is an added luxury to have love and happiness, too. The unhappy, unloving life still has most of the value of living and is worth living. That is merely to say that the principles of Jesus and Jefferson can become misused to make one think otherwise because they are insufficiently fundamental. They are not so basic as Dewey's, which gets down to bedrock, as it were.

How crucial this is to moral decisions can be illustrated in the case of the terminally ill. The person who is terminally ill and can no longer be happy or love others nevertheless has life. This life is still valuable for its own sake. It is right to prolong it. People detained in asylums because of mental deficiency or incompetency might be unable to be happy, but their lives are still valuable. Thus living is closer than happiness or love to the ultimate value.

The progression in this line of reasoning might become clearer through an examination of some quotations from Kohlberg in which he illustrated the stages in cognitive development in moral reasoning by showing how the value of life is defined in each:

1. The value of a human life is confused with the value of physical objects and is based on the social status or physical attributes of its possessor.

2. The value of a human life is seen as instrumental to the satisfaction of the needs of its possessor or of other persons.

3. The value of a human life is based on the empathy and affection of family members and others toward its possessor.

4. Life is conceived as sacred in terms of its place in a categorical moral or religious order of rights and duties.

5. Life is valued both in terms of its relation to community welfare and in terms of life being a universal right.

6. Belief in the sacredness of human life as representing a universal human value of respect for the individual.[9]

These statements show the argument is "stage six" and allow for its extension. Because living itself is so basic a value, there is a universal obligation to support any instance of human life. This means living is a human right, a right possessed by all human beings simply because they are alive.

The theoretical problem is to discuss the "sacredness" of human life in non-religious language. If one argues correctly that euthanasia, for example, is morally wrong because the terminally ill person has the right to live, it is not immediately credible because of the finality of the illness. The point is made in one of the statements Kohlberg quoted: "A human life takes precedent over any other moral or legal value, whoever it is. A human life has inherent value whether or not it is valued by a particular individual." Because human living has intrinsic value, it is right to continue it for its own sake.

The intrinsic value of human living is a special case of the intrinsic value of living, which nonhuman animals and plants also do, and this is merely a special case of the intrinsic value of existing, which non-living things also do. The duty to respect all living things because of the intrinsic value of their living is therefore a special case of the more fundamental principle to respect the existence of all things because each has its own value.

An action is right if it enables existing things to persevere in their being. One ought to let things be what they are, and who they are, in the flow of their becoming what their possibilities allow them to be. An action is right if it lets existing things be. The chief commandment is not to love one's neighbor but to love everything that exists, i.e., to love the universe insofar as one knows it.

---

[9] Quoted in Chazan and Soltis, p. 136.

The fundamental obligation to let things be supports the moral principles stated at lower levels of abstraction in the way the principles of Jesus and Dewey underlie them. Standard ethics does not include obligations to nonhuman living things like bears, puppies, crocodiles, pine trees, and rare and endangered species of flora and fauna, but the technologizing of the planet requires a new ethics of right and wrong regarding the treatment of all living creatures. Similarly, if the love for living things does not include obligations to the earth, sky, sea, rivers, rocks, hills, and the wind, the technologizing of the planet requires a new ethics of right and wrong regarding nonliving but existing things based upon an appreciation of their qualities. Perhaps the technological society in general and the technological consciousness in particular should adopt as an ultimate principle a respect for the existence of the things that are.

The claim about the intrinsic value of all existing things, however, is a principle of value, not moral value. It concerns good and bad, not right or wrong as these words have been ordinarily understood. It is a principle of value, not of morality. It is axiological, not deontological. If moral conduct is restricted to the interhuman domain, then the most fundamental moral principle would pertain to the relations between people. Then the claim that respect for persons is the most basic principle should be grounded in the intrinsic value of human living. The ultimate moral, or deontological, principle is grounded in the ultimate value, or axiological, principle when one claims that people should be respected because of the dignity of the human being as such.

One can value the dignity intrinsic to a human being without loving him, but one cannot love him without appreciating his or her unique value. The most fundamental moral principle is not love of one's neighbor but concern for the dignity of the individual person because this can be founded in the final claim that each person has his own value and dignity.

Intuitionism, rationalism, and empiricism have failed as theories of value because they have tried to answer the question of how we know values. This reifies "values" and the concern for knowing them ignores learning them. Because values are not self-subsisting entities, it is necessary to begin with valuable things and then ascertain how one becomes aware of valuable things. This involves becoming aware of their qualities through perceptual consciousness of them. One does not learn that each person has his or her own value and dignity by reasoning, not even through "sixth stage reasoning," but through the cumulative experience of multitudes of people, each of whom does in fact have his or her own value and dignity.

This may result in a positive, affectionate orientation toward others, but the ultimate principle cannot be to love others because this would consider the loving consciousness in narcissistic isolation from the beloved thing in an extremely complicated paradox. It puts the cart before the horse, as it were, because such love is the product of the discovery of the value and dignity of others, and the last thing one wants to do when one loves others is to focus attention on one's own subjective feelings. Such love is the outcome of experiences of the value and dignity of others similar to the way in which becoming aware of the qualities of existing things enables one to value them and come to love the world. For this reason the ultimate ethical principle that obligates one to act in accordance with human dignity is based on the value of all things that exist.

In any case, values cannot be learned through reasoning alone. There are ethical theories that instead of reasoning rely upon feelings, attitudes, character traits, and virtues, e.g., serenity, love, honesty, and industriousness, respectively. The development of these other characteristics in the realm of affectivity is a necessary condition of the adequate conceptualization of moral principles. It may even be valid to claim with Prichard that moral philosophy is based on a mistake.[10] At best it can help articulate at the so-called sixth stage what one already understands pre-theoretically as the outcome of moral living. One learns to value things by becoming aware of their qualitative characteristics on the level of perceptual consciousness. This axiological principle therefore underlies the deontological principle that one ought to treat each person according to his or her own value and dignity.

---

[10] H.A. Prichard, "Does Moral Philosophy Rest on a Mistake," *Mind* 21 (1912), reprinted in A.I. Meldon, ed., *Ethical Theories* (Englewood Cliffs: Prentice-Hall, 1955), pp. 469-481.

These foundational matters will be explicated more fully within appropriate educational contexts, where it will be seen that the things necessary to enhance the value and dignity of each human being as a human being are universal moral obligations. If the obligations to others are emphasized, they should be called "moral principles," but if the others' claims upon oneself are emphasized, they should be called "human rights."

IV. The Theoretical Approach

This study in the ethical dimensions of education is therefore a theoretical investigation of human rights in education. To contribute to educational theory understood as the theory of pedagogy, its methodology is guided primarily by the effort to be as reasonable as possible about questions emerging from educational practice in a technological society that concern human dignity.

The objective is to clarify the questions, sort out the contexts of their origin, understand and conceptualize the relevant educational phenomena, and find ethically adequate solutions to the questions. To achieve this aim, each chapter will conform as closely as possible to the following format:

Introduction,
I. Elucidation of the educational question,
II. Analysis of the question's moral term,
III. Justification of it as a human right,
IV. Resolution of the educational question,
Conclusion.

These first two chapters have already employed the general format of elucidating the question of the chapter, analyzing its relevant terms, justifying a substantive recommendation, and returning to the question to resolve it.

The approach is "inductive" in the sense that it begins a chapter with the educational question before resorting to the moral principle, then the specific human right is defined and justified in the educational sphere after the context is clarified through the analysis of the relevent moral terms. The consideration of the moral principle as a human right enables the resolution of the educational question to be made in terms of human dignity in as reasonable a manner as possible to attain the maximum objectivity possible.

To avoid the deductive approach, this chapter was restricted to illustrating "sixth stage" reasoning in an attempt to show how moral principles are used. It has not discussed or justified the moral principles of freedom, equality, fraternity, and human dignity as human rights. If these were first elaborated and then applied deductively to the educational problem, intellectual energy would be devoted to endless justification of the universal obligations that is more usefully directed to the educational questions themselves. Most of the discussion would have occurred outside of the educational domain to resolve philosophical questions, thereby allowing the educational questions to go begging.

By beginning each chapter with the educational question, the methodology is allowed to develop within theoretical reflection on the question. This lets the structure, content, and criteria of the theory develop in response to its requirements. This insures that the characteristics of the theory are largely determined by the phenomena of education in conjunction with the moral principles of so-called sixth stage reasoning, i.e., in domain-specific ways. The deductive approach begins in another domain, invokes its criteria of good theorizing, then imposes its methodology a priori on educational phenomena, rather like giving a ready-made suit to an odd-shaped man and asking him to change his shape to fit the suit. The approach through the educational questions tailors the suit to fit the man, as it were.

When Dewey said that education is the laboratory where philosophical distinctions are tested, he indicated that even his theory imposed those distinctions a priori on the educational domain in an ideological manner, but he did not indicate how his theory could fail such a test. On the other hand, it can be claimed that the approach through the educational questions makes education the laboratory wherein philosophical distinctions are discovered. Some very recalcitrant ethical problems can be resolved in the educational situation because of the relative simplicity of its relatively controlled context. For example, within the reflection on the question of freedom in education it is obviously necessary to justify freedom as a human right in an intellectually tenable way because this is found to be the most fundamental way to understand the phenomenon of moral freedom.

It is standard procedure in any of the sciences to develop the kind of theory required by the phenomena investigated. Criteria of good theory are not content-free but depend upon the class of phenomena concerned and the purposes of the theory. They are domain-dependent. The previous categorization of educational theory as philosophy of education has sometimes brought it a superficial, spurious intellectual respectability at the expense of imposing the doctrines and methods of the academic discipline of philosophy upon educational phenomena. Whatever value this has had, there is also the question of intellectual responsibility regarding educational questions. No theorist in any domain can afford to let an a priori methodology from another domain stand between him and the phenomena being investigated. Because the theoretician needs to be primarily curious about the class of phenomena belonging to his own domain and strongly committed to conceptualize them in ways most adequate to the phenomena and intersubjectively communicable, the inductive approach is necessary in any disciplined study of things in the world.

The approach through the questions of educational practice also facilitates the interdisciplinary study of education. For example, although historians and sociologists of education have been investigating problems of equal educational opportunity, and psychologists have been investigating discipline and punishment in schools, they frequently fail to recognize that these are questions of justice. The concrete approach through educational questions allows for interrelations to be made with these other approaches to the study of education. The focus directly upon educational questions therefore seems to be an absolute necessity in the study of education.

Conclusion

Human dignity is threatened by the encroachments of technology, particularly in respect to confidence in the capacity to know the world and to act as a moral agent. It is the school's responsibility, however,

to develop reason and moral sensibility, i.e., to develop the intellectual capacities that result from the acquisition of the theoretical
knowledge of the arts, crafts, trades, sports, professions and academic disciplines when it is learned in conditions conducive to the
development of the moral characteristics intrinsic to the school as an
institution of learning.

The ethical problems of educational practice ought therefore be
reasoned through with as much objectivity as possible. This means
that the questions of pedagogy should be considered as moral questions and reasoned through in terms of universal obligations
expressed as human rights. No ethical, political, social, religious, or
psychological ideology should be imposed upon these educational
questions, for these are manipulative, part of the problem, and an
affront to human dignity.

The educational questions deserve to be investigated and resolved
in terms of the value intrinsic to education as a unique human
undertaking, i.e., in terms of the human rights actually inherent in the
educational process itself. They will therefore be investigated as
belonging to a particular, unique domain that merits an indigenous
theoretical effort to understand itself in terms of its own inherent
normative characteristics.

Chapter Three

EDUCATION TO FREEDOM AS A HUMAN RIGHT

> A time of domination by authority will call out as response the desirability of great individual freedom; one of disorganized individual activities the need of social control as an educational aim.
> Dewey[1]

Fluctuations in educational ideologies between the emphasis on freedom or authority will continue as long as freedom is defined negatively and authority is presumed to oppose it. When freedom seems to be the absence of restraints imposed by someone in authority, each is posed as the negation of the other, and the pendulum swings back and forth between progressive and basic educational ideologies. Defining authority as the power to negate freedom and freedom as the negation of the negation, however, is adolescent. The technologizing of the planet requires a much more fundamental consideration of freedom as a positive, contributory aspect of the moral agency essential to human dignity.

I. The Question of Freedom in Education

The question of freedom in education is frequently raised in oppo-

---

[1] John Dewey, *Democracy and Education*, p. 112.

56

sition to authority, but this is neither its most significant feature nor its justification. To the contrary, when it is raised to oppose authority in a generalized anti-authoritarianism, it is often a self-serving ploy that has no justification at all. Personal involvement is necessary to want to raise the question, but this makes it difficult to consider it objectively. The personal ideology can be transcended by asking the questions of freedom and authority together to seek a balance that acknowledges rights and duties on both sides of the pedagogic relation.

The questions of freedom and authority in education, however, are not coordinate. The word "freedom" is a good word. It bears a positive, warm emotional tone when used rhetorically. To raise an objection against restraints imposed by authority in the name of freedom virtually assures that one will be perceived as being on the right side, regardless of the truth of the matter. The word "authority," on the other hand, has come to bear a negative, cold emotional tone. Exhortations to respect duly constituted authority are no longer heard. Everyone is for freedom, whether they are on the political left, right, or center, but someone who is "for" authority is perceived as conservative *ultra non plus*.

The question of freedom is raised to obtain more of it, but questioning authority desires less.

The lack of symmetry may be more obvious in substantive matters. Public funds used to support state educational systems furnish free educational facilities, but no one is free to refuse this free access to formal education. Zealots of freedom question the legitimacy of the authority of the state to compel school attendance, but the demise of the deschooling movement shows that the authority of the state to provide schooling with compulsory attendance cannot be successfully challenged. On the other hand, the question of freedom in the classroom cannot arise unless there is compulsory attendance. Otherwise the fitting answer to such questioning is to tell someone they chose to be in class of their own free will and they can leave if they do not like it.

The question of authority leads into macroscopic perspectives, but questions of freedom are relatively individualistic, raised when one's own "freedom" is in jeopardy. It is frequently an ad hoc response to particular infringements, without questioning the authority of the state to establish and maintain public schools or the authority of the teacher to be a teacher. That is, when a child or youth raises the question of freedom in the classroom, it is seldom raised on the larger scale that questions how classrooms in general should be conducted. It is for something specific, such as more freedom to move around in class, to be able to talk to other students, to use different instructional materials, to do something different from what everyone else is doing, to be less restricted by the time schedule, or to do something without having to ask permission first. These are requests for inchoate civil liberties: freedom of action, freedom of speech, freedom to read, freedom of assembly and freedom of the press. Their connection with learning and face-to-face relations with other students, however, involves the moral context.

When the question of freedom in education is raised because someone wants to be free to say, think, learn, or do something, it concerns freedom in the moral sense of the word. Whether it is accompanied by generalized claims about freedom of speech, assembly, action, etc., depends partly upon a level of cognitive development not widely prevalent in primary and secondary schools. The questions are, rather, about how much freedom students should have to say, read, write, and learn what they want. To what extent should they be free to do what they want? These are moral questions, for they implicate freedom as a moral principle.

It is not the same thing with authority. Teachers may indeed have legitimate authority to restrict students' freedoms in these respects, but whether they do or not, authority is not a moral principle. It can be exercised with moral responsibility, however, and is therefore a moral phenomenon related to moral principles.

The questions of freedom and authority are therefore not symmetrical because only the former can be raised in the name of a moral principle as such. This is the basis for the favorable connotations of the word and the sense of rightness that tends to accompany claims for freedom. Because authority is not itself a moral principle but can be exercised in conjunction with moral principles, it is always vulnerable to criticism originating in moral indignation. Advocacy of freedom is not. Moral outrage may be expressed against permissiveness or anarchy, but not against freedom. Be that as it may, the question of freedom in education is a moral question. It requires a moral answer.

For this reason, only after the question of freedom in education is properly put can the genuine question of authority arise. Properly understood, however, the former becomes the latter. When a pupil raises a question about the desirability of more freedom in the classroom, this implicitly questions the authority of the teacher. The question could be over some triviality, or pedagogic oversight, and the teacher might readily concede the point. Then there is no questioning of authority. If the point is not conceded and the pupil persists, the question of freedom becomes the question of the teacher's authority, logically and theoretically if not in fact. The questions of freedom and authority in education are the same question.

The consideration of either without the other deals with an abstraction. Once abstracted from the living totality of the classroom situation, the questions are no longer those originally asked, which are about the freedom of the pupil in the context of the authority of the teacher, and about the authority of the teacher in the context of the freedom of the pupil, or about both of these simultaneously. The original questions are about freedom and authority in the classroom as corresponding elements of the pedagogic relation.

At any rate, the questions are distinctly educational questions, indigenous to classrooms and schools as institutions of teaching and learning. They are mutually and reciprocally implicated in classroom situations. They are not about authority in society as it may be exercised by officers of the law, referees in sports, employers on jobs, or doctors in hospitals. Nor are they about freedom in society in the political, economic, or social systems. They are about authority in the classroom and about moral freedom in education.

II. Meanings of the Word "Freedom"

If the freedom to move, speak, write, read, and learn in classrooms concerns freedom in the moral sense of the word, i.e., moral freedom, it ought to be distinguished from other senses of the word and justified as a moral principle.

The most important distinction is between descriptive and normative senses. The word is used in the descriptive sense when the freedom-talk is about whether "human nature," "man," or "human beings" are free or not. It involves concepts and questions of free will, determinism, destiny, fatalism, and psychological and sociological conditioning. The normative senses are on a wholly different plane when the freedom-talk is about what ought to be, such as economic, political, social, and religious freedom as well as moral freedom. Because the latter are often obfuscated by the presence of beliefs concerning the former, the former will be considered first.

When "freedom" is used descriptively, it can refer to physical, physiological, psychological, phenomenological, intellectual, or metaphysical freedom. It is correct to say a person is physically free to leap tall buildings at a single bound but is unable to do so. If someone says they are not free to do what they are physically unable to do, the source of the apparent lack of freedom is their own free choice of a project that is physically impossible. Being unable to do things is not an absence of physical freedom. This is indeed lost when one is thrown into chains, put into a strait-jacket, incarcerated, trussed up with ropes by a burglar or kidnapper, etc. It makes sense, however, for paraplegics to say they are not free to do things others do. This means that freedom in the physical sense of the word is co-extensive with the kinds of things ordinary people ordinarily do. At least we can say a person is physically free in the absence of physical handicaps and actual physical restraints upon his body.

Freedom at the physiological level is more complicated. Digestion, respiration, and circulation, for example, occur at the prompting of the involuntary nervous system without conscious intervention, organically, perhaps mechanistically. Pavlov's dog was not free to refuse to salivate at the sound of the bell, nor at the sight of raw meat. Only a limited determinism can be argued, however, for although thirst, hunger and fatigue are "caused" physiologically, the person decides when to yield to them. He or she also decides what to eat, drink, and where to sleep. There is no doubt at all that anyone can eat, drink, and sleep less than needed. Or more. People who unknowingly receive morphine in hospitals do not become addicted, and nicotine addicts can always choose to live with the withdrawal symptoms until they disappear or seek medical advice to enable them to do so. The point is not whether there is physiological freedom in more complicated, narcotic addictions, but rather that if mild addictions can be transcended by a free choice, then the normal organic functioning of the healthy individual leaves even more room for freedom. Because the bodily needs that rise into awareness can be delayed, channeled, over-indulged or suppressed, some degree of physiological freedom can be attributed.

This is not to deny the reality of physiological conditioning. It shows that physiological causation can be transcended. More importantly, however, it shows that psychological and sociological conditioning must be less deterministic because they do not have the physiological basis. For example, Freud's theory of the "defense mechanisms" applies only to neurotic people and is accompanied by the talking-cure that enables them to transcend their psychological conditioning and become free in the psychological sense.

It can be said that someone is intellectually free if they can reason out a course of action, pursue complicated goals, and express and maintain beliefs appropriate to their projects. Intellectual freedom is manifested in the works of art, theatre, literature, architecture, science, technology, politics, and industry that make up the human heritage. Freedom in the intellectual sense is therefore partly a descriptive concept referring to the structure of mental processes involved in reasoning and mental creation. It is also a normative principle about a social climate tolerant of idiosyncratic and/or unpopular beliefs. If one believes in intellectual freedom one believes people ought to be free to believe in God, or that there is no god, or in witchcraft, or Santa Claus, or the flat earth, or the *Genesis* story, without persecution if this is where the evidence leads them.

Intellectual freedom overlaps freedom in the metaphysical sense because the mind, or intelligence or reason, is a central topic in metaphysics. More generally, freedom in the metaphysical sense depends on concepts like free will, chance, and determinism. There have been a few significant expressions of complete determinism: Stoicism, Spinoza, deism, Marx. Each of these has a path that leads to freedom. One should learn everything one can about the determinate world so that one can live in conformity to what will happen. As if one were intellectually free to do so. As if one were free to do otherwise. As if the freedom of consciousness that everyone experiences were genuine freedom. As if Kant were right to claim we are empirically bound but transcendentally free.

"Freedom" is also used in the descriptive sense to refer to economic, political, and social freedom. Economic freedom involves gainful employment of a desired kind and access to the goods and services available in society. Political freedom involves the right to vote, form political parties, and run for public office, whereas social freedom involves freedom to move about, live where one wants, "vertical mobility," and access to desirable people socially. The use of the concept of freedom to decide if a particular society embodies economic, political, or social freedom, however, uses a normative principle about what ought to be to make third-person evaluations about what is. Freedom in the political, social, and economic senses is essentially a normative principle, part of a social, political philosophy that often supplies elements for political platforms about what ought to be.

The moral sense of the word refers to the freedom to think about what one ought to do and then to go ahead and act on the basis of one's reasoned judgment. It is essential that there be freedom in all three aspects: reasoning, deciding, acting. It is necessary that whatever reasoning processes are involved are one's own, that the deciding be voluntary, and that the action be their result for it to be said to be done freely out of one's own moral conviction of what was the right thing to do. One would deny that someone acted freely in the moral sense of the word if she or he had not been free to act in accordance with her or his conscience, i.e., if someone violated his or her conscience due to pressure, cultism, or compulsion.

This does not imply that what anyone subjectively believes to be right is objectively right. It means only that freedom cannot be ascribed to an act unless it is in accordance with one's conscience, with the moral standards one does have, regardless of what they are. Merely because something is done freely does not mean it is morally correct, and simply because something is morally wrong does not mean that it was not done freely. Poor judgment, like poor taste, is quite compatible with freedom.

The reasoning processes, however, have to be about what ought to be done, about duties, obligations, or about doing the right thing, to

anything, for it is freedom in the moral sense. It is freedom to do the right thing.

Confusion on this point can result from the consideration of the one principle in isolation from others, for this fanaticizes consciousness, like staring at one color too long. To claim freedom of thought and action for oneself necessarily includes the acceptance of a set of moral rules or principles, such as those specified in the previous chapter or their equivalent. It is these other principles that channel one's choices within the parameters of doing the right thing. If one claims freedom of thought and action, furthermore, one is assuming an obligation to think with reasons that can be presented to others when the occasion requires it. In other words, the freedom that can rightfully be claimed for oneself is only the same that can be granted to everyone, including the person whom one might want to punch in the nose, but to whom one does not want to grant the freedom to punch back. The other person's freedom limits one's own. These limits are entailed by the very idea of freedom as a universal right. If it is universal, it is equal freedom.

That moral freedom is equal freedom is extremely important for the educational question. Contrast with another viewpoint will accentuate its importance. The distinguished philosopher of law H.L.A. Hart argued in a very famous essay that if there were any human rights at all, there had to be the most fundamental right that he stated as the equal right to freedom.[3] He did not claim there were any human rights, only that if there were then there was the equal right to freedom. The precise wording is extremely critical, and Hart's logic can be shown by a simple substitution. If everyone has an equal right to water, this is compatible with variable distributions of water, as long as everyone gets the minimal amount of water to which everyone has an equal right. Some people could get a great deal of water, others very little, yet their equal right to water would be honored. The words "the equal right to water" mean the right to some water, an indefinite amount. The words "the right to equal water," however, imply the same amount of water is everyone's due.

In other words, the logic of human rights does not work as Hart

---

[3] H.L.A. Hart, "Are there any Natural Rights?" *The Philosophical Review* (1955).

thought. To say something is a human right is to say that everyone has the right. It adds nothing to say that everyone has an equal right. A right is a right. It does add something to say that the right that everyone has is to equal freedom. Hart's claim leaves it open to there being different amounts or degrees of freedom by different people, just as the "equal right" to life is compatible with some people living longer, and just as in eighteenth century classical liberalism, which is not immune to the Marxist critique of being an implicit apology for capitalism rather than a statement of human rights. The logic of a human right is that everyone has it equally, of course, and it is not incorrect to point out as Hart has done that human rights are equal rights. This does not go far enough, however, for one should claim that everyone has the equal right to equal freedom.

The present argument also begins with the claim that if there are any human rights, then there is at least the one human right to moral agency, and then the latter is also argued to be the case. Then it is claimed that moral freedom is a human right, and the analysis of freedom in the moral sense shows it is necessarily "equal freedom."

Agitations for freedom are often self-regarding, although moral conduct is characteristically other-regarding. The legitimate situation is not to argue for freedom as such, but to want to do the right thing and then claim the freedom to do it because it is understood to be the right thing and morally obligatory. One is morally correct not to argue for freedom but for the framework in which one can do the right thing.

The reason this is true is that even after one accepts the principle of freedom, one is exactly where one was before, confronted with the necessity to reflect and decide upon one's obligations in particular situations. This is why freedom in the moral sense of the word entails doing the right thing.

No moral principle can do otherwise.

IV. Education to Freedom

Because freedom as a moral principle is justified by the right to moral agency, questions of freedom in education should be resolved within the perspective of the gradual development of moral agency. If moral agency is a characteristic of adult members of the species, without which one would hardly be human, then its development is one of the important aims of education.

What schools can do in this regard is much broader than the parameters of moral freedom. Physical and physiological health are important to the development of moral freedom because the energy available to someone in good physical condition and who can move freely helps overcome the languor that frequently impedes the assumption of responsibility for one's choices. The inclusion of sport in the curriculum promotes the development of physical and physio-logical freedom, which, if not a necessary condition of moral agency, at least facilitates it. Psychological health is also important, for a school system that induces psychologically caused behavior, for example, in developing neurotic defense mechanisms, compulsive or conditioned behavior, inhibitions, and lack of frustration tolerance, is functioning in opposition to the development of moral agency. These emotional disabilities have to be transcended, for it facilitates the growth of moral agency to be mentally free to consider alternative courses of action on a reasonable basis. Whatever the school does in respect to vocational and citizenship education that promotes eco-nomic and political freedom in adulthood also facilitates moral agency. In short, most of the ordinary school curriculum provides knowledge and skills that are a positive help to the growth of moral agency.

This context should not be forgotten when considering the educa-tional questions of freedom in the moral sense. Of special importance is the fact that although fully responsible moral agency is a character-istic of adult human beings and therefore lies outside the educational sphere, moral agency as such is a matter of degree. Even the very small child can be responsible for feeding himself, dressing himself, walking to school by himself, and so on. Children and youth, how-ever, cannot be fully responsible for themselves as a matter of defini-tion. It is part of the concept of the child or youth to be partly dependent upon responsible adults. It is also the legal situation wherever separate juridical procedures such as children's or juvenile courts are established in accordance with the concept of diminished responsibility.

This means that the freedom that should be given to children and youth in school should be appropriate to the degree of responsibility that can be undertaken. Too much freedom can result in anxiety and a flight from freedom; too little encourages passivity and an escape from responsibility. Because the moral agency that rightfully belongs to adults is acquired gradually through the progressive acceptance of responsibility, the progressive enlargement of freedom in education to enable this assumption of responsibility is necessary. It would not, however, have to occur in schools. It can be argued that the school's contribution should be limited to the knowledge and skills of the normal curriculum and that the development of responsibility is the task of the parents, who have a better grasp of the kinds of responsibilities their children are ready to assume than teachers ordinarily possess. On the other hand, it can be argued that the very existence of schools has induced parents to be pedagogically negligent and that their efforts are insignificant unless reinforced by the appropriate exercise of responsibility in schools. This requires a certain amount of freedom.

Their resolution is now very simple if the genuine questions of freedom in the classroom in the moral sense concern the desire to move around, talk with others, find different materials, study something different, set one's own learning tasks and goals, and the like. Students should always have as much freedom as they can bear responsibly. Only the individual teacher is able to decide how much responsibility can be delegated to a particular class, bearing in mind that the students still have to do the right thing, which is to accomplish the objectives pre-specified in the syllabus or curriculum guide. It would seem, however, that the teacher is correct to err on the side of too much freedom because the sphere of responsibility should be progressively enlarged, and whether particular students will rise to the occasion cannot be predicted. Youth also have to be free to learn to refuse responsibility for which they do not feel ready.

It is not true that people become moral agents overnight on their twenty-first birthday. Because they become them by degrees, gradually, correlatively with the extent of the responsibility they have learned to bear, the degree of freedom the pupil deserves as a matter of human right is that which gives him responsibilities he can manage successfully. By the same token, the degree of structuring of the classroom by the teacher that the pupil also deserves as a matter of human right is that which reduces the responsibility to that which can be managed successfully.

The students in any given classroom are not equally able to assume responsibility for their actions and learning. Some are more responsible than others. One third-grade teacher might be able to give her class a great deal of freedom in a way that induces responsibility, whereas another can succeed with much less freedom. A tenth-grade English class might function well with more freedom than a tenth-grade mathematics class with the same students, and a tenth-grade class in one school might be ready for much more responsibility than another tenth-grade class in another school in another neighborhood. A given student might be able to assume more responsibility some times than others. Some days a given class can be more responsible than others. Much depends upon the teacher's uniqueness, charm, enthusiasm, verbal facility, warmth, and manifest affection for children and youth. In the final analysis, the question of how much of which kind of freedom is appropriate to develop moral agency can only be decided by particular teachers in particular classrooms in conjunction with particular instructional content and particular pupils. Any definite prescription is necessarily wrong and ideological in the pejorative sense.

It is probably not necessary for the progressive enlargement of responsibility to be continuous. Life is not that way outside of school, where responsibility is learned in household chores, in working situations after school and during vacations from school, during family crises, etc. If growth in the capacity to bear responsibility occurs in fits and starts, episodes of considerable freedom and responsibility interrelated with periods of structured learning would also effectively promote the development of moral agency. This is an empirical matter. It suffices to suggest that it is probably wrong to assume that students have a right to the maximum freedom they can manage in every classroom throughout their school career. That is an ideological error and fanatical. There is no evidence it is necessary. It seems reasonable to assume that moral agency will be developed if some classrooms sometimes function on the principle of implementing as much freedom as the students can manage.

The situation is analogous to the idea that all teachers should teach reading, which does not mean they are all teachers of reading. It means teachers of various subjects should be aware that learning a new subject includes learning how to read its textbooks and its literature, and that some instructional effort should be oriented toward helping students understand certain features of the writing to aid in its comprehension. Similarly, although it can be said that all teachers should promote the development of moral agency through allowing as much freedom in the classroom as can be borne responsibly, it does not have to be promoted all the time. They are not teachers of responsibility.

To use a different analogy, children have a right to food, but it does not promote physical health for them to be eating all the time. Because they have a right to freedom, it does not mean it would promote a healthy development of moral agency to be free all the time. It can destroy academic motivation because students go to classrooms expecting to learn something there, not to be free to do otherwise as if it were not a classroom. Not many students really want to waste their time.

Besides, teachers have other responsibilities, not only to their employers and to the public but also to the student's own cognitive growth. The student's right to cognitive education has higher priority than the right to the development of moral agency as far as the school is concerned because the latter can also occur outside of school. It should not be forgotten that the "freedom dimension" of the classroom is only the means to facilitate in a more humane way the acquisition of the knowledge and skills for which the classroom exists. This is why freedom and authority in education ought not be defined in opposition to each other.

They are mutually implicated in classrooms, and the basic question concerns the balance between them. Existing, possible solutions can be placed on a continuum from authoritarianism to permissivism:

A	B	C	D	E
$\longleftarrow$				$\longrightarrow$
Teacher-centered, absolute authority		Ordinary humane practice		Student-centered, *laissez-faire* freedom

Pure dictatorship and pure anarchy exist only in the imagination of someone dedicated to refuting traditionalism or progressivism, respectively. Most classrooms can be located somewhere near the middle of the continuum, depending upon the structure provided by the teacher and options left open for students. An intelligently conducted conventional classroom might be located at B, whereas an intelligently conducted open classroom might be placed at D, although even the former will have free time, and even the latter will include some teacher direction. The practice of beginning teachers is sometimes closer to A or E than it will be with experience, and teachers who combine the best aspects of traditional and progressive practice conduct classrooms near the middle at C.

One advantage of this kind of continuum is that it encompasses all possible viewpoints. All existing writings on the topic can be located somewhere on it. This takes the issue out of the abstract, ideological plane by considering the various views as possible classrooms and by suggesting there is considerable scope for the teacher's choice. This is important, for although students raise the question, in practice it is the teacher's responsibility to decide whether the more structured or more open approach is more conducive to the acquisition of knowledge and skills and the development of moral agency, and to establish the conditions of learning in the most productive way.

The continuum, however, might suggest that the extreme positions are somehow wrong in principle. To the contrary, every point on the continuum has its own validity. For example, kindergarten children can be subjected to a teacher-centered classroom at story time, and they love it, but they can also have free time consisting of a *laissez-faire* situation. If most of their activities are structured by an approach from the middle of the continuum, this does not mean that centrist views are better, except for those activities. Similarly, teaching in the graduate school can vary from the formal lecture to the student-led seminar, and neither is better except for accomplishing its own cognitive objectives. Similarly, twelfth-grade mathematics might very well lend itself to a fairly structured classroom, whereas seventh-grade social studies might be better with fairly open parameters. Different teachers find the classroom works better for them one way rather than another.

Ideologies about this frequently serve as psychological compensation. For example, the teacher who says he or she believes in furnishing a good bit of structure might in practice be much more open and free than another who advocates freedom but is somehow unaware of how much his or her classroom is dominated by his or her personality. Ideologies also serve the need for social approval, as when teachers say they maintain a classroom that is either more or less structured than they actually conduct in order to promote a good image of themselves. Most of the literature on these questions advocates one view as if it were equally applicable everywhere in education. This is ideological, fanatical, and doctrinaire. It is totalitarian regardless of the view recommended. Only demagogues can afford such mistakes. Practicing teachers cannot.

The teacher is correctly concerned with the question of how the pupil's freedom should be related to pedagogic authority in this subject at this age level with this many pupils in class on this particular day. Which position on the continuum will serve as the best framework for the strategy in this specific lesson? The teacher is also interested in the problem of the shifting optimum degree of freedom, i.e., when the classroom ought to be more structured, and when less. Several major shifts can be organized to occur within an hour. A practicing teacher cannot decide things once and for all, and maintain one view throughout a career, irrespective of experience and the changing complexion of the student body.

The continuum is like a rainbow. All the colors are beautiful. The selection of a position on it is like choosing colors when painting. They are all good. Each is useful and productive in some context. The master teacher, like the master painter, can work with all the colors in the spectrum and need not, like Picasso, have a "blue period," although this need not be ruled out. Nor does a teacher need a "favorite color," as if one could have a preference in how one taught that took precedence over the content of instruction and the particular idiosyncracies of the unique pupils in one's classroom. One can rejoice in freely exercising pedagogic skill in the varieties of structures conducive to the achievement of the several aims of education.

To develop moral agency, however, the approach should be chosen to correlate the practice of freedom with the existing mental processes of the child or youth. It cannot be assumed that they can become free to think and act without nurturing the relevant mental processes to moral responsibility. This involves conscious attention to the needs of other students, commitment to the classroom as a place of learning, simultaneous foresight into several goals or projects, adherence to a chosen project in the midst of other people working on other projects and in spite of unforeseen boredom and difficulty, and so on, depending upon the context. It cannot be assumed that certain stages of conscious control of one's thought and action simply emerge without special pedagogic influence, as Piaget seems to have assumed about cognitive processes. Nor could any stages be postulated, for the subsequent application would be less congruent with the child's development than the teacher's judgment based on experience with particular children.

In addition to being openly tolerant of the freedom of movement, thought, and discussion needed to facilitate learning, the teacher can promote the growth of responsibility by helping the continuing expansion of foresight. The child's orientation to the future is stretched out as she or he becomes able to work on projects that require progressively longer periods of time, and hence greater foresight in their inception. Because it is the commitment to the project that enables the assumption of responsibility for its accomplishment, the project has to be freely chosen in order to engage this sense of responsibility for it. Projects do not, however, have to be constructive projects, nor of the pupil's own invention, as Kilpatrick apparently desired, nor do they have to result from collective, student-teacher planning, as Dewey desired, nor do they have to be derived through individualized pupil-teacher conferences or contracted negotiations. They can be developed through these means, but the teacher can also give a choice from two or three specified projects or assignments of one kind or another. For example, when studying colonial America, everyone could study all thirteen colonies, and each child could also be asked to study the history and geography of one of the colonies in depth for committee work and/or an oral or written report. This is two choices, one for the colony and one for small group study or written or oral report. If it were also accompanied by the study of all thirteen for breadth, the depth study of any one of the colonies would help attain the relevant cognitive objective, i.e., to understand and value one's own country.

This kind of choice between teacher-specified options, practiced wherever the cognitive objectives of the curriculum allow, can do a great deal to promote the growth of the mode of consciousness characterized by the acceptance of responsibility for one's choices. Although these choices occur in the cognitive domain regarding learning tasks, rather than in the moral domain, the sense of responsibility for continuing in a chosen course of action and accomplishing a chosen task may be more significant to the growth of moral agency than more direct approaches because it maintains a basic harmony with the main goals of classrooms and does not risk a perversion of its values.

It is also possible that the questions of freedom in the classroom should not be understood literally but interpreted. Perhaps they overstate the point. If all the students in a class are given the same assignment, or the same work, or learning task, time after time, they can choose only to do it or not to do it. To many, this will not feel like a choice, particularly if classroom routines are established by a teacher with a strong personality. Then a student who wants to taste the reality of a choice has to "rebel." The practice of freedom through the presentation of several teacher-specified projects, on the other hand, promotes the feeling of the experience of freedom to the extent that the alternatives are devised on a cognitive level appropriate for a particular class. If this is not the kind of freedom asked for, it may nevertheless be what is wanted.

It is not true that a choice is worth having simply because it is freely made. A choice from a menu listing garbage and offal is a wretched dinner, regardless of how freely chosen either is, whereas few would complain if the only choice on the menu was prime roast of beef. If free choosing from among teacher-specified tasks does not fully engage the freedom of students, there are three alternatives to pursue. The area of knowledge might simply require extrinsic motivation, more freedom could be practiced, or the educative attractiveness of the specified projects could be improved.

There thus seem to be three pedagogical principles to insure that the moral responsibility correlative to freedom and moral agency as human rights is acquired in education. Wherever students can choose among several projects or tasks within a given domain, they should be allowed to do so. Whenever they cannot choose among projects in a given subject, they should be educated to do so. Whenever the projects, tasks, and assignments within an area prove unworkable, attention should be devoted to the development of educationally attractive projects.

Conclusion

The kind of freedom that belongs in the classroom is freedom in the moral sense of the word, modified to make it age-placed, sequential, and developmental. The justification of freedom as a universally valid moral principle is based in moral agency as a human right. Moral freedom is itself a human right, but a direct justification of it as such can involve ideological definitions of freedom inconsistent with its universality. It suffices for the purposes of educational theory to justify it indirectly as one of the necessary conditions of moral agency, which is manifestly a human right.

Moral agency is a human right no matter how one defines any moral principle or morality itself simply because the human being is a moral being. People live their lives within the perspective of right and wrong, of obligations and duty. The specific aspects of what it means to be a moral agent may vary from society to society, but moral agency is a cultural constant. It is not necessary to define moral agency for the purposes of educational theory except for the involvement of personal responsibility for one's conduct. What one should be responsible for can be defined within the parameters of the cognitive domain because it is freedom within classrooms devoted to cognitive learning that is the main concern.

It is, however, a peculiar characteristic of moral agents that they assume responsibility for their actions, including the responsibility of assuming and defining this responsibility. Part of the educational process itself, then, is becoming aware of the kinds of responsibilities that belong to the exercise of moral agency in a given, social, historical context. The parameters of adult responsibilities cannot in the final analysis be defined by philosophers, theologians, or psychologists, nor by legislators, magistrates, or therapists. They have to be defined by each human being. That is part of what it means to be an adult member of the species. It is the adults of the species who decide these things. It is part of what it means to be free in the moral sense. Freedom therefore belongs in the educational process to enable people to learn how to be responsible and gradually become adult.

At each age level, in each subject, and every day, children and youth ought to be allowed the freedom they can manage because they learn to be free by being responsible for progressively larger, more complicated things. Because it is a necessary condition of becoming a human being, such an education to freedom is a human right.

Chapter Four

AUTHORITY AND EQUAL FREEDOM IN EDUCATION

Freedom (independence from the constraints of another's will), insofar as it is compatible with the freedom of everyone else in accordance with a universal law, is the one sole and original right that belongs to every human being by virtue of his humanity.

Kant[1]

Kant's authority for the idea of equal freedom is invoked because of its omission in Kohlberg's explanation of stage six moral reasoning. Its educational significance is that the implementation of conditions of equal freedom can liberate an authoritarian regime or structure a permissive one. It is beyond ideology. This will show in the investigation of authority that is necessary because a defense of freedom cannot benefit students if it undermines the authority of the teacher.

I. Meanings of the Word "Authority"

There is a great difference between being in authority and being an authority. A teacher is put in authority in a classroom because he or she is an authority. The first usage corresponds to the question, Who is in authority? Who is in charge? The second to, Who is an authority

---

[1] Immanuel Kant, *The Metaphysical Elements of Justice*, Part I of *The Metaphysics of Morals*, tr. John Ladd (New York: Bobbs-Merrill, 1965), pp. 43-44.

on this topic? What is the teacher an authority on?

A teacher can conduct a well-managed classroom, exercising authority in the first sense excellently, even though she or he is barely competent in the content of instruction. It is logically possible. Similarly, a teacher can exercise authority in the second sense excellently, teaching the subject superlatively, without being able to control the class. This, too, is logically possible. The first gets everyone to behave, but does not teach them much. The second teaches much to those who do behave. The exercise of managerial authority is clearly different from the workings of cognitive authority.

Criticism of authoritarianism can be directed against either kind. When the teacher's managerial activities are allegedly too directive, the class is said to be "regimented" because of the loss of freedom of speech and action. Opposition to alleged authoritarianism in the cognitive sense, on the other hand, uses the words "regurgitation" and "indoctrination" to highlight the loss of intellectual freedom. A given teacher can be authoritarian in the managerial sense but libertarian in the cognitive, and vice-versa.

Managerial authority is exercised in society by officers of the law, magistrates, politicians, foremen, executives, employers, referees, umpires, parents, and baby-sitters. A magistrate or politician, for example, might also be an authority on the law, but they do not have to be great jurists to carry out their ascribed social functions related to the exercise of power for managerial control. Police officers have to know the law, but they do not have to exercise their reason on behalf of truth or justice. The features of these legitimated uses of power, consequently, cannot be abstracted from their contexts and applied to the classroom without losing the uniquely educative features of the classroom. Teachers do not have the same power. They simply are not policemen, magistrates, parents, or baby-sitters, and it does not help to adopt aspects of their roles as if their exercise of authority could be emulated without their social power. The similarity is that, like these other functionaries, the teacher is given the authority of the office.

Cognitive authority is exercised in society by golf and tennis "pros" who teach at country clubs, by coaches in all sports, by professional people such as doctors, dentists, lawyers, and engineers, by experts in various areas of industry, by editorial writers, by authors, and by university researchers when consulting off-campus. Authority in the cognitive sense is powerless, so to speak, for it is "obeyed" only by acts of free intellectual assent. Its "power" is non-coercive. Cognitive authority is the result of one's own achievement. Through arduous learning processes, plus talent, one establishes himself or herself as an authority in some domain or activity. Because the way in which the authority is exercised depends upon the kind of knowledge possessed, it would not help to abstract the characteristics of these authorities for classroom use. The similarity is that the teacher's cognitive authority is acquired, or earned, through personal achievement and then recognized.

Managerial authority may be granted to someone because of his or her personal achievements, but it is not the result of those achievements. It is given to a role established by a group, institution, or society. The authority is exercised in the role on behalf of the institution, corporation, or society. To say that a policewoman is an officer of the law, for example, means she fills an office concerned with law enforcement. The uniform shows everyone it is not the individual but the officeholder who acts. It is the office that carries out the necessary social functions, so to speak. Through it legitimated power is exercised on behalf of society.

The managerial and cognitive authorities of the teacher will be considered separately. Then reflections on the normative exercise of each will be made under the topics of academic freedom and equal freedom to continue the explication of human rights in education.

II. The Authority of the Social Office

When the question of the student's freedom, as opposed to existing authority structures, was raised at the tertiary level in the 1960's, it was part of a worldwide movement toward student participation in decisions affecting them. Most well-known were their expressions in liberal democracies, where they have historical foundations in Rousseau and his formulation of what came to be called the New Education, i.e., so-called child-centered or student-centered approaches, and which was manifested in the movement called Progressive Education in the twentieth century. This movement was predicated upon advocacy of freedom and attacks upon authoritarianism in school practice.

One of the theorists who grew up intellectually with the disciples of Dewey in the Progressive Education Movement noticed that the anti-authoritarianism of the latter eliminated legitimate authority as well as its abuse. To avoid this but to reject authoritarianism, too, he asked the question about the legitimate basis of the teacher's authority. He sought for a non-authoritarian authority in teaching. Benne's work has become a classic in the sense that his basic view is considered in most subsequent treatments of the topic.[2] Benne was not a reactionary, although there were reactionaries when he was writing, not unlike the reactionaries of the late Seventies in the complex movement toward basic education. Benne was not a conservative, either, although there were legitimate conservatives in education at the time who wondered if children in progressive schools would learn to read and write. Benne agreed with the progressives' anti-authoritarianism, and he, too, rejected bossy, arrogant teachers, cruel and inhumane teaching practice, unfair and unethical practice, and the "know it all" attitude. That is, he rejected the whole constellation of rather ugly teacher behavior that anyone with any sensitivity, compassion, or kindness would reject. What he rejected, however, was not the teacher's authority but its abuse.

Ordinarily, anti-authoritarianism conflates the concepts of authority and authoritarianism. Both the legitimate exercise of authority and the abuse of authority are rejected because of the failure to distinguish them. This frequently results in the suggestion that the classroom is either democratic or authoritarian, as if there were no middle ground. To perceive classrooms through such stereotypes, however, is an authoritarian way of imposing meanings on the classroom, and to phrase the issue this way is a very ancient rhetorical ploy.

To avoid these traps, Benne simply searched for a non-authoritarian authority. His conclusions were similar to those of many practicing teachers. A teacher is hired to do a specific task, such as to teach third

---

[2] Kenneth Benne, *A Conception of Authority* (New York: Teachers College, 1943).

grade again this year. This means the teacher fills a social office to accomplish a specific task. To hire a teacher to complete a task authorizes him or her to complete it. Thus the authority to teach resides in the social office.

Because the idea was obtained from sociology, Benne did not also consider authority in the cognitive sense. His claim was that it was not necessary to fill the office of teaching in an authoritarian manner. Because it is the office that bears the authority, the teacher does not have to identify with it personally. One can exercise authority as inherent in the situation, as if one would be inclined to say, "This is not really why I am teaching, but it goes with the territory." Or one can adopt the managerial role quite willingly, as if to say, "I am here to see that they behave themselves." The flexibility in attitude toward the managerial functions of teaching enables teachers to create a non-authoritarian attitude toward their own role in maintaining a productive, educational atmosphere in the classroom.

An extremely important aspect of the teacher's managerial authority is the pupils' state of diminished responsibility during the years of school attendance. There is no avoiding certain aspects of the *in loco parentis* doctrine in any role that involves the supervision of children. This sharply distinguishes the teacher from other authorities in society. Unlike the police officer, umpire, or employer, the teacher is the adult in charge. As such, she or he is responsible for the safety of the children. He or she has to keep them from hurting each other and prevent them from hurting themselves. It is not too much to say, in fact, that in the face of an imminent mishap, a very caring teacher will not hesitate to become extremely authoritarian to prevent it. The end can justify the means on the odd occasion and in the short term. The precise parameters of the teacher's responsibilities can be defined by the community, perhaps through the courts. It suffices to say that because the teacher is responsible for the children and their safety, she or he needs the authority to bear this responsibility effectively.

It goes without saying that students do not like to be told they cannot do something because they might hurt themselves, and of course the teacher should avoid overprotection and be as non-authoritarian as possible. In the final analysis, however, what matters is that the teacher is responsible for establishing the safety of the classroom in the effort to promote learning. It is most important that he or she fully assumes this responsibility as the adult moral agent present.

Because the social office is created by the community, however, it is probably valid to claim that the mode of exercising managerial authority in schools should be appropriate to modes prevalent within the community. A liberal community expects classrooms toward the *laissez-faire* end of the continuum, whereas conservative communities expect more highly organized discipline. A strict teacher might not succeed in the former, nor a liberal one in the latter, unless they adapt to the role expectations students bring to the classroom. This is no problem for teachers willing to accept pupils as they are and prepared to function from the location on the authority-freedom continuum required by the situation.

III. The Authority of the Canons of Inquiry

Control of the classroom shifts from managerial to cognitive authority as the children grow older. The increased importance of the teacher's cognitive achievement at the secondary and tertiary levels of schooling correlates with an increased affiliation of the teacher with other teachers of the same subject matter. Cognitive authority is dependent upon the community of scholars in the discipline rather than upon the local community in the neighborhood of the school. The teacher is also responsible to this extended community, for she or he ought not teach, e.g., bad biology or untrue history, and only its members have the intellectual knowledge necessary to hold the teacher intellectually responsible.

The authority of the social office is vested in the teacher in order to accomplish certain tasks related to the transmission of knowledge and skills. No one, however, teaches knowledge in the abstract. They teach biological or literary or scientific knowledge about something in the world. The body of knowledge about these things in the world, accumulated from their previous disciplined study, is preserved, transmitted, and enlarged by a group of qualified investigators. This creates an ambiguity in the basis of the teacher's authority in the cognitive sense. It is due to personal achievements in learning, but these are possible only because of the prior existence of a group of researchers who subscribe to specifiable canons of inquiry that make it possible to decide what is admissible evidence about the things they study. Without canons of inquiry held in common by some group of investigators, there is no intersubjectively valid, cumulative knowledge about things and no basis for any cognitive authority for any teacher. As a teacher acquires knowledge, two different things gradually occur. He or she becomes a member of the group of qualified investigators, and he or she adopts its canons of inquiry as the basis for his or her own disciplined thinking about the things in the domain.

It is not the method to discover knowledge nor the conclusions obtained by the method but the canons of inquiry that link these together that enable the group to accumulate knowledge about the phenomena studied. These canons are then the ultimate basis of the teacher's authority in the cognitive sense. The members of the group may use different methods of investigation from time to time, and their conclusions may vary, but there remain certain common standards of judgment for deciding what is a legitimate object of study within the domain, what is admissible evidence about that object, what are acceptable inferences from the admissible evidence, and what counts as cogent reasoning about the things in the domain. There is a commonly accepted expectation of scrupulous acknowledgement of one's sources, intellectual honesty in reporting one's findings, and personal integrity in making the proper qualifications when stating conclusions. These canons of inquiry allow fellow investigators to assess the worth, certitude, and general quality of the contributions to knowledge in the domain.

Someone who knows only the tested knowledge within a domain cannot teach the method by which it was obtained, nor the valid reasons why it is valid knowledge. Similarly, someone who knows only the methods for the discovery of knowledge in a domain cannot teach the *raison d'etre* of the method in the study of the things in the domain. In neither case can the teacher teach the knowledge as knowledge, i.e., with awareness of the epistemic characteristics it possesses that make it be the type and kind of knowledge it is. The students could not learn its precise status as knowledge, its degree of certitude, etc. These things require cognizance of the canons of inquiry that unite method and content in the disciplined study of things in the world.

Knowledge of the canons of inquiry and loyalty to them are therefore part of what qualifies a person as an authority who can teach in a given domain. Acquiring them in such a way that one also feels obligated by them is tantamount to adopting the relevant group of investigators as one's reference group. Because the canons enable one to distinguish between good and bad evidence, experiments, reasoning, and theory, they become normative for one's own thinking when learned as canons of inquiry. They discipline one's thinking about the things in the domain. The effect is to transfer cognitive authority from the person of the teacher to the canons of inquiry. Something is valid not because the teacher as an authority said it but because the teacher adheres to explicit canons of inquiry that require anyone who accepts them to believe it. Then the teacher can be a non-authoritarian authority insofar as the knowledge or skills that are taught contain some canons of legitimacy within them that serve to regulate communication within the area.

It may seem to exaggerate to speak of canons of inquiry in the area of skills, but even in the first year of school, the child learning to read and write acquires norms of correctness in the process. Learning to speak and listen in the first years of life at home also involves the acquisition of norms of pronunciation, syntax, and meaning while communicating with older people whose talk embodies these norms of correctness. Perhaps no one can teach anyone anything with cognitive validity without such canons.

This analysis is neither authoritarian or non-authoritarian because it does not concern classroom procedure as such. Any place on the authority-freedom continuum has to involve such canons of inquiry. Saying that the teacher's authority in the cognitive sense is based in the canons of inquiry is neutral toward the exercise of authority in the managerial sense. On the other hand, the social office is legitimately established by the community only if there are such canons of inquiry to purify, refine, and discipline the knowledge of the things in the world.

IV. Academic Freedom

If it is true that the teacher's rightful authority in the cognitive sense is based upon the canons of inquiry, then teaching and learning in accordance with those canons is not miseducative. It may be irrelevant to consider whether such teaching is authoritarian because authoritarianism in the pejorative sense occurs in the cognitive domain when there is indoctrination that violates the canons of inquiry. Indoctrination as the imposition of beliefs without consideration of the evidence to substantiate them is not necessarily miseducative if the canons of inquiry are not violated, i.e., if the beliefs are true. Indoctrination that violates the canons of inquiry is miseducative because it promulgates false doctrine. The question of authoritarianism in the cognitive sense, i.e., indoctrination, is basically about truth and falsehood.

It is difficult to understand how indoctrination into truth can violate the student's freedom in any important way. On the other hand, there can be no more pernicious evil in teaching than the indoctrination of falsehood. Nothing can more thoroughly betray the social office and the respect and trust in their teachers given by the young. The issue, however, is not indoctrination but truth.

The genuine questions of academic freedom arise when a teacher is advised not to teach some subject, topic, theory, or point of view that is not acceptable to someone, particularly someone with vested interests that need protection from the truth. The justification for academic freedom for teaching concerns the teacher's allegiance to the relevant canons of inquiry and the necessity to teach the truth and only truth even if unpopular or contrary to someone's personal interest.

Academic freedom cannot be rightfully claimed simply to teach what one wants, or to indoctrinate students into some political party, sectarian religion, fashionable cult, private code of ethics, or ideological perspective, no matter how important one's own views in this regard seem to be. One can, in fact, claim the right to intellectual freedom in any of these respects only if one grants the same intellectual freedom to everyone else, including one's students. Someone who will grant intellectual freedom to his own students will be reluctant to announce his own views on such partisan matters. Intellectual tyranny can therefore be avoided by emphasizing not the freedom to teach but the freedom to learn the truth. The student's academic freedom is honored by a refusal to indoctrinate anything but the canons of inquiry themselves.

Requiring allegiance to the canons of inquiry is not indoctrinative in the pejorative sense because they are the only means to distinguish teaching in epistemically valid ways from indoctrination in the pejorative sense. If one does not accept current canons of inquiry in a particular area, one has no basis to argue against indoctrination. In any case they have to be accepted tentatively in order to transcend them, discover better ones, and communicate them to adherents of the established canons. Without allegiance to canons current in a domain there can be no disciplined study of its distinctive phenomena and no question of indoctrination.

The appeal to the canons of inquiry does not resolve all the issues of academic freedom, however, for they can conflict with the other basis of authority. The social office does not exist in the abstract but is defined in a finite community. The teacher is employed to teach X and Y in a particular situation and is granted authority necessary. In this role the teacher is authorized to manage the classroom to insure that conditions of learning prevail, i.e., to set assignments, schedule recitations, evaluate student achievements, and assign grades to certify the quality of the academic achievement. If these things are somewhat peripheral to the instructional tasks of teaching, they nevertheless indicate the kinds of powers granted to teachers placed in authority in the classroom.

The teacher's authority in the cognitive sense, however, is rooted in the competency in the content of instruction. This very competency is (a) the reason for employment, and (b) something the employer does not have. Merely by obeying the relevant canons of inquiry the teacher can accidentally teach something the employer, some parents, or the community do not expect, e.g., a significant novel, some finding in one of the natural sciences, or perhaps a concept in the social sciences. Then they complain that the teacher is not employed to teach that. Its excellence, or truth, as judged by criteria within disciplined study is disregarded because it is unknown. Other criteria of value are utilized. If these other criteria are valid in their own sphere, there is a genuine conflict because the authority granted to the social office requires a decision that differs from the teacher's choice made on the basis of the canons of inquiry sustained by the community of investigators in the particular domain of knowledge. This is an honest conflict that ought not be oversimplified.

The particular community that supports the social office need not have any loyalty to the canons of inquiry. They need not even know them, e.g., they might want secondary school subjects to prepare students for tertiary schools without having the slightest idea of their content. That is why an authority who does know them is employed. Even though a community employs specialists in the physical sciences, for example, it does not mean that it wants their canons of inquiry to be applied to their children's belief in Santa Claus, or to destroy their belief in the spirit of Christmas. They might even want to claim it is not the teacher's concern if the people in the community want to believe in Christmas, the *Genesis* story, UFO's, premarital chastity, etc.

They are partly right. It is not only a question of truth. It is also a matter of which knowledge belongs in the curriculum. The canons of inquiry in any domain cannot prove that the knowledge discovered through their use is important to know. It requires value judgments to decide which knowledge is valuable.

It also requires a value judgment to decide that one's beliefs should be based on evidence, etc.

It seems that a teacher has no obligation, and perhaps no right, to root out false beliefs unless they interfere with the cognitive learning required by the canons of inquiry in the subject taught for the students present. This is precisely what would happen if the story of the first ten chapters of *Genesis* were given "equal time" in a class in biology or earth science. The teacher would have the duty, i.e., the moral obligation, to apply the canons of inquiry rigorously in the pursuit of the truth of the matter. Anything less would be tantamount to a lie. That this would result in the destruction of so-called creation science should be pondered by its advocates.[3]

---

[3] It seems the important part of *Genesis* is the story of Abraham and his encounter with what he believed was deity. *Genesis* may still be the best source of knowledge of this historical event, but it would not belong within the natural sciences if it belonged in the school curriculum.

A clearer illustration is the study of the history of one's own country, which belongs in everyone's education to enable them to become at home in it and exercise citizenship duties when adult. The histories of Holland, Canada, Australia, etc., are very important school subjects in the respective countries regardless of their importance to world history from the viewpoint of the objective scholar. In other words, when choosing between domains of knowledge, the canons of inquiry within them is not determinant for the question of which knowledge is most important educationally.

They are not always determinant within a domain. Although the teacher should always be free to teach the truth according to the canons of inquiry in a domain, this is not self-justifying. Its objective and justification is to enable the student to learn the truth. It is the basis for the student's intellectual freedom and necessary for developing moral agency. It is the student's human right. There is a peculiar anomaly, however, resulting from cognitive dissonance and a greater pedagogic principle regarding the promotion of the conditions of learning. One always has to teach within the framework of existing attitudes and motivations. These can cause learning interference. For example, anyone studying theology in a Christian context sooner or later has to resolve the problem of believing in the divinity of Jesus without violating the commandment about not worshipping any likenesses of deity. Introduction of the problem too early will not serve truth, and there is no point to it. Similarly, a community controversy over some particular books studied in English Literature may destroy part of the value of reading those books. Changing books might be advised merely to maintain the conditions of learning in the classroom. The logic is that A, B, or C will serve to attain the objectives, X, Y, and Z. Once controversy is aroused by A, it may be more conducive to the attainment of the objectives to switch to B or C. It would not seem politic or pedagogic to fight a battle over one means to a goal when another will suffice. It is the objectives for which the battle of academic freedom should be fought. The anomaly is that the authority to establish the objectives does not reside in the canons of inquiry. It belongs in the social office. After the community decides literary appreciation is a worthy objective, the teacher ought to be sufficiently competent to select reading materials that will attain the objectives in educationally productive, pedagogically desirable ways that are also morally acceptable to the community. Competent discretion is better than valor. The student's freedom to learn is not enhanced by a raging community controversy that tells him that significant adults believe he is studying something not worth learning.

The problems are different in different parts of the curriculum. The general principles regarding the authority of the social office and the canons of inquiry do not themselves indicate which should take precedence, or when. The general societal norms that support and are supported by the social office of teaching are probably the more important the younger the child; the canons of inquiry, the older the student. The canons of inquiry are more clearly defined in the natural sciences than in the social sciences or humanities. The actual case to be made for academic freedom in the primary and secondary schools should therefore be made in conjunction with a particular subject matter in a given place in the curriculum. It concerns the necessity for the students to come to adopt the relevant canons of inquiry in order to learn the truth.

What is clear is that a teacher cannot make a justifiable moral claim to teach his or her own opinion, beliefs, or values if these are only matters of opinion. A teacher who ventures to express values, opinions, or beliefs that are logically independent of the canons of inquiry of the subject taught is in fact authoritarian in the pejorative sense. The willful pronouncement of *obiter dicta* is undisciplined and mis-educative. In other words, teachers are non-authoritarian in the cognitive sense if they submit their views to the canons of inquiry, and this stance is essential to promote the academic freedom that is the student's human right.

V. Equal Freedom in Education

The teacher has legitimate cognitive authority as long as the relevant canons of inquiry govern instructional efforts, for then she or he freely consents to be limited by the pupil's right to intellectual freedom to follow the evidence and argument in the pursuit of truth.

The situation regarding managerial authority is similar, with one sharp difference. If managerial authority is regarded as limited by the pupil's freedom of action, then authority and freedom are set into opposition. The teacher's legitimate cognitive authority, however, is not directly limited by the student's freedom to learn. Cognitive authority rightfully limits itself by the canons of inquiry. Managerial authority ought therefore be limited by the behavioral parallel to the canons of inquiry. These are the norms and rules necessary to establish equal freedom in the classroom and school.

Because the freedom that belongs to each person as a matter of human right is not the freedom to do what one wants but to do the right thing, the basic limitation to the student's freedom should be the freedom of other students. This should be defined and codified into rules that establish equal freedom. It is not relevant to the policy issue to wonder if the rules should be formulated by students or faculty, or by each class. This is a matter of pedagogy. The concern of policy is that if the rules are formulated so that they establish the conditions of equal freedom, then the teacher's efforts to gain obedience to them will be non-authoritarian in principle. It will use authority to promote freedom.

For example, the ordinary kindergarten teacher frequently needs rules like, "No hitting!" "No running!" "No shouting!" If one of these rules is stated quite pointedly at a propitious moment it might seem authoritarian to someone who isolates it from its context and interprets the episode as a bit of teacher-student opposition. Many children would not see it that way, however, and in any case the freedom to hit, run, or shout is not defensible on moral grounds. It is not an infringement of anyone's freedom in the moral sense to have to follow rules against hitting, running, and shouting. Just as freedom to learn can only be justified as freedom to abide by the canons of inquiry to learn the truth, so can freedom to act be justified only by the freedom to abide by the rules of equal freedom to do what is right.

If a teacher is unnecessarily harsh and abusive when enforcing the rules of equal freedom, this is quite a different thing from being cantankerous or moody when enforcing arbitrary rules. The latter is authoritarian in the pernicious sense. The former can also be said to be authoritarian, but this epithet confuses it with the latter and makes it quite difficult to distinguish the legitimate use of authority from its abuse. Enforcement of the rules of equal freedom should be retained.

Perhaps it would be better to say they should be enforced with dignity, restraint, and compassion than in non-authoritarian ways. Care ought to be taken to avoid undermining the authority of the teacher. If rules are necessary to establish equal freedom, it is better to enforce them without dignity than not to enforce them at all. Criticizing their undignified enforcement as authoritarian will do more harm than good if it results in loss of the rules or a sense of their rightness.

It is not necessarily true, furthermore, that a teacher who sometimes enforces the rules of equal freedom in undignified ways is *ipso facto* authoritarian. A temporary loss of dignity is a temporary loss of dignity. There is no reason to ascribe authoritarianism to it if it is not prompted by insensitivity or cruelty. It is also a loss of dignity to make third-person moral judgments about other people's temporary loss of dignity. If an occasional loss of dignity, when the student errs, is confused with a willful, persistent, arrogant attitude toward students worthy of the authoritarian epithet, it becomes much more difficult to establish the appropriate basis for dignity in education.

To begin in good faith, one ought assume that every morally responsible person wants to know where his freedom ends and where his moral obligations to the freedom of others begin. It is not necessary to have correct intuitions, or to be able to reason it out on an individual basis. It can be established and codified in rules and laws. Any rule or law that designates what is required by equal freedom is a just rule. Every morally responsible person wants to live in a community of laws that establish the conditions of equal freedom and are worthy of respect.

If the situation of children is different because of their status of diminished responsibility, it does not follow that there should be any modification of the criteria of just rules in the classroom. The rules themselves need to be grade-placed, but not the criterion of equal freedom. With children there might be more need for additional administrative or safety rules, but otherwise the only just rules are those that establish equal freedom, and it is contrary to justice to avoid enforcing just rules.

The point is so important it ought to be substantiated with Kant's words. The principle of equal freedom was argued on its own merit in the previous chapter, independently of its origin in Kant's ethics, because the point is not its origin but its validity. Kant's words, however, might attest to the presence of sixth stage moral reasoning. He said, "Justice is therefore the aggregate of those conditions under which the will of one person can be conjoined with the will of another in accordance with a universal law of freedom."[4] By universal law of freedom, Kant meant that which is universalizable, i.e., freedom as a human right, or equal freedom. The "aggregate of conditions" that enable people to cooperate freely with each other as distinct moral agents should be called "justice." These are established by the rules that allow each person to freely interact with the free interactions of other people. Therefore justice is equal freedom. The concept was stated more directly when Kant said, "Every action is just that in itself or in its maxim is such that the freedom of the will of each can co-exist together with the freedom of everyone in accordance with a universal law."[5] An act is therefore just, or right, if it is compatible with everyone else's freedom. Because a rule governing this action is in accord with justice, it is worthy of respect.

Conversely, an act is wrong if everyone cannot choose to do it simultaneously. How this might work itself out at the adult level does not have to be deciphered for the educational application. Running, hitting, and shouting are wrong at the kindergarten level because all the children cannot do them at the same time. They are wrong elsewhere in school, too, but if the principle is operative at this level, it is patently independent of the degree of responsibility that can be borne. Very small children are perfectly capable of understanding the point of the question, What if we all shouted at once? The rule against it can be perceived as just and worthy of respect in kindergarten. As children and youth are expected to learn the canons of inquiry in the cognitive domain, so, too, can they be expected to learn and respect just rules as part of their growth toward the moral agency of adulthood.

Finally, Kant also said that if someone's use of freedom proved a hindrance to the use of freedom by another, it was just to use coercion to prevent that hindance to rightful freedom.[6] This use of coercion

---

[4] Kant, op. cit., p. 34.

[5] Ibid., p. 35.

[6] Ibid., p. 36.

does not constrain freedom. It protects it. If the managerial authority functions through the maintenance of just rules, it is therefore justified by freedom itself. This is why it is better if just rules are enforced badly than not at all. Of course it is better to enforce them gently, and with dignity, but this is another matter. For the present it suffices to say that the exercise of authority in the managerial sense is not authoritarian in the pernicious sense when it serves to enforce just rules. Del Vecchio put it quite straightforwardly when he said, "The possibility of enforcing the observance of a right is an integral and characteristic part of the right itself."[7] The teacher's managerial authority is justified by freedom as a human right.

Conclusion

The teacher's authority in the managerial sense of the word is justified by the pupil's need to learn to act according to just rules. If it is exercised according to the norms of equal freedom, it is basically non-authoritarian because it augments the moral freedom that is a human right.

The teacher's authority in the cognitive sense of the word is justified by the pupil's need to learn to reason according to domain-specific canons of inquiry. If it is exercised according to the norms of truth, it is basically non-authoritarian because it augments the intellectual freedom that is a human right.

Whether the exercise of authority in either sense is compatible with human dignity makes a difference, but this is not so important as whether it is guided by the conditions necessary to establish equal freedom and truth, i.e., whether its exercise is limited by just rules and canons of inquiry. It is more important for the classroom to be a miniature community of law in both the moral and intellectual senses than that it always be maintained as such with the dignity appropriate to learning, although there is nothing inherent in such a community of scholars under law that is incompatible with maintaining it with dignity. To ask how one can maintain discipline with dignity, however, is to ask another question. That question presupposes an answer to the question of the teacher's legitimate authority.

---

[7] Giorgio Del Vecchio, *The Formal Basis of Law*, tr. John Lisle (New York: Macmillan, 1921), p. 193.

The present effort to avoid undermining the authority of the teacher seeks to establish the rightful role of pedagogic authority in the development of moral and intellectual freedom. It tries to find the non-ideological way to formulate the theory of the moral and intellectual characteristics inherent in the institution of education to enable their enhancement as appropriate for a heavily technologized society. These moral and intellectual characteristics are developed when pupils learn to act in accordance with rules needed to establish equal freedom in the classroom and when they learn to reason according to canons of inquiry needed to establish truth. They are developed when the classroom is a community of scholars under law. Access to classrooms that are such communities of scholars under law is therefore a human right.

Chapter Five

EQUAL EDUCATIONAL OPPORTUNITY

> The only universal right is the right to equal consideration. This is not a right in the ordinary sense. Its existence cannot be established by referring to law, for it is presupposed by the idea of law.
>
> Benn and Peters[1]

Freedom in education is an individual's concern. Equality in education is characteristically the concern of a group of people. The former is about pedagogy, but the latter is about policy needed to obtain a fair share of the provisions made for education. The question of equality is basically about distributive justice in its general provision, and it is usually expressed in terms of a desire for equal educational opportunity.

I. The Question of Equality in Education

The groups who ask for greater educational justice can be classified as private, different, disadvantaged, or discriminated. The first category seeks to acquire public tax money for private, free-enterprise schools not open to the general public without qualification. It includes religious, independent, and alternative schools. Although the first article of the Bill of Rights appended to the Constitution of the United States is generally understood as forbidding the use of

---

[1] S.I. Benn and R.S. Peters, *Social Principles and the Democratic State* (London: Allen & Unwin, 1959), p. 110.

public funds to support church schools, in Canada the Separate Schools (Roman Catholic) are tax-supported and in Australia all non-government schools receive financial support from the national government. This suggests that the particular policy of a given country is not necessarily the fairest solution. One question is whether public funds should be given to schools or to children, i.e., whether children should receive public financial support for their education regardless of the school they attend. A second question is whether parents who choose to send their children to non-government schools should also support public schools, i.e., whether they are entitled to tax rebates if they are paying tuition elsewhere.

The word "different" is used to denote the second category, comprising students who want secondary and/or tertiary schooling different from university preparation and university attendance and who are not otherwise disadvantaged or discriminated against. It includes those who leave high school before graduation; who are enrolled in non-academic tracks in secondary schools or in technical, trade, or specialized high schools or adult education centers; who attend junior colleges, municipal colleges, colleges of advanced education, or polytechnical institutes instead of universities; who study by correspondence; or who have specialized curriculum needs in non-academic areas such as art, dance, music, drama, sport, and vocational or business subjects.

This category evokes questions of educational justice for children and youth who are not necessarily benefitted by the prestigious, academic track of the secondary school because they are not going on to the university, or the professions, or to the upper-middle socio-economic class. It is a question of justice for working-class children and youth. It asks the second of two significant questions of equality in education. Do all children have an equal opportunity to compete for university places? Do the children who cannot benefit from academic subjects or who believe they can benefit more from non-academic tracks have an equal educational opportunity?

The word "disadvantaged" is used to designate the category of children with physical handicaps who are not otherwise discriminated against, i.e., who are deaf, mute, or blind, paraplegic or hospitalized, mentally retarded or disturbed, etc., including students in isolated or rural circumstances. Their impediment to normal school learning is not the result of their own choosing, as in the two categories already discussed, nor is it the result of social circumstances, as in the following category. The need for compensatory measures is generally acknowledged and non-controversial.

This category, however, has considerable significance for an explicit understanding of the principle of equality in education. If one says that blind children, for example, need materials printed in Braille, and Braille teachers, to have an equal opportunity to learn to read, one makes a normative claim about a moral obligation to provide different, unequal, and probably more costly educational resources to compensate for the handicap. It is the principle of equality that is operative because one is assuming that all children have an "equal right" to learn how to read. This is the "same right," i.e., simply the right to learn to read. It is expressed in the words "equal opportunity," however, because there is an implication that the disadvantage requires something different to create the opportunity, yet it is the same opportunity given to sighted children. They cannot have the same thing, so they should have one equal to it. "Equal" here means the same, not literally but substantially the same opportunity. The use of Braille materials by blind children gives them the same opportunity to read that sighted children have.

There is also an implication that the use of different materials and instruction tends to equalize things between groups. Precise equalization is not expected. Nor is it important to decide whether it is their education or opportunity for it that is "equalized." The ordinary understanding is that the compensatory measure tends to equalize things, and this suffices to establish justice. It is assumed that reading in Braille is a rough equivalent to sighted reading, but a rough equivalency tending to equalize things suffices to allow one to say they have been given an equal education.

There is no implication of any equality in the factual sense between blind and sighted individuals, blind and sighted groups, or between individuals within either group when one claims that blind children should receive, or have received, an equal education. Strictly speaking, the issue is not equality but educational justice. Equality cannot be attained. Everyone knows this and it is not aimed for. What is desired is only some rough equivalent or close approximation to "normal" education. In this context the principles of equality and equal opportunity are not meant to be understood literally. They are invoked to state and justify a belief in what is required for justice.

The word "discriminated" is used to refer to the groups often said to be culturally, economically, or educationally disadvantaged or deprived, or exploited or oppressed, not excluding but not only including people who have been consciously discriminated against in their personal and institutional encounters. They are disadvantaged not in the physical but in the social sense. The general social circumstances have seemed to disadvantage them in respect to schooling in the dominant culture. At any rate, the category includes the poor, blacks, Hispanics and Chicanos, other ethnic minorities, aboriginal populations such as American and Canadian Indians, Eskimos and Australian aborigines, and women. Because these groups have rejected the names used for this category that are judgmental, they are referred to by a word that is judgmental against the dominant group. The name is irrelevant. The point is to avoid "blaming the victim" and further discrimination in the search for educational justice.

These groups raise the question of equality in education because they believe themselves to be either economically, socially, politically, or educationally disadvantaged, and they use the principles of equality and equal opportunity in education to state their view that justice requires that they receive an education equal to that of anyone else, i.e., equal to that of the dominant group. For the most part, they want an end to institutional discrimination.

In other words, the question of equality in education is raised when someone feels unfairly treated and asks for educational justice. In the case of the different and physically disadvantaged groups, this requires a different kind of treatment that is somehow equivalent to the standard provision. The goal is to establish some kind of opportunity in education that is in some way similar to the standard academic track.

The reverse occurs in the case of discriminated groups, for here justice requires being treated the same as everyone else, i.e., to have a chance at an education equal to that available to members of the dominant culture without discrimination because of race, social class, gender, or other irrelevant factors.

The former want differentiated treatment to obtain virtually the same educational benefit, whereas the latter want the same treatment in education in order to secure a fair share of the social and economic benefits that seem to accrue to people with that education.

This is oversimplified to sharpen the contrast. Discriminated groups may also want differential treatment to overcome educational disadvantages alleged to inhere in early childhood growth when the parents are severely economically disadvantaged.

What is clear is that when schools are governmentally financed, their facilities ought to be shared fairly. It is also fitting that people who feel they are not getting their fair share raise the question of equality in education. This question, however, has clear corollaries. What kind of education should be provided equally to everyone? What is good, common education? When justice seems to require differential provision, should it be equivalent or equitable?

When does justice in education require equality, equivalency, or equity?

II. Meanings of the Word "Equality"

Jefferson's immortal words, "All men are created equal," show the necessity to sort out the senses of the word "equality." His mistake was grammatical, not factual, for he did not believe people were equal. He believed there was a "natural aristocracy of genius and talent" that should be educated to leadership regardless of social class origin. So did Plato. The expression, rather, makes a political, ethical claim that in certain respects people should receive equal consideration, i.e., be treated equally. It should be paraphrased to say that all propertied, white, adult males should receive equal political rights, among other things like the right to life, liberty, and the pursuit of happiness. That is what Jefferson meant. In its context in the Declaration of Independence, he was clearly arguing for representative government, i.e., for equality at the ballot box and in the opportunity to run for governmental office. He used the word in the political and moral sense. And he was a bourgeois, racist, male chauvinist.

When the question is whether people are actually equal, the word is used in the factual sense. Everything depends upon the dimensions concerned. If one refers to physical, physiological, or psychological aspects of the human's bodily being, then of course people are as different as the measuring devices that can be invented, i.e., in respect to height, weight, intelligence, strength, dexterity, visual acuity, tonal acuity, memory, metabolic rate, pulse, excitability, aggressiveness, and so on. They vary in respect to whatever is determined by gene pools, the physical organism, and the state of health.

There are aspects of the factual human condition, however, in which people are virtually equal. They have common basic needs for adequate nutrition, exercise, rest, and shelter that have to be satisfied merely to maintain physical well-being. These are perceived as differences if measured quantitatively, or as similarities if their satisfaction is emphasized as necessary to maintain health. Certain elemental emotions, such as affection, love, hate, sorrow, loneliness, grief, and concern for one's mortality also seem to be common aspects of human facticity. Nothing in the human condition itself compels anyone to believe the differences are more important than the similarities. Or vice versa. One is free to emphasize differences in an elitism or equalities in egalitarianism. One can have it both ways by believing that everyone has their own value and dignity. One can refuse to have it either way by claiming people are neither equal nor unequal because they are incomparably unique.

It may help clarify the distinction between equality in the factual and normative senses to note that only the left hand column of the following diagram has been discussed:

	Factual sense	Normative sense
Inequality	weight height metabolic rate intelligence strength etc.	equity

	Factual sense	Normative sense
Equality	basic needs elemental emotions human condition uniqueness own value	moral legal political economic theological

There are several normative senses of the word "equal" that belong together in the right-hand column. It is virtually axiomatic that people should be treated equally in the moral sense. For example, if truth-telling is a valid moral principle, one should tell the truth to everyone, not merely to one's friends or benefactors. Legal systems assume that people should be considered equally before the law, i.e., all violators of a particular law should be prosecuted equally, every defendent should be presumed innocent until found legally guilty, etc. Democracies assume that people should be considered equally politically, i.e., everyone is eligible for office and entitled to one vote. Some people believe in economic equality, i.e., that everyone should receive the same wages, although it is more defensible to claim there should be a minimum wage, or a minimum annual wage, or that there should be equal pay for equal work. Finally, to claim that all people are equal in the sight of deity involves the theological sense of the word "equality."

There are counterclaims made that people should not be treated equally, i.e., that fairness, or justice, requires unequal treatment. As Aristotle said, complaints about injustice arise as much when unequals are treated equally as the reverse.[2] He may have been echoing the view of distributive justice presented in the *Republic*, where Plato recommended that everyone should be educated to do

---

[2] Aristotle, *Ethica Nichomachea*, tr. W.D. Ross (New York: Oxford University Press, 1942), 1131a 23-24.

that for which he or she was best suited. This supposedly insures the existence of justice, understood as giving each person hir or her due. An equally famous definition of distributive justice was expressed by Marx in the Gotha program. "From each according to his ability; to each according to his need." The hero of latter-day egalitarians, Marx himself formulated this principle of the need for equity. The concept of distributive justice is that the distribution of goods is not fair unless it occurs unequally according to a criterion of need, merit, desert, or right. For Marx it was to each according to need; for Plato, to each his due.

Neither of these principles claims people are equal or should be treated equally in the sense of sameness. For Marx, each person is equally deserving of having his needs satisfied, but the needs vary as well as the means by which they should be satisfied. The moral and social equality inherent in his maxim becomes manifest in the image of the society in which everyone is equally able to fulfill their needs. The attraction of his Utopian vision is precisely that in it each person is equally able to secure enough goods to satisfy his needs, irrespective of his socio-economic class. Everyone should be happy because they see justice done, but it is equity rather than equality that obtains in Marx's "classless" society.

The kind of equality that does exist within a basically equitable distribution of goods can be seen in the family situation. If three children in the same family of different ages, appetites, and metabolic rates receive the same amount of food, it would be said to be unjust, especially if one left food on the plate and another went hungry. Distributive justice occurs when each child has enough to eat relative to appetite and nutritional needs. Each child is then treated differently in respect to quantities of food, but the same in the sense of having enough to eat. Strictly speaking, this is a situation of equity, but if one of the children was systematically denied enough food to satisfy his or her appetite, he or she might feel unequally treated and express the complaint in terms of the lack of equal treatment, or even as wanting the same treatment as the other children, meaning by the "same" enough to eat, not identical portions.

Thus equality in the normative sense sometimes requires that people should be treated equally, and other times, equitably. Strictly speaking, it is justice that requires equal or unequal treatment in order to establish equity but the principle of equality is invoked to claim that someone should be considered equally even when what is claimed is something proportionate to need, merit, or desert, rather than the same thing.

This does not leave the concept of equality in a confused state. The concept is not involved. It is the moral principle of equality, and the situation is not confused. It is complicated. Justice is a complicated matter.

Perhaps there can be further clarification through a comparison with criminal justice. Although criminal law assumes that everyone should be treated equally, justice in its enforcement requires that only people who violate specific laws should be punished. Criminal law thus requires both equal and unequal treatment. The inequality in the distribution of punishment (only to the guilty) is in fact necessary to establish equality before the law. So are unequal punishments.

Or blind children, for example, need "unequal" education in order to have an equal education. It is indeed the principle of equality that justifies the use of different kinds of reading materials. Different resources are required to produce equal outcomes when the principle of equality requires equivalent outcomes.

It would seem that Plato's and Marx's interpretations of distributive justice should be understood this way, i.e., as the use of differential means to produce equal outcomes. The inequality of treatment is merely the technological aspect of the means required by the principle of equality of consideration that is clearly implied in the claim that everyone should receive their due or have their needs satisfied without any partiality shown to anyone at all for any reasons such as social class, race, religion, gender, etc. The point is that everyone, without exception, is entitled to justice. Then it happens that justice requires different treatment. This different treatment should not be misunderstood as "unequal" treatment, for it is, rather, roughly equivalent treatment.

When all the children in a family receive enough to eat, for example, they can be said to receive equivalent treatment. It is technologically unequal treatment because it involves different amounts of food, but morally speaking it is the same treatment. It is equal treatment in the moral sense of the word "equal."

Distributive justice, i.e., justice in the distribution of goods, therefore requires a technology of unequal means in order to obtain the justice of giving everyone equal consideration. Giving everyone their due and/or satisfying everyone's needs is merely the economy of equality in the moral sense. The principle of equality thus requires that everyone is equally entitled to justice, their own due, without exception. That is what the word "equality" means when it is used in the moral sense. Its justification is another matter.

III. Equality as a Human Right

Benn and Peters said equal consideration is presupposed by the idea of law in a context in which they deny it is either a natural or human right. This seems somewhat disingenuous, or at least like trying to eat one's cake and have it, too, for they are as enthusiastic for equality as Kant was for freedom and even claim it is a universal right. Their view is worth examining in detail. Its criticism will show that equal consideration is a human right. Their disagreement is with explicit details of previous theories of natural rights and human rights, not with the substantive moral principles involved. They simply do not wish to say that equality is based in human nature, natural law, or some characteristic of human beings as human beings, but this does not detract from the force of their claim that equal consideration is a universal right applicable to all people in total agreement with the main point of both natural and human rights theories. It is prior to positive law and belongs to everyone. When they say it is presupposed by law, however, they take the existence of laws for granted. They should justify their existence. Law is found only in human society (physical laws are something else entirely). Everyone, presumably, has a right to live in a society under law, only humans have this right, and they have it universally.

Because Benn and Peters assume this without explicating it, they beg the queston. To justify equality, they say that law presupposes it, but it is because people have the right to equal consideration that they enact laws. If equality justifies laws, then laws cannot justify equality as a universal right. They seem to fall into their circular argument because of their erroneously truncated theory of meaning. They begin by claiming that when rules prescribe conduct, they indicate rights and duties. Rights are not compelled, but duties are prescribed.[3] Rules, rights, and duties are all bound up together. The right of one person is the duty of another, and one receives a duty to create a right for another. For example, if it is the right of every child in kindergarten to hear the teacher, then obedience to the rule of no shouting becomes the duty of each. Thus rules that fairly indicate rights and duties are worthy of respect. Benn and Peters are too far out on the linguistic limb, however, when they claim that the use of the word "right" is meaningless unless the corresponding duties are clearly stated in a rule. There is something in what they say, but not what they think. The word "right" has to be meaningful before a rule is made in order to justify the rule. For example, people who seek a law against abortion claim there is a right to life, and that this use of the word "right" is very significant and meaningful even without such a law. It is because all children have a right to hear the teacher that there should be a rule against shouting in class. What Benn and Peters mean is that a belief in a particular right is most likely to be nonfunctional in society unless it is enacted into law. They err in starting with law and trimming their theory of meaning accordingly.

The fallacy involved can be shown through a consideration of a similar point made by Ross when he claimed that the concept of equality involved in law is a matter of simple logic:

> The idea of equality as such simply means the correct application of a general rule (irrespective of which one). The general concepts or characteristics employed in the rule define a certain class of persons (or situations) with regard to whom a certain treatment should take place. The equal treatment of all those within this class is then simply the necessary consequence of the correct application of the rule.[4]

This is reasonable within its restricted parameters, after a rule or law is adopted. It gives no reason why a law should be enacted, or

---

[3] S.I. Benn and R.S. Peters, *The Principles of Political Thought* (New York: The Free Press, 1965), p. 101.

[4] Alf Ross, *On Law and Justice* (London: Steven, 1958), p. 273.

respected, and either of these requires a belief in equal treatment in one or more relevant respects to justify the rule or law. Justifying this belief that there ought to be a law to enforce such equal consideration is the important question. The concept of equality may be "simply" the correct application of a rule, but this is "equality" in the logical sense of the word, not in the moral sense. Equality in the moral sense is simply the moral principle that allows the enactment of new laws to specify rights and duties not presently functioning in society. If there are no such rights and duties before a law is passed, the law will not make them right. Later on, however, Ross was remarkably correct when he said, "A general unqualified demand that all shall be treated equally means only that the treatment accorded to each person shall follow general rules,"[5] for this implies that the person making the demand wants justice through the enactment of a new law. It is not "only" a logical claim but a socio-moral-political claim made in an historical context.

The existence of particular laws cannot be taken for granted. Neither can the existence of law in the generic sense. Although considerations of equality and justice frequently trace their origin to Aristotle and/or Plato when inequalities are to be justified, concern for equality and justice occurs much earlier in the first books of the Old Testament. As Friedrich said,

> The sanctification of each member of the community who obeys the laws of Yahweh implies an equality of all men. The laws of the Old Testament can be obeyed by anyone who is of good will. This markedly egalitarian spiritual attitude toward the law that one finds in ancient Judaism stands out in sharp contrast to the legal thought of the Greeks.[6]

Friedrich claimed that this egalitarianism was revived by Jesus in his struggle against priestly elitism. It is the meaning of his claim to be fulfilling the law of the men of old through considering rich men and thieves, virgins and prostitutes, equally, i.e., each with respect and

---

[5] Ibid., p. 285.

[6] Carl J. Friedrich, *The Philosophy of Law in Historical Perspective* (Chicago: University of Chicago Press, 1963), p. 11.

dignity. That this egalitarianism is not original with Jesus can be clearly manifested in two quotations. Strict impartiality in administration of the law, or equal consideration before the law, is prescribed in *Leviticus* 19: 15, "You shall do no injustice in judgment. You shall not be partial to the poor or defer to the great, but in righteousness shall you judge your neighbor." A few verses later (19: 17-18) this is accompanied by the admonition Jesus was to quote centuries later: "You shall love your neighbor as yourself." The egalitarianism in this maxim is as startling as it is overlooked.

There is little doubt that the basis for such impartiality of judgment is part of the principle of equal consideration as Benn and Peters interpret it. They claim that what all men have in common is their citizenship. All men are equal as citizens.[7] Presumably it is in human nature to be a citizen, or it is necessary to be a citizen to be a human being. It is either a natural right, human right, or both, but they do not say so. Be that as it may, they support their claim by quoting Carritt: "Equality of consideration is the only thing to the whole of which men have a right."[8]

After Benn and Peters elaborate by showing that equality of consideration is presupposed by law, they claim, "Equality of consideration is implicit in the idea of justice."[9] True. This use of the idea of justice, however, is as disingenuous as the use of the generic idea of law, for the idea of justice and/or law as something distinct from specific laws is the heart of theory of natural or human right. Whether it is Plato or Kant, or Aristotle or Aquinas, credence given to the idea of justice as distinct from positive law accepts the concept of law as such, i.e., a concept of right as such, i.e., the theory of natural or human right. Whether it is called natural law, natural rights, or human rights is a contingent matter, dependent upon current fashion in the canons of inquiry in philosophy of law and ethics. The idea of justice, and the idea of law, is the idea of right in the moral sense of the word "right." Benn and Peters find the connection between equality and justice that Kant found between freedom and

---

[7] *Principles of Political Thought*, p. 125.

[8] Ibid., p. 126, n. 5.

[9] Ibid., p. 127.

justice. This connection with justice suffices to show something is a human right. When Benn and Peters say that equality of consideration is implicit in the idea of justice, they unknowingly say it is a human right. For them, justice requires that each person be considered equally as citizens, presumably as morally responsible citizens. This presupposes adult human beings are moral agents, and that the moral agency required to be a responsible citizen in a given, historical context is a universal right.

In Chapter Three it was claimed that this kind of moral agency is the most fundamental human right. It presupposes freedom in the moral sense, which is therefore also a human right. Moral freedom is equal freedom, which presupposes a community under law, which is therefore also a human right. The community under law in turn presupposes equality of consideration, which is therefore also a human right. Equality in the moral sense of the word is therefore a human right.

Kant claimed freedom was the most fundamental human right, whereas Benn and Peters claim the one universal right is to equality of consideration. The emphasis upon freedom is the corollary of Kant's focus upon the inward, ethical aspects of human conduct such as good will, moral intentions, perceived obligations, and felt duties. It is the corollary of deontological ethics. The emphasis upon equality is the corollary of Benn and Peters's focus upon the outward, legal aspects of human conduct, such as consequences to other people, that is characteristic of pragmatic, utilitarian ethics. It is the corollary of philosophy of law.

Human conduct, however, is equally inward and outward, individual variations notwithstanding. A holistic, non-ideological view requires cognizance be taken of both inner and outer aspects. The emphasis upon one or the other ought to be transcended in educational theory by maintaining that freedom and equality are distinct human rights, reciprocally necessary to moral conduct and developing moral agency.

The argument for equality as a human right can be stated simply, without reference to law. Moral obligations are owed to other human beings simply because they are human beings, i.e., to all other human beings. If promise-keeping is a valid principle, one ought to keep his promises to whomever they are made, without discrimination. To decide there is a category of people to whom this obligation is not due is a moral error. Similarly with truth-telling. One's veracity is due to all others, irrespective of who the other is. All other people are worthy of being considered as reciprocating moral agents. This is their right as human beings. It is their human right. Equality is therefore a human right.

Kant's saying that human beings are empirically bound but transcendentally free can be paraphrased. They are empirically different, but transcendentally the same. Human beings are empirically unique, but they should be treated equally as moral agents and fellow citizens.

IV. Equal Educational Opportunity

At the very heart of its existence, schooling at public expense is the provision for people who cannot afford private schools an education equal to that offered by them. High schools in the United States were provided through the tax structure beginning in the 1870's to supply education for the working classes equal to that received by youth from well-to-do families. The expansion of schooling in the twentieth century in industrialized societies happened concurrently with the general democratization of society because of the steady pressures from the working classes for equal educational opportunities.

That public schooling as such is an attempt to provide equal education for working-class children has been strongly criticized by "revisionist" historians of education. They say the claim is a myth perpetrated to disguise the way in which the schools have been instruments of oppression, used by the economic system in an organized scheme of exploitation to fulfill its manpower needs. There is something in what they say, but three points can be made to challenge them. First, the school can be used this way only if it is not a dominant institution. It is not. It always receives its major orientation from the dominant institutions, i.e., from political and economic institutions. The complaint is trivial. Second, many people who want access to schooling to improve their opportunity in life want to get into the economic system that prevails in their society. They do not want to acquire knowledge for its own sake, for self-realization, to learn how to think, or to change economic systems. They even think efforts to educate for these things instead of a job are wasteful and exploitative. More than vertical mobility, furthermore, they want the knowledge and skills for a certificate or credential that will be honored by employers or for entrance to a tertiary school that will provide them with such a credential. They will frequently settle for a job of a quality similar to that of their parents or neighbors. They would be quite happy if the schools reproduced current patterns of social stratification, for this would mean they would avoid downward mobility and joblessness. The revisionist critique is not only trivial, it is beside the point. Most important, however, is that the pressures for the development of the public schools have come from the working classes themselves in strenuously organized efforts to improve their chances in life. It would make an interesting study to weigh the evidence for the thesis that public schools are an organized system of exploitation against the evidence to support the thesis that they have been wrested from the "ruling classes" by the working classes, for this would show whether the Marxists or Marx was correct. Its outcome, however, would affect nothing, for the use of tax money to provide schooling is *ipso facto* a provision of schooling for those who cannot afford private schools. This is quite independent of the question of whether the schools are engaged in liberation or oppression. Regardless of these contingent matters, where there are public schools, their facilities ought to be shared fairly. Whatever is distributed to the public in terms of educational goods ought to be distributed fairly. It is a matter of justice.

There are two questions. One is whether the people who attend public schools do receive an educational opportunity that is approximately equal to that which they might receive in a private school. The second is whether people attending public schools receive an educational opportunity equal to that of other people attending them.

The first question ought not be forgotten or conflated with the second one. It is stated factually to make an extremely important point. If a reason for the schools is to furnish an educational opportunity equal to that of private schools, one can certainly ask if they do so. This is nonsense, however, for it is like asking if the education of the blind child is equal to that of sighted children when Braille materials and instruction are provided. One does not really know how it can be equal or even comparable. There is a prima facie case for claiming it is equal, or perhaps roughly equal, or equivalent, if the academic subjects offered in the public school are the same as those taught in private schools. The claim that there is equal educational opportunity is warranted if a student can become as well prepared for university in the public schools as if he or she had attended a private high school. This is logically possible. The probability of it happening is not relevant to the question of whether the opportunity is there.

The second question is similar. Since the Smith-Hughes Act of 1917 furnished federal funds for the teaching of agricultural, industrial, and home economics subjects in American high schools, there has been continuous expansion of vocational, business, and general tracks in the high school curriculum to provide equal educational opportunities to students who are not preparing for tertiary schooling. To ask if the education in these tracks is equal to education in the academic track is also like asking if the education of the blind child is equal to that of the sighted. It is incomparable. It is different, but again there is a prima facie case for claiming it is equal, i.e., for holding it is "roughly equal" or equivalent.

It is necessary to retain this commonsense grasp of things. It may be the view closest to justice. Many people who graduate from non-academic tracks believe their education is fully equal to that offered in the academic track, which they have also sampled. Many regard the high school diploma as sufficient evidence that they have had an equal education, and they are satisfied that the curriculum studied gave them an opportunity equal to that received in the university preparation track. They might even say that whenever they sat in the same classroom together, they learned the same things as their friends who went on to tertiary schools.

This commonsense view of the matter should be called the equal access view of equality in education. It is a rather vague, indefinite belief that tax-supported, multi-track high schools furnish equal educational opportunity, and even equal education, providing that everyone has equal access to it through to the completion of the high school diploma. It regards the comprehensive high school as the ideal way to furnish education to everyone, and it believes there is no major injustice when everyone has access to some curriculum perceived to be suitable for their different aptitudes, interests, abilities, and futures, i.e., providing everyone has access to the several tracks without discrimination for reasons of social class, race, or gender.

Equality of consideration here means that the available curriculum tracks offer suitable choices, the decision is made by the student on the basis of knowledge of his or her own aptitudes, interests, abilities, and futures, and occurs late enough to be as realistic as possible and not irreversible, but early enough to be vocationally satisfactory. Under these conditions there can be said to be equal educational opportunity.

It is called the "equal access" view of equality in education because of the belief that a differentiated curriculum roughly correlated with ability and interest provides equal education. It might be called the "vague view" because it is not stated with sufficient precision to use words like "equivalent," "equitable," or "equal opportunity." It is assumed that there is such a thing as personal responsibility for learning outcomes, and that having the same number of years of schooling available to everyone provides equal access to education and equal education. Its lack of precision is its excellence, for it is like the belief that "mainstreaming" children with physical handicaps will give them an equal education. It is an extremely vital insight.

When the focus of attention is shifted from having equal access to the same programs to the characteristics of the programs, educational justice becomes understood as requiring equal resources, or a fair distribution of resources. It can then be maintained that vocational and academic tracks provide equal resources for education, or they provide equal educational opportunities in the sense that resources are provided for students equally, regardless of whether their needs are for vocational or university preparation. It is then considered fair to have two or more tracks, providing they are equivalent in terms of equipment, materials, teachers, class sizes, number of years in the program, etc. These things insure that the opportunities are equal. It should be noted that it is correct to say the opportunities are equal if instructional resources are adequate in each case. For example, shop materials and laboratory materials should each be adequate, although they might not cost the same. The opportunities are considered equal, furthermore, in terms of the adequacy of the resources, not in terms of the value of the content of the knowledge and skills to the students in their later lives.

It is sometimes held that equal educational opportunity requires the provision of the same resources for each student, i.e., the same textbooks, the same subjects, the same amount of time per subject, the same per capita expenditure, the same class sizes, etc. One of the reasons for the statewide use of a textbook is that it insures that no child uses an inferior one. This interpretation of justice in education attempts to provide equal education in the literal sense of the word. It does provide a minimum level of achievement in each subject each pupil is exposed to, but it is usually accompanied by an assessment system that helps the system and the students to select themselves for tertiary schools. It is therefore the fairest attempt to give students an equal opportunity to succeed scholastically and be selected for tertiary schools on achievement in school, regardless of social class, race, or gender.

Equal resources are therefore the conditions for equal opportunities to compete for the system's rewards. There are two aspects of distributive justice involved. The resources are supplied to everyone equally. Secondly, the opportunity for tertiary education is supposed to be granted solely on the basis of academic achievement and promise, without regard for social class, race, gender, or other irrelevancy.

The desire for equal access to schooling is a desire for equal education. The desire for equal resources, on the other hand, is a desire for equal education at one level in order to earn the right to receive unequal education at a subsequent level. The latter is held to be in accord with justice if higher grades, awards, etc., are distributed solely on the basis of ability and merit as evidenced in actual achievement in schools when measured by impartial criteria, providing everyone has equal access to the same resources. It is held that the bestowal of awards and tertiary school admission on the basis of what is learned under fair, competitive conditions provides justice defined as equal educational opportunity. This view assumes there are abilities and achievements necessary to succeed in tertiary schools and that the fairest way to ascertain who has these abilities is success in secondary schools. It also assumes it is fair for the most academically able to be selected for higher education, providing the rules and conditions of competition are scrupulously fair.

When it is said that the "equal access" view is a view of equal education, this means it is not an interpretation of equal opportunity in education. It is an interpretation of equality in education.

The "resource view," on the other hand, is an interpretation of equality in education that does not want equal education as much as it wants equal educational opportunity to acquire the rewards of the system in terms of tertiary schooling and admission to the professional classes.

Equal access to education is required by equal consideration as a human right. It is not incompatible with equal opportunities to compete for admission to tertiary schools if the latter are societally necessary and if it is true that not everyone can benefit from them. The same arguments for equal access apply to higher education. Municipal colleges and state universities furnish equal education to the academic elites who cannot afford to attend private institutions of higher learning.

Equal access to schooling and equal educational opportunity within it are therefore both required to secure justice in education. They are its necessary conditions for students who want a curriculum to prepare themselves for higher education, for those who want a curriculum to suit different vocational and other needs that is equal to the former, and for physically disadvantaged children. The necessity to provide additional measures to compensate for physical handicaps, including voluntary, segregated schooling, cannot override the obligation to grant equal access to common schooling and equal educational opportunity within it in order to provide justice in education.

These are the necessary conditions, but not the sufficient conditions for discriminated groups, particularly for the children of the poor. The particular problem of these children has been unfortunately referred to by such words as "cultural disadvantage," "cultural deficit," and "cultural deprivation." These get at something real that requires compensatory measures, but the words have lost favor because they have been applied to members of minority groups who were also poor. When children come from culturally different groups, the difference ought not be misinterpreted by diagnosing it as a deficit. For example, the child who comes from a Spanish-speaking home does not necessarily suffer from a cultural deficit simply because his school instruction occurs in English. He knows how to talk. He does suffer from a disadvantage, but it is a lack of equal access to schooling unless bilingual teachers are present to compensate for the cultural difference. The problem is only a bit more complicated for the children of the poor, independent of ethnic group membership, when the poverty is correlated with factors that prevent the child's normal cognitive growth, i.e., that prevent the child from developing cognitively in ways helpful to success in schools when compared to children from middle class homes. If the parents do not talk much, fluently, or readily with the child, e.g., then for the child to have equal access to schooling the compensatory measures involved in programs like Homestart, Headstart, Follow Through, Upward Bound, and so on are required for the same reasons bilingual teachers are needed by children who receive instruction in school in a language they have not learned at home.

In other words, when social and domestic circumstances fail to establish readiness for schooling by the time schooling age is reached, compensatory measures are required to establish equal access to schools. Phrases like "cultural deficit" may be satisfactory explanations for the lack of schooling readiness found among the children of poverty, but they ought not be used without careful diagnosis of specific circumstances. Otherwise they lend themselves to the creation of an expectation that the children cannot learn, which is pedagogically destructive. One does not have to know why a child is blind to prescribe instruction in Braille. Not all children from poor families suffer from a "cultural disadvantage," etc., and explanations for detected lack of readiness for school learning may not always be needed in order to prescribe the appropriate educational measures. It is the duty of the educational psychologist to define precisely what constitutes schooling readiness and to develop diagnostic tools to ascertain its lack and perhaps also to make the prescriptions to compensate for what should be called a "schooling disadvantage" in order to enable the children who lack readiness for schooling to have equal access to education, but this is merely the technology to provide such access. The conceptual point is that the child's homelife does not have to be investigated, or discussed, but schooling disadvantage resulting from the lack of schooling readiness requires appropriate compensatory measures in order to establish equal access to schooling in the same way physical handicaps require them. Whatever specialized vocabulary is necessary for diagnosis should not be allowed to obscure the fact that it is the lack of schooling readiness and schooling disadvantage that deserves to be compensated for in order to establish equal access to schools that can then furnish equal educational opportunity.

Equality of consideration as a human right would seem to require that these compensatory measures be taken in order to establish equality in education. They are required for educational justice. The tools to diagnose the lack of schooling readiness should be developed to the point where the schooling disadvantage due to environmental handicaps are as obvious as those due to physical handicaps and then compensated for with the same concern for the child's elemental right to an equal education, irrespective of social class, race, gender, etc.

Conclusion

General confusion over equality has occurred because of the confusion of factual matters with the simple belief that people should be considered equally irrespective of their social class, race, religion, gender, and physical or mental handicap. People deserve equality of consideration because they are human beings quite independent of their social class, race, gender, etc. It is their human right to be considered as human beings.

Educationally, the right to equal consideration means the right to access to the public institutions of education possessed by everyone in the society: it means everyone should have equal access to all the programs in the schools irrespective of their social class, race, religion, gender, handicap, or other educationally irrelevant factor.

It also means the right to equal educational opportunity within the schools, i.e., that all grades, awards, and honors should be distributed strictly for achievement in learning, without regard for social class, race, gender, handicap, or other irrelevant factors.

It also means that children have the right to compensatory measures to overcome the educational effects of physical, mental, and environmental handicaps and thereby gain effective access to educational programs provided for the general public.

It also means everyone is entitled to equal education, which means they are equally entitled to the same number of years of access to various curriculum tracks in which they are free to specialize without regard to their social class, religion, race, gender, handicap, or other educationally irrelevant factors.

It also means access to state-supported higher education on an equal access basis, i.e., without regard for social class, race, gender, etc. Although there is no injustice to restrict access to higher education according to previous relevant achievement, compensatory measures at the tertiary level to overcome the effect of environmental handicaps at the secondary level can serve justice when they insure that students with ability and motivation thereby acquire the knowledge and skills necessary to have effective access to higher education.

In other words, equal consideration in education means that public education ought to be open to the public without regard to social class, religion, race, gender, handicap, or other educationally irrelevant factors.

Chapter Six

EQUAL EDUCATION AS A HUMAN RIGHT

Our objective in dealing with the issue presented in this case is to see that school authorities exclude no pupil of racial minority from any school directly or indirectly on account of race.

Burger[1]

It was not until 1954 that the United States Supreme Court decided schools should be racially desegregated under the equal protection of the law clause of the fourteenth amendment to the United States constitution. The decision gave legal standing to equal consideration as a human right within the context of equal access to schooling. Then in 1964 the U.S. Congress ordered a survey to ascertain the status of equal educational opportunity for minority groups in the United States. When sociologists re-interpreted the ethical principle to suit their research capacities rather than inventing methods to investigate the problem, serious misunderstandings arose.

I. The Sociological Error

At least four errors resulted from the application of pre-existing research methods to problems of equal education. The first was the inability to diagnose the lack of schooling readiness in children from poverty backgrounds as an educational disadvantage, for the use of the cultural deficit model tended to deflect attention from the preparation of children to succeed in schooling to which they are supposed to have equal access. Two of the errors occurred in the research

---

[1] Swann v. Charlotte-Mecklenberg, 1971.

Congress commissioned Coleman to do to ascertain the extent to which minority groups received equal educational opportunities, and the other in the interpretation of his results.

An investigation to find out if any groups, minority or otherwise, were receiving equal educational opportunities should examine the programs available, admissions criteria and practice, composition of successful enrollees, incidents of manifest discrimination, allocation of resources, use of state and federal equalization funds, and the like. This would determine if schooling practice and policy supported principles of equal access and equal opportunity. It should use projective techniques and questionnaires to ask teachers, principals, and superintendents if they acted upon the principle of equal opportunity, to ask students, parents, and community action groups if they were denied access or opportunity anywhere in education, and so forth. Had Coleman explored the problem this way, his finding that the school attended did not make any difference would not have contrasted so strongly with the Federal Court decisions that ordered busing to achieve racial balance and equal access to schools for racial minority groups.

Instead of investigating the actual educational problem, Coleman acted like a sociologist. He set up a magnificent random sample and used nationally standardized achievement tests to get readily quantified "data" for massive "data-processing." This is the right procedure to get quantitative data, but it was the wrong data. The tests were largely vocabulary tests and were so remote from the data needed to answer the question about equal opportunities that Coleman's own words need to be quoted:

> The test battery in grade 1 consisted of the picture vocabulary test, which was used as a measure of verbal ability, and the association and classification tests as the non-verbal ability measures. In grade 3 the picture vocabulary test was again used as the verbal ability measure and classification and analogies were the non-verbal measures. Similar non-verbal measures were also used in grades 6, 9, 12, and 13. Grade 3 students were also given the reading and mathematics tests. Similar tests were also used in the higher grades of 6, 9, 12, and 13. Grade 6 used a similar battery as grade 3, with the exception that the sentence completion and synonym tests were

used in place of the picture vocabulary test. These types of tests were continually used in grades 9, 12, and 13. In grade 9, however, the general information test was added and also used in grades 12 and 13.[2]

The tests bear little resemblance to teacher-made tests designed to test for the kind of learning the teachers were trying to promote. They bear little evident relation to the curriculum materials the children in the sample would have been using. They cannot be considered as tests of actual school achievement, regardless of their names, and they bear remarkable resemblance to tests one might devise to assess the acquisition of white, formal English and the general middle-class culture that can be learned outside of school. Children should learn these things, but their measurement is not a measure of school learning. Instead of measuring school achievement, Coleman measured the acquisition of the dominant culture.

Coleman also gathered "data" regarding the students' backgrounds, i.e., social class, race, parental occupation, and career expectations. When he processed the data, he thought that schools did not make much difference in respect to providing equal opportunities in education, but he actually found that the culturally different are culturally different. He was looking for correlations between compensatory programs and subsequent school achievements, but egregiously assumed the tests actually measured the school achievement made possible by such compensatory programs. Even worse, the study was not longitudinal. It assumed the children measured in each of the grades 1, 3, 6, 9, 12, and 13 received the scores that would have been received if he had traced one group of age cohorts through thirteen years of schooling and measured them at the stated intervals. He treated a synchronically horizontal cross-section as if it were a longitudinal study. Since he was trying to measure the effects of innovative programs, the results are disastrous, for it is doubtful that anyone in the upper grades in the sample, taken before 1966, would have been the beneficiaries of Headstart, etc.

---

[2] James S. Coleman, et al., *Equality of Educational Opportunity* (Washington, D.C.: U.S. Office of Education, 1966), p. 575.

The worst blunder, however, was to proceed to talk about realities on the basis of inferences from the "data" simply because the "data" had certain names. The scores on the achievement tests have an unknown relationship to students' actual achievements, but this is forgotten once one calls the tests "achievement tests" and refers to scores as if they were achievements. The effects of compensatory measures might have been very powerful in dimensions of schooling achievements Coleman did not measure, and he had no basis for inferences about them. He did not in any case prove that Headstart, etc., did not work, for he did not even know how its beneficiaries managed in the upper grades compared to how they would have managed without Headstart, particularly since they were not into the upper grades by the time of the study.

His first error was research design. He neglected to research the actual allocation of resources and practices of equal access to existing programs to see if opportunities for learning were being equalized. When he tried to measure achievements instead of opportunities, he committed the second error, which was to use the moral principle as a criterion to make third-person judgments about the morality of the system, i.e., about its quality as compared to what the principle seems to require. This shifted concern from equal access and equal opportunity to equal education in the literal sense without giving the latter explanation or justification. This was conservative in effect because it reinforced existing curricula, which everyone is supposed to get equal portions of, although it had a progressive, salutory effect on minority groups expectations, particularly in regard to tertiary school admissions, which came to be understood as an indicator of equality of opportunity in primary and secondary schools. It had a polarizing effect as pessimists became glum, optimists militant, and conservatives cheerful when they heard Coleman's words that the kind of school one attended made no difference. The effect was probably counterproductive when it was supposedly shown that compensatory measures did not work, for then their costs could be curtailed without guilt.

These results were merely the effect of using the first-person moral principle as a basis for making the third-person moral judgments about society from the viewpoint of the disengaged spectator, over-distanced from the specific action of pedagogic situations. This happened unknowingly simply when the random sample was set up to measure the outcomes in terms of achievement. This was *ipso facto* an effort to make a moral judgment. The pseudo-scientific paraphernalia were simply the technical means developed by the technological consciousness to disguise the fact that the quantitative vocabulary was being used to express a moral judgment.

Judging an existing situation by a universal moral principle as if it were an absolute principle is like judging a glass that is half-full against a full one. One notes it is half-empty and regrets it is not full. One can also compare it against an empty glass, note it is half-full, and rejoice it is not empty. Had Coleman compared actual achievements with what they might have been without compensatory programs or without schools, he might not have concluded that the kind of school one attends makes no difference.

What Coleman seems to have meant was that the schools seem to make no difference in students' learning when one compares lower-class children to children from professional families. School learning seems to correlate with social class background in such a way that compensatory programs make little difference. To say that the schools make no difference means they are unable to provide vertical mobility for lower-class children. This is the sense in which they do not seem to provide equal opportunity, i.e., it is not an open contest after all. This impression, however, is precisely the sociological error. It results precisely from taking the outside, macrocosmic view of things to make the moral judgment. Before it is adopted, one ought to make one concrete suggestion about how a specific teacher can implement or promote vertical mobility. It is not something teachers do, or can do. What cannot be done in the classroom cannot be done in schools, for there is nowhere else in school to do it. On the other hand, an individual with drive and ability can get to tertiary schools from any primary school even if his or her parents are unskilled, laboring-class people. Coleman did not collect data about this kind of reality. Or, for another example, if teachers in relevant neighborhoods are bilingual, it will help to provide equal access and one knows this for a fact regardless of research into learning outcomes. In this case there is no point to asking if they provide opportunities that are really equal if the children are receiving instruction in a language not learned at home. There is no doubt that the opportunity will be more equal with bilingual teachers. The glass gets closer to half-full, like the education of the blind child learning Braille. Regardless of outcomes, the provision of compensatory measures is equitable when schooling disadvantage is demonstrable. Just because one cannot get the cup half-full does not mean one should stop pouring.

The ultimate error is to take the mistake made in the research design and claim there has been a change in the definition of the moral principle. This fallacy has since become known as a cover-up. Coleman claimed there was a shift in the understanding of the principle of equal opportunity from a concern for inputs to a concern for outputs, i.e., from equal resources to equal benefits.[3] It may be necessary to assess outputs to evaluate the justice of the system, which it may be desirable to do, but it does not follow that the research done to monitor the system should require a corresponding re-interpretation of the word "opportunity." Indeed, it cannot do that without failing to monitor the system.

In any case, education is not a cybernetic system, despite the misleading words "inputs" and "outputs." There can be equal opportunities without equal benefits. Every Olympic Games is full of them. Each event can have only three medalists or the point of the Games is lost. This is not an analogy but a conceptual clarification about the meaning of "opportunity." Measuring benefits to ascertain whether there have been equal opportunities in schools is rather like measuring the health of soldiers to see if they have had equal opportunities after they ate together in the same mess hall for a year. Positive health benefits would count as evidence for it, but the lack of good health would not count against it. There are too many interfering variables.

II. Equal Educational Benefits

The main value of equal educational opportunity does not lie within the educational realm, for education is only the putative

---

[3] James S. Coleman, "Responsibility of the Schools in the Provision of Equal Educational Opportunity," in *Education for Whom?* ed. Charles A. Tesconi and Emanuel Hurwitz (New York: Dodd, Mead, 1977), pp. 101ff.

means to available social, economic, vocational, and other goods. The point of the principle is to establish fair competition for the economic goods and benefits contingent upon educational outcomes. It is not an attempt to promote economic equality, but equal economic opportunity. Distributive justice requires fairness in the distribution of economic goods, the putative means to which is education. The competition for these economic goods is supposed to be fair, i.e., without being dependent upon the wealth, social class, race, etc., of one's parents. To have an equal opportunity to compete for them is like a horse race. All horses have an equal chance to win, although only one can. Plato embodied the principle of equal educational opportunity in *The Republic* and Jefferson put it into his 1779 Bill for the More General Diffusion of Knowledge.[4]

Social and economic justice, however, would not have to depend upon equal opportunities in a competitive system, nor upon educational outcomes.

It is the belief they do, or should, that results in the shift from inputs to outputs Coleman specified. This same case was argued by Green, who claimed there were two "interpretations" of equal educational opportunity, the resource view and the benefit view.[5] One claims there ought to be equal or equitable resources available to everyone in education, and the other claims there ought to be equal benefits available to all groups in education, without discrimination because of class, race, gender, etc.

The second view can only apply to groups, within which there are differential benefits, or it becomes a principle of equal education. Only the average members of one group should have an education equal to the average members of any other group. This view should be understood as the result of the diffusion of the Coleman report and/or an adamant refusal to believe there are equal opportunities unless they are manifested in the fair distribution of benefits to discriminated groups.

---

[4] Thomas Jefferson, in *Crusade Against Ignorance*, ed. Gordon C. Lee (New York: Teachers College Press, 1961), pp. 83-92.

[5] Thomas F. Green, "Equal Educational Opportunity; the Durable Injustice," *Philosophy of Education 1971* (Edwardsville: Studies in Philosophy and Education, 1971), p. 128.

The shift to the benefit view seems inherent in the idea of educational justice. When efforts to promote justice through the equitable distribution of resources seem unable to promote equal opportunities, it seems quite reasonable to shift attention to benefits.

When Coleman alleged the "evolution" of the shift began in the 1954 Brown case, then changed sharply in his own research of the Sixties, he granted his own opinions the force of historical reality. There was no such shift in the Brown case, however, as can be seen if one pays close attention to what was said:

> In these days it is doubtful that any child may reasonably be expected to succeed in life if he is denied the opportunity of an education. Such an opportunity, where the state has undertaken to provide it, is a right which must by made available to all on equal terms.

> We come to the question presented: Does segregation of children in public schools solely on the basis of race, even though the physical facilities and other "tangible" factors may be equal, deprive the children of the minority group of equal educational opportunities?[6]

The first paragraph argues for the necessity for equal access to schools, the second, for equal opportunities within schools. The second is for resources, not benefits, but in the intangible things. It claims that the resources are not accessible as opportunities under conditions of segregated schooling. This belief is then supported by a quotation from one of the four cases the court was considering that claimed that segregation is demoralizing and has detrimental effects on learning. The court said, "The effects of this separation on their educational opportunities were well-stated."[7] The word "effects" here refers simply to the opportunity to learn in the classroom, and there is no shift to benefits. In any case, the decision by the court to guarantee access to all schools irrespective of race is a decision for equal

---

[6] Chief Justice Warren delivered the opinion of a unanimous court. In Richard Kluger, *Simple Justice* (New York: Knopf, 1976), p. 781.

[7] Ibid., p. 782.

resources, and there is nothing in the court decision to suggest that anything more than desegregation is necessary to create the educational opportunity that the court said should be made available to all on equal terms.

The shift to the benefit view, then, was part of the developing concern of the Sixties for the general improvement of the poor and minority groups. Because this would be effected through political means, rather than education, by anyone who wanted it and had the political power, it is not possible to do it through education. This means it is reasonable to maintain a sharp distinction between social goods and benefits and educational goods.

It is also necesssary to maintain a sharp distinction between educational resources and benefits, as indicated in the following diagram:

Educational Goods

Resources		Benefits	
Ancillary	*Pedagogic*	*Achievements*	*Awards*
classmates	teachers	knowledge	grades
buses	books	skills	honors
lunch	classrooms	tastes	certificates
health care	libraries	appreciations	credentials
etc.	etc.	etc.	etc.

The crucial point is that educational achievements such as knowledge and skills are the outcomes of learning. They are not given to one, but are the outcome of effortful study and practice. On the other hand, awards such as grades, honors, certificates and credentials are given to one in recognition of achievements. Thus there are two categories of outcomes, or benefits. Only one of these is distributed in the ethical sense of the word.

Advocates of the benefit view such as Coleman fail to distinguish between the two categories of outcomes. The importance of the oversight appears when one realizes that the fundamental issue is not equal opportunity in education. It is educational justice, to secure which schools with equal access and equal opportunity were devised. The issue is whether the general provision of education is equitable, and how manifest inequities can be conceptualized. Nothing depends upon distorting the concept of equal educational opportunity.

All educational goods are not matters for distributive justice. For example, some of the ancillary resources such as food, medical care, and time and space for exercise can be furnished for children and are candidates for distributive justice, but health is not. Health is partly a result of the use of the things that can be furnished, partly a personal achievement, and partly a matter of the nature of the body in response to these things. It is unfair if someone does not get enough to eat, but it is not if their body will not assimilate food. The latter is unfortunate, but not a matter of justice. Similarly, educational resources and awards are candidates for justice in their distribution, but educational achievements cannot be handed out. Differential achievements are therefore neither just nor unjust. They simply are not a matter of distributive justice. It is the very fact that the differential outcomes of education in terms of acquired knowledge and skills are a matter of individual initiative, effort, motivation, inherent ability, self-discipline, and achievement that it is vitally important to have equal educational opportunities.

The desire to establish equality between groups in respect to the outcomes of education that are the result of personal achievement is contrary to justice. To insist that minority groups need more than equal access and equal educational opportunities to achieve at the same level as other groups, in fact, assumes they are scholastically inferior even when schooling disadvantages are duly compensated. It would therefore seem that the shift to the benefit view of equal educational opportunity involves condescension if not racism.

An example might help. Suppose it is established that the children attending a specific school are characteristically two or three years behind children in other schools in their reading scores, and/or other educational development. As Green put it, our sense of injustice is instantly aroused. We assume that these children may be getting equal educational opportunities but are not benefitting from them.

Instinctively, we want the children to benefit equally, i.e., to find ways to bring their reading level up to standard, and so on. This would be totally wrong, however, for it unconsciously assumes that the teaching staff in that school is incompetent, lazy, or both. This is not known. It could be a dedicated, hard-working, competent staff, who are in fact doing a superlative task in the circumstances. The children could be enjoying above average educational opportunities, from which they are unable to benefit. If so, the feelings of injustice are misplaced, the situation is misunderstood, and moral outrage makes things worse because it prevents an adequate diagnosis of the situation. The error is assuming the macrocosmic, sociological perspective in which one is unable to see the trees for the forest, and then being unable to accept the reality that schools, like hospitals, are simply not able to help everyone equally. They, too, can have successful operations while losing clients.

The word "distribution" has been thoroughly ambiguous in discussions of equal educational opportunity.[8] If one says that achievement scores are distributed according to a normal curve, or that one has placed them in rank order to see how they are distributed, one is using the word "distributed" in the statistical sense. No one is giving out anything, and there is no matter of justice except for computational accuracy. There is no issue of distributive justice in the ethical sense. The conversion of raw scores into grades, however, does distribute something in more than the statistical sense. It gives out grades for achievements. The achievements themselves are not handed out, or there would be no point to giving out grades for them. To say that learning achievements are distributed thus uses the word in the statistical sense. It means only that they are different from each other, not that they are handed out.

Educational achievements are therefore not candidates for distributive justice. Distributive justice involves the delivery sense of the word "distributed." Something has to be actually handed out, given over, delivered, and it has to be valuable and in short supply, to be a

---

[8] This was noticed in the response to Green by Gerald Reagan and mentioned by Lois Weinberg, "A Radical View of Educational Justice for Women," *Philosophy of Education 1975-1976* (Tempe: Arizona State University Press, 1976), p. 145, but neither followed the matter up.

candidate for distributive justice. Educational achievements are not only not handed out, they are not "scarce." One person's knowing something does not prevent someone else from also knowing it. Everyone in a swimming class can learn how to swim, and a teacher can get all the children to learn something. Because one person's knowing does not prevent another's, it is as if the "supply" were inexhaustible, except there is no "supply."

This means that the benefit view of equal educational opportunity is not a view of distributive justice. It is a conceptual mistake, caused by the technological consciousness that would accept learning achievements as outputs of a closed system, rather than being the achievements of human beings, each with their own value and dignity. The conceptual confusion seems not wholly innocent, for the attention it directs toward the achievements that are necessarily undeliverable is diverted from the benefits that are candidates for distributive justice, i.e., from grades, honors, diplomas, certificates, credentials, and degrees. These are the benefits upon which subsequent economic opportunities seem to depend.

Justice would go astray, of course, were awards distributed without due regard for the appropriate achievements. The issue in the whole context, however, is social justice rather than educational justice. One can make the following deduction. From the social and economic goods to which everyone should have an equal opportunity, one can deduce that the educational benefits upon which they depend are matters of distributive justice. This includes certificates and credentials, and the achievements upon which they directly depend.

These particular achievements, then, are indirectly a matter of distributive justice, for they insure that minority groups receive their fair share of legitimate certificates and credentials. The allocation of resources to insure that these achievements are acquired is therefore a matter of justice. So are all the compensatory measures necessary. This includes the credentials needed to gain proportionate admission to tertiary schools. It would not necessarily include the achievements Coleman tried to measure. Greatest priority would go to the resources to provide the achievements recognized by the certificates and credentials needed to gain entrance into the economic system.

In other words, the historical struggle for justice by minority groups depends upon an equitable distribution of certificates and credentials that serve as permits into the occupational, social, economic, political system. These benefits of education are matters of distributive justice, and they are necessary to insure that there is equality of educational opportunity in the critical sense.

III. Education as a Human Right

If educational achievements are not matters of distributive justice because they are not handed over from a short supply, their intergroup comparison cannot ascertain if equal opportunities existed. The groups might have had opportunities that were not exploited for reasons not revealed in comparative achievement scores. If the data shows females scoring lower in mathematics than males, for example, it does not show that the system involves gender discrimination. It may, and this is indubitably the first hypothesis to check, but it requires different data. The low achievement in mathematics can result from completely rational choices to develop in areas not involving mathematics. By itself, it does not signify inferior education.

Achievements in the acquisition of knowledge, skills, tastes, and appreciations are not a matter of distributive justice, but they are a matter of justice. These are not things one has been allocated or possesses. They are things one is. They enable one to be the human being one is, and are therefore a matter of human right. For example, reading comprehension is not a thing one has but something one can do, and the acquired skill is a human right if it can be argued that everyone has a right to this skill.

The child's right to education received emphasis in the International Year of the Child, 1979, along with the right to nutrition, love, medical care, a name and nationality, and special care if handicapped. These rights of the child should be considered together to contextualize the human right to education as a right of children. Celebrations like the Year of the Child invite proclamations, but they have to be articulated because someone might argue that the child does not have a right to these things. They are, for example, freely given to it by its parents. This is true because when the parents have adequate means, the obligation rests very lightly. It is a joy to do what in unfortunate circumstances can become a difficult duty, but this does not signify the obligation is not present. The condition for something to be a human right is that it is necessary to enable the person to become a human being as such. To claim that a child has a right to love, nutrition, medical care, and education, then, means (a) the child will not grow up to become a normal adult member of the human species without them, which is true, and (b) adults are morally obligated to supply them to children simply because they are children. This is also true.

Liberal democracies consider it morally negligent for parents to refuse to feed, clothe, shelter, and love their children, unless they are destitute. Civil authorities are empowered to take children from negligent parents and place them in foster homes. This shows legal recognition of the obligations of society, i.e., of adults considered collectively, to care for all of its children. All children are assumed to have a claim on adult society in respect to the means to become an adult member of the society, i.e., of the species. This means they are human rights.

One might argue there are children only a mother can love. This means that the child does not have to earn his mother's love. She gives it unconditionally simply because the child is a child. It may be because it is her own child, but this is largely a contingent matter. Children are equally beautiful, but in any case their beauty is not relevant to whether they deserve enough to eat: the argument would violate the principle of equal consideration and impartiality of judgment.

To say that education is a human right means that just as the child has the right to food and shelter when it is too young to sustain itself at normal growth patterns, so, too, does it have the right to an education that will enable it to sustain itself as an adult in the society into which it is born. It means society is obligated to its young to educate them to participate in the activities characteristic of the adult members of the society. If it is unable or unwilling to assume this obligation, it should not have children.

It therefore accords with what is right, with justice, for each child to be educated to adult status in the society of birth. The kind of education to which there should be equal access, and in which there ought to be equal opportunity, produces outcomes that are a human right. They are those achievements, or acquired skills and competencies, necessary to maintain adult status in a specific society.

This right supplements but does not replace the claim that distributive justice requires that minority groups receive their fair share of certificates and credentials. It therefore includes the achievements necessary for certificates and credentials, but it also includes achievements related to adult life outside of occupational structures in personal, social, leisure, and civic activities.

The importance of the consideration of education as a human right can be seen through a different diagnosis of the problem Coleman addressed. If a white, upper-middle-class, sheltered but mature professional person would have actually visited a classroom or two in a racially isolated, ghetto high school about the time Coleman did his research, he or she would have been exposed to the raw data regarding equal opportunity. The trauma would have made the use of a battery of achievement tests to quantify the raw data morally unacceptable, for it would have appeared to be unnecessary and an avoidance technique. Nor would she or he have drawn the conclusion that the kind of school one attended made no difference. He or she would have been quietly grateful he had not attended that sort of school and thought that the kind of school one attended made all the difference in the world. Not very much would have been made of the claim that the important variable was the neighborhood and social class of the parents. True as these things may be, they merely divert attention from the raw data. In that situation the morally sensitive person would have been simply appalled by the waste: the waste of time in class, the waste of the previous lives of the students, and the waste of the lives to which they were obviously destined.

This kind of waste cannot be explained away by blaming someone. It is not the fault of the students, teachers, schools, neighborhood, society, or the system. The battery of tests was superfluous. Supplying a few remedial teachers or teacher's aides does not confront the problem, which is to promote the most effective use of school time. The low scores on so-called achievement tests are merely a sign of the loss and destruction of human possibility. This is not corrected through raising test scores but through finding ways of letting children use their time productively while they are in school.

The abandonment of the so-called benefit view because of the recognition that achievement cannot be handed out eliminates the belief that the worth of compensatory programs should be judged by results on so-called achievement tests. Dysfunctional resources do not furnish equal educational opportunities regardless of equal or compensatory aspects. The kinds of resources that actually engage the children in learning activities are required for educational justice, even if they do not directly produce outcomes easily measured for intergroup comparisons. The worth of compensatory materials and programs is rightfully judged by their ability to engage children in productive learning. The criterion is not productive learning but engagement. What is crucial is that the time is not wasted, i.e., that the children make the most of their developmental time.

The time of schooling is taken out of the lives of young people to enable them to develop educationally as well as biologically before they enter into society as adults. The basic criterion of educational justice is therefore whether the time allocated for education is used productively. Application of the criterion requires a consideration of the uniqueness of the particular child and whether the individual is enlarging his or her own possibilities in ways that are compatible with the certificating, credentialing processes that lead to the social and economic goods and benefits that ought to be fairly distributed.

When the injustice incurred by educationally disadvantaged children is interpreted as the waste of their developmental time, it can be understood simply as the lack of education. This is almost tautological, except it allows one to say that the fifteen-year-old young man who reads, counts, and thinks like a twelve-year-old probably acts like one, although he is of normal intelligence, and this allows one to see that he is not only lacking achievement along some of the measurable dimensions but lacking educational maturation appropriate for his age. Resources that enlist an engagement in learning can promote the maturational processes that occur in schools through the years because of the engagement in learning even if the scores on the dimensions measured are not "equal" to those of people in other groups. Racist, classist, and sexist criteria of achievement will always yield racist, classist, and sexist results. What is needed are the resources to promote the engagement in learning that results in the educative development of human possibility. The resources that do allow this development during the time allocated for education therefore belong to each person as a human right, i.e., irrespective of race, gender, etc.

This right is more fundamental than the right to education. It is the right to become a human being through education. It is the right to be.

The Brown Case should have been understood through the language of human rights, rather than through the spurious shift in the concept of equal educational opportunity. Its explicit statement that black people were denied the equal protection of the law by segregated schooling actually defends the human right to equal education. The explicit claim about the detrimental effects of segregation on learning is that it prevents an active engagement in learning and is tantamount to saying it is dehumanizing. Finally, it manifested a concern for education as a universal human right, i.e., one that was not open to abrogation by majoritarian legislation.

Because equal access to education should have been granted everywhere in the United States when the court announced its decision in 1954, subsequent discussion about justice in education should have been unnecessary. Where it was needed it should have focused on the substantive obligation that underlies the procedural obligations regarding equal access to education in which there are equal educational opportunities. It should have focused upon the human right to education, which is the right to use one's developmental time as a child and youth productively so that one can assume a position in society as a morally responsible, free citizen, i.e., as a moral agent. Although the amount of time allocated to development is relative to a particular society, equity requires that everyone be granted the resources that will enable them to use that educational time most productively.

IV. Equal Education as a Human Right

The question of equality in education can now be understood in the context of human rights. The idea developed historically that to obtain equal educational opportunities, people need equal access to education, i.e., they need to be provided with resources equal to those purchased for their young by wealthy people. This has come to mean that at the secondary school level it is fairer to furnish equivalent resources in a differentiated curriculum than the same resources for everyone, i.e., that different but equal education should be provided in non-academic tracks for people with specialized needs. This supplements but does not replace the common, general education in the academic subjects that insures the acquisition of an equal education.

Minority groups have explicitly and actively expressed their claim for educational opportunities equal to those of the dominant group. Their claims may have been confused when expressed in the language of equal opportunity possessed by the dominant group. As important as busing, racial balance, integration, and equal achievements are, their point is to establish equal access to educational programs without discrimination because of race, gender, etc. It is a matter of elemental human rights, of being given equal consideration without regard for race or gender.

The point seems to have been adequately if concisely stated in the relevant article of the Universal Declaration of Human Rights adopted by the United Nations in 1948, the first section of which says:

> Everyone has the right to education. Education shall be free, at least in the elementary and fundamental stages. Elementary education shall be compulsory. Technical and professional education shall be made generally available and higher education shall be equally accessible to all on the basis of merit.

What it means to say that higher education should be equally accessible to all on the basis of merit can be understood in the light of the Declaration's second article, which claims that everyone is entitled to the rights specified in the entire document "without distinction of any kind, such as race, colour, sex, language, religion, political or other opinion, national or social origin, property, birth, or other status." Merit necessarily means previous achievement. It might also involve ability and promise, but these are difficult to assess apart from actual achievement, which cannot exist without them. It is clear that merit does not include preferred religious, political, national, or economic status. The point of saying "on the basis of merit" is not to establish a meritocracy but to deny the relevance of these other kinds of factors.

The content of technical, professional, and higher education has to be decided in context by qualified experts. This leaves the content of elementary and general education at the secondary school to be specified, but clearly required by the next sentence in the document, "Education shall be directed to the full development of personality and to strengthening of respect for human rights and fundamental freedoms." This implies that a common, general education is needed to develop the human being as such, i.e., that equal education is a human right.

Because the Declaration also maintains that participation in the economic system is a human right (Article 23), it has to be understood as implying that specialization in technical, professional, or higher education is a human right, which would substantiate the claim that equity requires a fair distribution of certificates and credentials. If education is to assist in the full development of personality, however, such specialization ought to be balanced by common, general education, and the right to this is the human right to equal education.

It is extremely difficult to argue that any particular knowledge or skill is necessary for human development. If at least one adult without it who seems quite human can be found, such a claim is refuted. Illiterate adults in advanced industrial societies, for example, can compensate by the development of other endearing, valuable qualities that forbid hasty generalization about the knowledge and skill necessary to become human. There is also a matter of practicality. One cannot say primary school education should be compulsory everywhere as a human right if other such rights deserve priority.

On the other hand, universal literacy and numeracy are generally accepted ideals of education. Illiterate adults can become more fully human by learning how to read the newspapers and assuming citizenship responsibilities at a more complex level and by becoming a moral agent at a deeper degree of responsibility.

Most of what is accepted as the human world by modern societies is not accessible except to literate, numerate people. A prima facie case can therefore be made out that it is necessary to gain access to this modern world through literacy and numeracy in order to become a human being. Equal access to the world requires an equal education to literacy and numeracy. This does not allege that illiterate adults are not equally human, for they may very well have access to the human world through one or more of the practical activities of the arts, crafts, trades, or sports. Making and doing things, and playing, may be as humanizing as the reasoning that literacy and numeracy make possible.

The curriculum for the common, general education designed to promote the full development of personality would therefore seem to require the learning of at least one art, craft, or trade, and at least one sport. Each gives a particular kind of access to the world. The mode of access to the world, of knowing the world, involved is a necessary part of the education of everyone who aspires to become fully human. Particularly if they are not going to practice an art, craft, or trade as a full time occupation as adults, they should learn one as a hobby or artistic skill in order to gain the solid grasp on the world through their hands that these practical activities involve. This enables one to know the world and to feel secure in it in a precise, irreplaceable way. It also enables one to have a proper appreciation for the contribution to society made by people who work with their hands. To this should be added some reasonable level of achievement in at least one sport, or dance, in order to come to know the world through a holistic bodily grasp on it and a full bodily immersion in it, i.e., to gain access to the world through holistic play. It also enables one to play throughout one's life.

To the bodily but cognitive development that occurs only through some degree of achievement in some art, craft, or trade, and in sport, or dance, should be added the development of the conceptual processes that occurs in the acquisition of literacy and numeracy. The standard, human rights justification is that literacy and numeracy involve symbolic processes essential to become a human being. They do, but it is more fundamental to indicate that symbols are symbols of things in the world. They therefore constitute a mode of access to the human world not otherwise obtainable. One should learn to read, write, and calculate for the same reason one should learn at least one art, craft, or trade, and at least one sport, or dance. Each is a unique, distinctive source of knowledge about the world that is necessary for humanization. Each gives a mode of access to the world not otherwise obtainable. It follows that learning at least one art, craft, or trade, at least one sport or dance, and acquiring basic literacy and numeracy are human rights.

Consideration of the intellectual part of general education should begin with the observation that the world does not belong to anyone. Everyone can have conscious access to the things in the world without depriving anyone else of them. If Niagara Falls wears out, for example, it will not be through the gazes of millions of spectators who have come to know and value its beauty. It is the function of common, general education to give people this kind of cognitive access to the things of the world that they may know and value them through the content drawn from the natural sciences, social sciences, and humanities.

It probably cannot be argued successfully that learning the natural sciences is a human right. On the other hand, the child becomes aware of the things in the natural world through ordinary experience—of physical things, growing things, living things, changing things, moving things, celestial things, etc. He explores the natural world, the plant world, the animal world, the chemical world, and the physical world in ordinary, childhood play activities, and comes to learn the common sense objects in each of these sub-worlds. Much adult activity is dependent upon the refined, disciplined knowledge of the things in the natural world that the child or non-literate adult knows only as common sense objects because it is the natural world that provides the basic resources that sustain human life. One's access to these things in the natural world is greatly increased by the methodology and conceptual schemata of the respective natural sciences. These should be exploited to enable people to become aware of the things in the natural world as the things they are when submitted to disciplined study to form a generally accurate picture of reality, i.e., an image of the universe as several billion years old, of the planets as revolving around the sun, aware that the constellations of astrology do not exist, knowing that UFO's do not exist, either, cognizant that non-living and living things exist in dynamic interplay because living things have evolved through adaptation, that nutrition is basically a bio-chemical process that can be guided by knowledge to promote health, that medical science is different from sorcery, shamanism, and the witch doctor, and so on.

Similarly, the child becomes aware of the things in the social world through untutored experience, but the moral agency of adulthood requires learning about the economic, political, legal, and social systems of society in general education. That is, one ought to gain a disciplined, conceptual access to the things in the economic world, the political world, the civil world, and the social world, such as the market, unemployment, inflation, representative government, political parties, civil and criminal law, the court system, and so on, i.e., to the major phenomena in one's own society. Only the disciplined study of these things as they are made accessible through the conceptual schemes of the relevant disciplines can integrate the person into society and enable one to function fully as a moral agent.

Finally, one also gains a disciplined access to the human world through poetry, literature, drama, music, history, ethics, religion, and philosophy. Through the conceptualizations of the humanities one becomes aware of the things of the lived world such as love, suffering, jealousy, conquest, adventure, mystery, cultural and scientific inventions, the struggle between good and evil, catastrophes, revolutions, and human aspirations, hopes, and tragedies in a manner sufficiently disciplined to bring some order to one's own feelings, hopes, and aspirations.

Each of the natural sciences, social sciences, and humanities has its own mode of knowing things, its own mode of access to the things in the world, but all of them cannot be included in any finite general education. What is important to general education is that the things in the natural world, the social world, and the human world that one becomes aware of in common sense experience are studied in disciplined ways in schools through the use of the conceptual schemes of the disciplines to establish a progressive enlargement and deepening of perceptual reality.

Common, general education should therefore include significant, disciplined study of the most important things in the major regions of the world. These may be classified together with their curriculum correlates and objectives as follows:

Elements of Common, General Education

1. things in the written world: reading (literacy)
2. things in the quantified world: arithmetic (numeracy)

3. things in the fabricated world:	at least one art, craft, or trade
4. things in the play world:	at least one sport, or dance
5. things in nature:	natural sciences
6. things in society:	social sciences
7. things in the lived world:	humanities

Each of these categories concerns the exploration of a unique region of the world and a particular mode of access to the things in that region. These various modes of knowing nurture specific intellectual powers as their conceptualized schemata come to structure conscious awareness of the things in the region through their disciplined study. It can be argued that the development of these various intellectual abilities is a human right in the standard defense of "liberal education," but this argument is insufficiently fundamental. The various modes of awareness of things become differentiated modes of knowing because of the use of the differentiated schema involved in their disciplined study. These become differentiated because of the differentiated characteristics of the phenomena studied. The acquisition of the various modes of awareness is therefore secondary to the access to the things in the world. This means that the reason these curriculum strands should be available to all human beings in the course of their educational development is to insure they have equal access to the things of the world.

These things are accessible to everyone in the course of ordinary experience, for they have access to them through the perceptual consciousness of them structured by the schemata of ordinary language. The presence of the conceptual schemata in these seven strands can discipline the study of these things and give greater access to them. Education is this conceptual acquisition of perceptual reality. Equal exposure to the study of the things in the major regions of the world in education therefore provides equal access to reality.

Equal access to the world is required to establish educational justice. In this sense equal education is a human right.

Conclusion

The question of equality in education concerns what should be equalized in the provision of education to insure justice is done. Educational resources can be equalized by allowing everyone to have equal access to educational programs and equal opportunities within them. Educational benefits can be equalized by insuring that socially and economically disadvantaged groups receive their fair share of school certificates and educational credentials even if it requires compensatory measures to achieve this result. The number of years devoted to schooling can be equalized through adjustment of compulsory attendance laws. The productive use of school time can be equalized through the development of differentiated ("compensatory") materials that effect an engagement in learning about the things in the world. Finally, education itself can be equalized through the provision of a common curriculum consisting of elements that disclose the regions of the world to which education should give equal access.

One or another of these things is emphasized by various ideologies. Justice requires them all.

Chapter Seven

DISCIPLINE AND DIGNITY IN EDUCATION

> Both the classical rights of the individual which protect him from the intervention and encroachments of the power of the State and also the political rights which assure to the individual a share in that power, derive from the principle of human dignity.
>
> Schneider[1]

The teacher is obligated to maintain the classroom as a community under law to insure that students have equal opportunities to maximize their learning. This aspect of equality was noted in the justification of the authority to establish the rules needed for equal freedom. Equality of consideration requires the enforcement of these rules to maintain the discipline of learning. The question is how to maintain discipline without the loss of essential dignity.

I. The Question of Discipline in Education

The myth invented by some educational psychologists that good teachers do not have discipline problems is a recommendation to take a positive approach through concentration on the tasks of good teaching. An enthusiastic, flexible, prepared, congenial teacher who

---

[1] Peter Schneider, "Social Rights and the Concept of Human Rights," *Political Theory and the Rights of Man*, ed. D.D. Raphael (Bloomington: Indiana University Press, 1967), pp. 91f.

varies voice, method, and materials and succeeds in enlisting pupils in learning activities will have fewer discipline problems than a boring pedant. The first question is whether good teaching can suffice to eliminate problems of discipline. The answer is affirmative. Many teachers have none because of their good teaching.

Their absence, however, does not necessarily indicate good teaching. Nor can it be said that good teachers do not have to give attention to questions of classroom management. To the contrary, conscientious teachers often reflect on ways to avoid confrontations, minimize upsets, and mobilize pupils' energies toward the maximization of learning. They also take things in stride and handle them so adroitly they no longer perceive them as discipline problems.

There is a difference between discipline problems and the problem of discipline. If one sees Jenny is out of sorts today but will be all right again tomorrow, or that Johnny is excited and needs reminding to use his "inside voice" again, one can deal deftly with these very minor problems and move on quickly. These problems emerge unpredictably. Resolving them in educative ways requires an understanding of the more general problem of discipline, i.e., of maintaining the classroom as an orderly place in which learning occurs, to avoid having minor discipline problems coalesce into a problem of the discipline of the class. The difference is between having discipline problems in a classroom and having a discipline problem with a class. The former concerns behavioral problems, i.e., matters of individual conduct, but the latter concerns the maintenance of the classroom as a community of scholars devoted to maximizing their learning. It concerns this kind of community under law.

Consequently there are two different questions of discipline in education. One concerns irregular individual conduct; the other, the general conditions of learning. The former is a perennial question that emerges from time to time quite unpredictably. The latter often arises in times of perceived permissiveness. It is not a question of the meaning of the word "discipline," but a concrete question of whether the learning in a specific classroom, or in classrooms generally, can be improved with more discipline. It emerges when permissiveness allegedly interferes with learning and more discipline is desired.

There is seldom any complaint about too much discipline in the classroom. The relevant objection is against regimentation and authoritarianism. People who raise the question of discipline, however, do not advocate regimenting classrooms in authoritarian ways. They merely want teachers to fulfill their obligations to promote learning. Someone who finds their concern or approach morally objectionable is obligated to provide morally acceptable ways to maintain classroom discipline.

To be morally acceptable, it ought to insure that students make progress toward moral agency by becoming increasingly aware of their responsibilities. This means the classroom should be perceived or experienced as a community under law dedicated to the maximal learning. Under any form of leadership—*laissez-faire*, democratic, moderate, or directive—students ought to learn to act willingly in accordance with the rules needed to establish the necessary discipline. These rules should be just, i.e., necessary to establish equal freedom, and students should have as much freedom as they can bear responsibly.[2]

Under these conditions the question of discipline cannot arise. It emerges, then, when the rules to establish equal freedom are not operative, or when the teacher inadvertently allows more freedom than can be managed, or when the students reject the rules and/or responsibility. Investigation of the question, furthermore, is independent of any specific model of pedagogy. Regardless of the teacher's stance on the authority/freedom continuum, the final criterion of a morally acceptable solution is the maximization of the student's disciplined learning.

A morally acceptable way also retains the concept of discipline. One of the goals of education is the acceptance of the responsibility for one's own learning, i.e., self-discipline. A fully responsible moral agent is capable of self-discipline. For an education to freedom to occur through as much self-discipline as possible, the concept of discipline has to be available to students as a moral principle to enable them to understand that it is good to be able to persevere in learning activities regardless of temptation or distraction.

If a stern disciplinarian engages in a morally undesirable practice,

---

[2] This paragraph summarizes earlier arguments.

it is not because he restricts the pupil's freedom, nor because he is undemocratic, nor because he imposes discipline on the classroom. His actions are morally undesirable when and only when they diminish learning or violate the student's dignity as a human being. Discipline that does not violate human dignity is morally superior to the psychological manipulation that bypasses moral agency and is therefore contrary to human dignity.

Although the people who raise the question of discipline in education usually see it as a good thing, those who raise the question of punishment usually want to eliminate it. The former might be accompanied by a punitive attitude, but the latter is often raised to challenge the legitimacy of punitive attitudes in education. All punitiveness has to be transcended, of course, to ask either question with human dignity.

When one asks about discipline in a specific circumstance, one is looking for a programmatic answer and might settle for a system of punishments to enforce discipline in the classroom. Conversely, asking about the conditions under which punishment is justifiable in education seeks some of the parameters of the question of discipline.

With or without punishment, discipline is a continuing question in education. Theories settle the problem, but actual school-keeping remains complicated. Perhaps the most enduring problem of pedagogy is that of effective discipline.

This is as it should be, for it is "the other side of the coin" of freedom. The most important educational question concerns freedom, but because they are co-extensive with it, the questions of discipline and punishment are equally fundamental. Freedom and discipline are dialectically related in education. If the teacher has authority to promote the conditions of equal freedom and equal opportunity to learn, he or she has the authority to maintain the requisite discipline. The most that can be asked is that it be maintained in a manner compatible with human dignity. The question is how to maintain discipline and dignity in education.

II. The Meaning of the Word "Dignity"

Freedom is the central ideal of eighteenth century versions of democratic ideologies, now known as classical liberalism, or plain liberalism in England and Australia. Equality is the central ideal of nineteenth and early twentieth century versions, now known as modern liberalism, or plain liberalism in America. The shift in emphasis in the democratic ideals from liberty to equality was a wide-ranging, profound, historical shift in the cultural ideologies as they continued to become democratized in the search for social and economic justice.

Human dignity has now become the central ideal as the result of an equally momentous shift toward fraternity and human dignity that has been occurring since World War II. Whereas the words "natural rights" are found in the ideologies of the seventeenth and eighteenth centuries, and the words "civil rights" and "welfare rights" in the ideology of modern liberalism, the words "human rights" have been used increasingly since the Second World War. Human rights were even mentioned in the inaugural speech of the American President in 1976. This emphasis upon human rights is itself an index of the shift toward an increasing awareness of the dignity of the human being as a counterpoint to the development of the technological consciousness.

When liberty is considered most basic, the principle functions to defend a person's claims against society. It is therefore thought to be a natural right, inherent in human nature, or in the natural state of man, prior to a voluntary contract to participate in society. The discovery that natural rights are highly dependent upon the society in which one lives leads to calling them civil and political rights. These are the same rights, but they are defended in a different way. The additional discovery that they are dependent upon one's humanity, irrespective of one's society, which is largely a contingent matter, finally leads to calling them human rights. First they were thought to inhere in human nature, then in human society, then in the human condition. In one sense the name does not matter. As Raphael has pointed out, the intent in any case is to establish a sense of right, law, justice, and obligation on an ethical basis as something explicitly distinct from positive law.[3]

Calling something a human right is therefore sometimes intended to contrast sharply with the right established by a statute law that

---

[3] D.D. Raphael, "Human Rights: Old and New," in *Political Theory and the Rights of Man*, p. 54.

seems contrary to justice. When Martin Luther King, for example, sat in the seats of the theater reserved for Caucasians, he might very well have said it was his human right to do so, and the force of the word "human" would have been to convey the message that the specific law in question violated his sense of his own worth as a human being, i.e., his human dignity. It was contrary to justice, and King was obliged to violate it to maintain his own dignity as a human being. It is in this kind of context that the resort to the expression "It is my human right" implies that something is deserved simply because one is a human being, only because one is a human being, in order to maintain oneself as a human being.

The concern for human rights based in human dignity seems to be something quite new since World War II. It grew out of the reaction to the Holocaust, but the failure of the Communist countries to be egalitarian has caused the principle of equality to lose its lustre much as the gross inequalities of wealth under *laissez-faire* economics caused the principle of liberty to become tarnished. Perhaps it can be said that Third World countries do not want equality with industrialized nations as much as they want to be treated with respect and dignity. Similarly, although rights movements like women's liberation are concerned with liberty and equality, they are motivated even more with the idea of human dignity that underlies expectations of equal consideration. Gender discrimination violates one's dignity as a human being. The complaint about being the "second sex," or about treatment as a sexual object instead of a person, is an assertion of human dignity. When left-wing feminists argue that pornography and prostitution are degrading to women it is based on a sense of human dignity.

The shift to human dignity, however, is not a shift to an emphasis upon a third ideal analogous to earlier emphases on freedom and equality. That would lead to a stress on fraternity, which, too, has become tarnished because of the left-wing and right-wing totalitarianisms of the twentieth century. It is, rather, a shift to another, more fundamental level. This is stated in the sentence by Schneider quoted at the chapter's head when he said that the classical rights of liberty and the political rights of equality are based on human dignity. As he also said, all rights such as political rights, economic rights, and social rights "serve to develop the principle of human dignity."[4] This point is also made in the first clause of the Preamble of the Universal Declaration of Human Rights:

> *Whereas* recognition of the inherent dignity and of the equal and unalienable rights of all members of the human family is the foundation of freedom, justice, and peace in the world....

The claim to recognize dignity and rights means it is understood that dignity is not itself a right and is therefore on a different plane. Then the first article of the Declaration says,

> All human beings are born free and equal in dignity and rights. They are endowed with reason and conscience and should act toward one another in a spirit of brotherhood.

The first sentence seems ambiguous. It seems to make two points: (a) All human beings are born free. (b) All human beings are equal in dignity and rights.

To say they are "born free" is to make a claim like Jefferson's "created equal." It means that moral and political freedom are things that belong to human beings as such, i.e., that freedom is a human right. Then it says people are "born" equal in dignity and rights. Dignity is different from rights. It does not say that people should be treated with dignity, or with equal dignity, as if some kind of dignified treatment was a human right. It may be, but what it says is that we are all equal in dignity.

All people "have" dignity because they are human. Their very humanity is their dignity. As they are equal in their humanity, in their humanness, in their being human, so they are equal in dignity. Then, in addition to this dignity, they have these rights. Equally.

The second sentence explains the first. People should be treated with dignity in a spirit of brotherhood because they all have reason and conscience. Because reason and conscience are the human dignity, other human beings are reasonable, moral agents and should be addressed as brothers and sisters.

---

[4] Schneider, op. cit., p. 92.

As shown in Chapter Two, the principle of human dignity is more fundamental because it is the principle of value and goodness upon which the principles of human right and morality depend. It is the axiological principle upon which the deontological principles depend. Freedom and equality are deontological principles, i.e., they specify obligations. We are obligated morally to let each other engage in responsible, moral action and to give all other people equal consideration. These are primordial duties.

The principle of dignity entails this kind of duty only in a minor sense, i.e., we are morally obligated to treat each other with dignity. To be treated with human dignity, with the dignity that becomes a human being, is a human right on the same plane as other human rights.

There is another sense in which the principle of dignity does not express a duty but makes a judgment of value about every human being, i.e., that each is equal in dignity, or that every person has his or her own dignity and value.

This judgment of the value of every human being underlies all deontological principles because it is the basis of morality itself. If one does not value other people, the only reasons to become concerned about obligations to them are self-seeking ones such as those characterizing the first three Kohlbergian stages. This judgment of the value of each human being is required to enable one to see that other people's rights are human rights, due to them simply because they are human.

This judgment of value is based upon the qualities that are experienced as inherent in the "object" valued. This "ultimate" value should be explicated without reference to the UN Declaration. To say that a person has a certain dignity simply because she or he is human, or that all human beings have a certain dignity, each their own, states it as a factual claim that each person has his or her own dignity and value. One's dignity is enhanced by any and all rights that human beings have as human beings. To say that human rights enhance human dignity makes a corresponding normative claim. Just as it requires nutrition, rearing, medical care, and education to become a fully developed human being even though one is a human being at birth, so, too, does it require a set of rights operating in society to develop one's fullest humanity. Whatever is required is in fact a human right. We all deserve as much of what is required to become a human being as anyone else. All human rights develop one's humanity, i.e., one's humanness, or one's dignity as a human being. Human dignity is therefore more fundamental than such principles as freedom or equality.

It is so fundamental that it errs to refer to it as a principle or right. Strictly speaking, to treat another person with human dignity requires one to accord him his human rights. That is why they are human rights. They are rights that accord the individual his or her human dignity. They are human rights only if there is a certain dignity inherent in the human being as a human being. Human dignity is the necessary condition for human rights.

Human dignity is the value perceived in a living creature when it is understood to be human. It is not attributed to it by an act of consciousness but is perceived out there within its own sentient possibilities, just as the value of a Rembrandt or the Ninth Symphony or the sunrise is perceived out there within the "object." Perhaps the chief characteristic of other people that one learns to value is the quality of their sentience, i.e., of the way in which their reason and conscience operate through their outlook on the world. The structure of the other person's sentience, his or her affective, conscious access to the world around him, is the quality found at the core of the experience of the dignity of a specific individual. It is the quality of the other person's sentience, of his or her interiority and its exteriorization, comprising his or her reason and conscience, that is his or her uniqueness, i.e., his or her own value and dignity.

It is this quality that evokes respect for the other as a person and creates the desire to do what is right by him or her as befits another member of the human race, as befits the dignity of a human being. This connection between respect and dignity was noticed by Kant in the following passage:

> Every man has a rightful claim to *respect* from his fellow-man and is *reciprocally* obligated to show respect for every other man.

> Humanity itself is a dignity, for one cannot be used merely as a

means by any man (either by others or even by himself) but must always be treated at the same time as an end. And it is just this that comprises his dignity (personality).[5]

Treating each other as ends in themselves means treating each other as moral agents capable of setting one's own goals (ends). If Kant was right that this comprises human dignity, then moral agency is the human dignity. A person is the "thing" that realizes value within itself, which is the basis for respect as a universal principle. If one appreciates the dignity of the person, one respects him or her as a person, i.e., as a moral agent with certain human rights.

The problem of discipline in the classroom could be approached through the principle of respect for persons rather than through the concept of dignity. It could be argued that students ought to learn to respect each other as persons by having the classroom structured by rules they can respect. Respect for persons, however, is a rather abstract principle for children and youth to apply to people whom they do not respect. Even without respect, however, another's value and dignity can be recognized. If it is argued that the teacher ought to observe the principle of respect for persons when engaged in specific disciplinary actions, this is very much like the psychological doctrine that prescribes that one ought to continue to accept students as persons when it is necessary to disapprove of specific actions. This can be done sincerely, however, only if one believes that in spite of a current misdeed, the child or youth still has his own value and dignity.

The axiological principle regarding human dignity is therefore more fundamental than the deontological principle of respect for persons. Be this as it may, if it is desirable for students to learn to respect each other as persons, each with his or her own dignity, it is necessary to establish rules they can respect and to enforce them with the highest regard for human dignity. Before the enforcement of rules can be addressed directly, however, conceptual clarity regarding the phenomenon of punishment is necessary.

---

[5] Immanuel Kant, *The Doctrine of Virtue*, Part II of the *Metaphysics of Morals*, tr. Mary I. Gregor (New York: Harper & Row, 1964), p. 132. Emphasis his.

III. Retributive Justice as a Human Right

In contrast to the concern for freedom in education, which is about the internal regulation of conduct through the gradual assumption of responsibility, the concern for discipline in education shifts attention to the external regulation of behavior. The characteristic mode of the control of behavior is through the use of reward and punishment, i.e., through retributive justice.

The practice of punishment in adult society and the "discipline" imposed by law occurs without regard for internal agreement with laws. Someone who pays the fine for speeding, for example, is free to speed another day and take his comeuppance again, according to law. There is no compulsion to agree that there should be a speed limit, that the law is just, or that its violation is morally as well as legally wrong. The administration of the penal system is not concerned with the offender's inner being. Efforts at rehabilitation are supplemental rather than essential to the practice of punishment (although the technological consciousness might fuse them together in the compulsion to get results). When considered from this proper concern with outer behavior only,

> Punishment is the correction of a violation of the law, which says beforehand to everyone subject to it: Give yourself no pains to interfere with the law or to transgress it, for everything will be adjusted, whether it be in the form of a liberal reparation or of some other substitute therefore.[6]

When explaining this definition, Stammler included amnesty and pardons among the ways in which the violation of laws can be corrected to show that any correction whatsoever falls within the category of punishment, objectively considered.

Such a definition, restricted to the province of law, i.e., to the external regulation of behavior, contains no reference to internal, subjective occurrences such as the desire to inflict pain or unpleasantness or the actual feelings of suffering or discomfiture in receiving

---

[6] Rudolf Stammler, *The Theory of Justice*, tr. Isaac Husik (New York: Macmillan, 1925), p. 47.

the punishment. It is not necessary for these things to be involved for something to be an instance of punishment in the sense of corrective justice. It is called "punishment" even if the sentencing judge and prison warden are totally devoid of any desire to inflict pain or unpleasantness, i.e., if they are merely doing their job as the law demands. Similarly, it can be called "punishment" even if the criminal enjoys staying in jail where it is warm, secure, and the food sufficient, if not choice. No special things have to be occurring internally for the punishment to occur objectively as a correction of a violated law. They are not an essential part of punishment.

This distinction between internal and external regulation of conduct makes it possible to consider all instances of the correction of the violation of the rules of the classroom or school together as instances of "punishment," i.e., as corrective justice. Then one can become concerned about how the administration of corrective justice can disclose moral obligations in educationally desirable ways. This in turn leads to the question about the kind of rule the student can respect, or the just rule. If the rules embody justice, the necessity of their enforcement can be taken for granted while the modes of enforcement are investigated.

An objective definition of punishment as corrective justice, particularly understood as "liberal reparations," is virtually unknown to the educational literature of liberal democracies. The culture is instead permeated by the much narrower view of punishment as the intentional infliction of some sort of suffering or pain, i.e., punishment in the painful sense of the word.

This common sense view of punishment is so prevalent it is necessary to submit it to an ideological critique in order to abstract and preserve its essential truth. Insofar as it is compatible with human dignity, it is an essential human right, strange as it may seem. Then it will be transcended in favor of "liberal reparations" in the maintenance of school discipline in the next chapter.

The standard definition among English-speaking philosophers that punishment is the deliberate infliction of pain, unpleasantness, or suffering upon someone who has violated a rule or law by someone in authority is set out as if it were a value-free definition obtained solely by analysis of the normal usage of the word "punishment."

Why ordinary usage should be the arbiter of something as serious as crime and punishment is not clear. That it involves ideological distortion can be seen in Peters's presentation of the position.[7] After stating the so-called descriptive definition of the nature of punishment, he analyzed various justifications, i.e., retribution, reformation, and deterrence. This enabled him to say that punishment was retributive by definition, insmuch as it was a return of something to someone for some reason, but then to reject the retributive justification in favor of deterrence. This, however, smuggled his own value judgment into the definition, for another definition without retribution is possible, e.g., Stammler's. The value judgment in the definition itself is only superficially denied when the deterrent theory is used to defend social control, for this obfuscation enabled him to retain retributive justice while seeming to deny retributivism.

He said a normative relation was built into the concept of punishment because it is not a law of nature that suffering is inflicted upon people who commit offenses.[8] It is odd that he then rejected the retributive justification that offenders deserve punishment simply because they broke the law, for it is not a law of nature for law enforcement to involve punishment. Because he takes this for granted, Peters quite obviously smuggles his own values into the "normative relation" he projects into the concept of punishment. "Smuggles" is the right word because it is a retributivism that is ashamed of disclosing itself.

The concept cannot be defined apart from the practice in adult society that in the course of several thousand years has given rise to the normative relation of retributive justice that is now built into the concept of punishment. Only in this century has it become unfashionable to say that criminals deserve punishment. If they do, then so much the worse for fashion and the patronizing, pseudo-psychological, pseudo-sociological "explanations" of a criminal's behavior that are mistaken for moral justifications and divest him of moral responsibility for actions which are legally, objectively wrong. However commendable it may be to try to understand his motiva-

---

[7] Peters, *Ethics and Education*, pp. 267-272.

[8] Ibid., p. 269.

tions, they are logically unrelated to a general understanding of punishment as a social practice. This requires one to accept Stammler's distinction: "The aim of ethical theory is perfection of *character*, while the institution of law has to do with the regulation of *conduct*."⁹ The general consideration of punishment has to occur not in the ethical domain but in the legal sphere, where one is obliged to assume full responsibility for culpable offenses. In law one is entitled to assume that offenders are in full possession of their faculties when they knowingly violate specific laws. In this context legal sense and common sense coincide in believing that offenders merit punishment.

It is not clear why this notion of retributive justice should be unpopular. Perhaps its detractors come from sheltered backgrounds and lack contact with life, or perhaps they are criminals themselves. More likely is its mistaken identification with the slogan "an eye for an eye," which in turn is mistakenly identified with revenge and retaliation. It should also be noted that alternative emphases on reformation and deterrence have contributed greatly to the rationalization and humanization of penal codes.

There is no reason to use punishment to reform a criminal offender, however, for pleasant methods of rehabilitation are superior on benevolent grounds. It is therefore not rational to argue that criminals should be punished to reform them. If they ought to be punished for a more cogent reason, however, the punishment should be calculated to maximize its reformative effect.

And Kant seems permanently correct to note that the deterrent justification would use the power of the state to make an example of offenders. It refuses to say that the criminal deserves punishment, but then contends he deserves to be made into an example. He is not punished for his own crime, but for the potential crime of others. In addition to being contrary to justice, this uses him as a means to the goals of others, rather than as an end in himself, and is thus contrary to human dignity.

---

⁹ Stammler, p. 40. The distinction is also found in Kant's "Introduction to the Metaphysics of Morals," *The Metaphysical Elements of Justice*, Part I of the *Metaphysics of Morals*, tr. John Ladd (New York: Bobbs-Merrill, 1965), pp. 19-21.

These moral objections to reformative and deterrent justifications cannot be overcome. It will always be contrary to human dignity to punish a person to reform him if pleasant ways are available or to punish him as an example to others.

Objections to the retributive justification that it involves feelings of vengeance, sadism, etc., are misplaced. These are morally bad, but they can accompany any of the justifications, as when someone hits their child and says, "This will teach you," thinking to reform him, or when a child is scolded publicly so that other children will behave. These feelings are morally reprehensible in any case. They confuse the issue of justice and make law enforcement incompatible with human dignity.

Kant's view was that a person who violated a law deserved punishment, i.e., that punishment was morally deserved simply because the person broke the law. Peters seems more correct to say that punishment must involve retribution because the word "retribution" means doing something to one in return for something else. This means that the person is punished because he broke the law.

This, however, is exactly why people are punished. It is all the justification necessary. One does not have to believe it is deserved, or that it will reform or deter. If someone violates the law, she or he should be punished because she or he broke the law.

It is not clear why some philosophers could think there should be a better reason. Perhaps the simplicity of this absolutely clear view of retributive justice should be explained.

Something equally obvious was claimed by Kaufmann when he pointed out that a law that prohibits people from doing what they want to do requires a penalty for its enforcement.[10] Without a penalty the law is ignored. Because the punishment for its violation has to be attached to a statute when it is enacted, one cannot agree that retribution is part of the concept of punishment. It is part of the concept of law.

For a law to be a law, its violators must receive retributive justice. Thus the justification for a particular punishment is identical with the

---

[10] Walter Kaufmann, *Without Guilt or Justice* (New York: Dell, 1975), p. 61.

justification for the particular law. For example, the need for a speed limit on highways justifies the punishment of speeders, who should be punished because they broke the law. Whether or not they deserve punishment rests wholly on whether they are found legally guilty. Legal guilt justifies the penalty. If the person is not proven legally guilty, he does not deserve the punishment. It would therefore be very odd to say that someone was found legally guilty but does not deserve the punishment prescribed by law, unless mitigating or exonerating circumstances are also cited. In the absence of the latter, the particular punishment is justified because the particular law is violated, which means it is justified by the need for the particular law. There is therefore no need for a justification of punishment in general, as if this existed apart from specific instances. What needs to be justified are particular laws, the violation of which entails punishment in their enforcement. This is not a deterrent justification of the punishment, however, for it is clear that the person is supposed to be deterred not by the punishment but by the law itself.

It is the law itself that deters people from its violation. At least people at Kohlbergian stage four or higher need only to know the law to sense its rightness, which evokes respect for it. To obey the law out of respect is very different from being deterred by the punishment. People at lower stages are not deterred by the punishment, either, for as Del Vecchio said, the penalty imposed for violating a law obviously did not prevent the offender from violating it, and people who do not violate it do not receive the penalty. The penalty attached to a law therefore does not coerce anyone into its observance. In fact, Del Vecchio seems right when he claims that the use of punishment presupposes that such coercion is impossible.[11] It does not help to shift the deterrent view to claims about the threat of punishment, for it can be safely hypothesized that most people are unaware of the punishments for specific laws.

Particular laws are just laws if they are necessary to establish equal freedom. For example, laws prohibiting physical injury to the person, such as assault, rape, and murder, protect the freedom of potential

---

[11] Giorgio Del Vecchio, *The Formal Bases of Law*, tr. John Lisle (New York: Macmillan, 1921), p. 203, n. 24.

victims, i.e., of everyone. Punishment for their violation is justified by the reason for the laws, i.e., to promote the enjoyment of equal freedom. Since this freedom is a human right, the punishment of the violators of just laws is a human right of the victims of the violators.

Retributive justice is a human right. If laws needed to promote equal freedom are just laws, their enforcement is a matter of justice. As Del Vecchio said, "The possibility of enforcing the observance of a right is an integral and characteristic part of the right itself."[12] Someone who violates a just law ought to be punished because justice ought to be done. The offender ought to be brought to justice. If there is a need for a general justification of punishment, it is simply this need for justice. This is why the retribution entailed by the normative relation is not built into the concept of punishment but into the concept of law. A defender deserves any penalty meted out because the law works that way. No penalty, no law. It is part of the concept of law, or justice, that violators of particular laws will receive retributive justice. It is their just due. It is their human right.

Retributive justice is a human right because only humans have law and because the protection of the law is required to become a fully human being. It is the right of the victim to be protected from the predators in society. It is the right of the offender to be held morally responsible for his actions by being properly instructed in the limits of equal freedom even when it means learning the hard way. It is the right of all human beings to receive equal consideration as moral agents who are responsible for themselves. This includes acceptance of liability for punishment, i.e., the acceptance of punishment as one's due if one violates a law.

Standard explanations of retributive aspects of punishment do not always emphasize the positive aspects of particular, just laws and their educative role in specifying right action to the general population. This is necessary if one is to maintain perspective and a sense of value. If a congeries of human and social conditions makes a law necessary, the candid justification is that the offender deserves to be punished. Why? Because he broke the law. No special importance need be attached to the word "deserves" when it is said he deserves

---

[12] Ibid., p. 193.

punishment. If he does not deserve punishment simply because he broke the law, the law ought to be repealed.

If the person does not deserve punishment, he certainly does not deserve being made into an example, and the punishment cannot reform him.

This explication of retributive justice does not justify punishment for the sake of retribution. It is justified for the sake of law, *das Recht, le droit*, the right, human right, i.e., for the sake of justice qua justice.

It offers no excuse for revenge or cruelty, and it is quite compatible with the acceptance of mitigating and exonerating circumstances, various criteria of diminished responsibility, variable and suspended sentences, and amnesty and pardons when magistrates seek the justice of the individual case. All these things, however, pertain to judicial proceedings, not to the general principles concerning the objective correction of the violation of law.

When the guilty person himself pleads mitigating or exonerating circumstances, he thereby assumes responsibility and admits objective guilt in a plea for mercy as opposed to justice. A plea for mercy admits the punishment is deserved and just.

The explication of retributive justice is also compatible with "liberal reparations." When Kant argued it was immoral to punish someone so that others would not violate a law, he also claimed it was contrary to human dignity to use the punishment to try to reform him, as if the punishment itself were not sufficient to inform him of the error of his ways. Acceptance of the punishment as his due enables the criminal to accept full responsibility for his action and subsequently re-enter the community as a moral agent on equal status with everyone else. According to Kant, this is a necessary condition of the restoration of the moral climate, or moral equilibrium, of the community that was disturbed by the violation of the law. This concern for the moral equilibrium of the community goes beyond retribution to reparation. It ought to be investigated separately before applying the concept of retributive justice, or punishment, to the problems of the schools.

Conclusion

The educational significance of the idea of retributive justice is that punishment ought not be used in schools to reform or to deter students.

Although any punishment meted out in schools should be done with concern for its reformative and deterrent consequences, to maximize them, it is morally wrong to punish a child or youth to keep him or others from violating a particular rule again. These things can be achieved in more educative and benevolent ways.

People who believe that punishment in adult society is justified by its consequences usually apply this belief directly to the educational situation without regard for the age of the child or the pedagogy involved. Whether the explication of punishment as retributive justice can be applied directly to education is not immediately clear.

It is right for members of society to be held legally reponsible for their actions in adult society, for it is clear that for adults Bradley was correct when he stated that responsibility and liability for punishment were convertible terms.[13] It is equally clear that societies that legally define children and youth as in a state of diminished responsibility accept that they are undeserving of the punishments attached to violated statutes.

If children and youth ought to be treated with as much responsibility as they can bear, there is some reason for attaching penalties to rules necessary to establish the classroom and school as the community under law that insures there is equal freedom to learn. If responsibility is a matter of degree, so is liability for punishment. Although punishment in schools can be justified, the retributive justification also seems morally unsatisfactory for people younger than the age of legal responsibility.

If none of the justifications of punishment in the painful sense are morally satisfactory in education, a renewed attention to the maintenance of discipline without punishment and to the justification of punishment in education compatible with human dignity is required.

---

[13] F.H. Bradley, *Ethical Studies* (Oxford: Clarendon Press, 1927), p. 26.

Chapter Eight

REPARATION AND PUNISHMENT IN EDUCATION

Evil which has been done ought to be undone, as far as possible, by the one who is to blame for it. There is no doubt that this is the first and elementary requirement of justice. From this, obviously, is derived the obligation of reparation of damage.

Del Vecchio[1]

Corrective justice requires a readjustment of the situation to what it was before the violation of law. The purpose of punishment in the narrower, painful sense is to repair the damage to the moral equilibrium of the community otherwise irreparable. In this perspective of reparative justice, the questions of discipline and punishment in education become focused on the maintenance of the moral equilibrium in schools by enforcing rules necessary to insure the equal freedom to learn.

I. The Question of Rule Enforcement
The teacher's main efforts to promote learning are not directly related to the rules needed to establish a community under law devoted to learning. In their first year or two of teaching, however, many teachers devote considerable attention to doing those things that establish harmonious relationships and a working climate. These

---

[1] Giorgio Del Vecchio, *Justice; An Historical and Philosophical Essay*, tr. Lady Guthrie (Edinborough: University Press, 1956), p. 211.

gradually become habitual aspects of their presence in the classroom as routines become established and enthusiasm generated without reference to rules or conduct. For example, if a class begins to become noisy when addressing it, one stops talking for a second and a half and then proceeds precisely when the hum stops, or one glances around more quickly to give each student more eye contact. If a group in one corner begins to buzz, they get enough of a stare to let them feel watched, but no more, or one walks quietly over that way, without staying longer than necessary. These sorts of things come to function in the teacher's behavior while the explicit attention is given to the content of instruction, for they become part of the teaching personality, so to speak. Experienced teachers can therefore quite truthfully say they never have any discipline problems, but this does not mean they are not constantly enforcing the "rules" that enable the classroom to be a community of scholars under law.

Equally important is the explicit enforcement of rules in ways other than punishment. Although a penalty is a presupposition of a prohibitive law in society, this is not true in schools. Enforcement need not require a penalty. The kinds of disturbances teachers worry about when concerned about the discipline of the classroom are those that interfere with the learning of other students, e.g., talking among themselves during a presentation, general discussion, recitation, or study time, or otherwise disturbing others through clowning around, boisterousness, etc. This is the area in which it is good to begin by following the psychologists' advice to run a more rapidly paced classroom, use better materials, give more attention to motivation, and be better prepared for the lesson oneself. Or one can secure engagement in freely chosen projects to elicit responsibility. When these things do not suffice, then methods of enforcing necessary rules other than punishment should be used first. There is, for example, the simple reminder. When children get excited and start shouting, they might need only a very gentle reminder to use their "inside voices." At another time it might suffice to say clearly, "No hitting!" The tone of voice can be varied to suit the occasion. Children forget things quite easily, especially when what they are learning excites them as it should. They can be reminded again and again. There is nothing wrong, for example, in saying, "Shhh!" five or ten times an hour if each time it obtains results for five or ten minutes, and if one keeps smiling. The simple reminder often enforces classroom discipline with the seriousness it deserves, and it often obtains an instant restoral of the equilibrium of the classroom, if the children like the teacher. When it does not, there is the warning, which cites the rule, too, but also mentions the penalty. Many children need only one warning to be able to remember a rule and obey it. Clever teachers can use a second warning ("I told you last time...") to good effect. If the third warning shows only that the rule will not be enforced, it becomes a wordy reminder. Third and fourth warnings can enforce a rule without punishment, however, if spaced far enough apart in the pupil's memory. It partly depends upon the importance of the particular rule.

When warnings are unheeded, one can also have a small "heart to heart" talk in which one simply reminds the student of the presence of other students and their right to use the time and place for learning, requests his cooperation, and reminds him of his obligation to himself to join in and learn things as long as he is there anyway. This relies on the right reasons to restore the moral equilibrium as such, shows confidence in the pupil's reason and conscience, and creates the expectation of reasonable conduct.

Some "offenses" are self-correcting or too trivial for punishment. In the first year of school, for example, children might void their bladder in the classroom (accidentally), break a water glass, or spill the paint. Because they are still learning to control their bodies and use their fingers, these children need a good hug to prevent them from crying. Giving them emotional support repairs the only serious damage that can occur, the injury to their own dignity. Older children, too, sometimes do careless things of which they become quickly ashamed and wish they had not done, and correct themselves by not repeating the action unless they cannot help it.

Some offenses are too serious for punishment by school authorities. These include bringing a gun to school, selling drugs on campus, assaults on teachers or other students, molesting female students, attempted rape, rape, murder, etc. These are not matters of school discipline, for they disturb the moral equilibrium so badly its restoration requires immediate, preventative detention of the culprit outside the school's jurisdiction. The distinction between a misdemeanor and a felony is useful to understand the point that some misbehaviors that occur in schools, i.e., felonies, are not matters of classroom or school discipline. Just as a judge cannot tell someone who has been determined to be guilty of felonious assault, "No hitting!" so, too, a high school principal cannot punish a student guilty of such assault. It would be harboring a fugitive from justice. The school is not a sanctuary from law. When fighting on the school grounds is more than hitting and less than assault, however, it is the kind of disturbance of the moral equilibrium that can and should be treated as a matter of school discipline.

The question of rule enforcement in education, then, concerns those disturbances of the equilibrium of the classroom and school that cannot be taken care of through well-planned routines and enthusiastic, dedicated, conscientious teaching; that cannot be dealt with in passing by reminding, warning, asking, etc.; and that are neither too trivial nor too serious for pedagogical concern. The question concerns two modes of enforcing schools' rules, the repair of damage by the offender himself and punishment in the painful sense. The use of reparation and punishment to promote discipline and dignity in education will by considered after reparative justice is shown to be a human right.

II. The Origin of the Concept of Reparation

The use of the word "punishment" in the narrow, painful sense reifies the word, isolates it from particular laws and its legal context, and considers it individualistically, as if it were something done to the offender to give him his due in retributive justice, as if it were only of concern to him and the courts.

Corrective justice is broader than that, as indicated in the more objective definition of Stammler's. Stammler's view also allows more responsibility to be attributed to the offender because it includes recognition that she or he knows she or he will have to pay the penalty if she or he violates the law and is caught. She or he can count on the punishment in advance, which will therefore have to be at least equal to, or greater than, the damage done by the violation. If it is not at least "an eye for an eye" the potential violator can decide to risk the trade-off. She or he then has nothing to lose if caught, everything to gain if not, and would be actually encouraged to commit the crime the law was designed to deter. The rational offender, furthermore, ought to accept willingly the punishment, or other means for adjusting things, to complete the agreement tacitly made when violating the law. Accepting it acknowledges personal responsibility, perhaps even in an effort to make things right again. In civil law the damages are often completely repaired through monetary payment, even when there is a violation of law. This suggests that it is less important to give an offender her or his due than to oblige her or him to give the offended parties their due.

Reparative justice seems not to have been widely discussed in the history of ethics, perhaps because of its proximity to retributive justice, with which it can easily become confused. This seems to be the reason for the misunderstanding of the oldest sources of the conception, which will be consulted to bring the concept back to light.

Reparative justice is associated with the expression "an eye for an eye, a tooth for a tooth" in both the Code of Hammurabi and the Mosaic Code. That expression is itself mistakenly understood when it is supposed to be a symbol of retribution. *Exodus* is thought to be closer to Moses than the other books ascribed to him. In its twenty-first chapter, the textual Moses is laying down the law for the wandering tribes of Israel during their sojourn in the wilderness of the Sinai Peninsula. He considers the treatment of slaves, then announces the death penalty for murder, kidnapping, and striking or cursing one's parents.

Then he says that if someone is bedridden after a fight, because of it, the medical bills and lost time should be paid by the person who hurt him. This is monetary compensation for injury, without punishment, and it clearly exemplifies reparative justice regarding criminal law (assault with grievous bodily harm). Reparative justice is also prescribed in the next statute. When men are fighting and cause a pregnant woman to have a miscarriage but no other harm, the guilty party is supposed to pay compensation to the husband for the lost child. Then it adds that if harm be done, there should be given "life for life, eye for eye, tooth for tooth, hand for hand, foot for foot, burn for burn, wound for wound, stripe for stripe." Immediately following are statutes about wayward oxen, stealing oxen or sheep, negligence regarding where one's cattle grazed, and so forth, all of which are to be rectified by monetary compensation. They are discussed in terms of repairing damages done, not in terms of retribution. There is no specification of whether the "eye for an eye" series is intended for reparation or retribution. The context allows only a reparative interpretation. The lost child is paid for to repair the loss, as if it could, and if harm occurs, then these reparations will be made. Someone who puts out another's eye makes things right again by sacrificing one of his own. Does this repair the damage so the other can see? It repairs the damage to the community. This might make not much sense to modern sensibility, but that is not relevant to the matter of ascertaining what Moses meant. It would make sense to many children today, who readily feel that if another child hits them, they have a right to hit back, and granted their hit, feel that justice has been done. The equilibrium regarding the privacy and sanctity of one's own person has been restored.

Everything else in the chapter enunciates the principle of reparative justice, and if Moses does not mention monetary compensation in regard to maiming, neither does he mention revenge, retaliation, punishment, or retribution. He does not mention reform, deterrence, or desert, either, because he is not presenting a theory of punishment or a theory of law. He is codifying in writing the practice he has developed as a working magistrate. When the phrase "an eye for an eye, and a tooth for a tooth" is used to attribute vindictiveness, etc., to Moses, Mosaic law, or such, it is a bit of anti-Semitic nonsense. Vengeance, retaliation, and retribution have to be read into the text in sharp contradiction to its explicit reparative justice. One could even argue that the concept of reparative justice permeates Mosaic law, as one might expect on the flight from the oppressors in Egypt, and as stated in the following speech by the textual Moses:

> If anyone sins...by deceiving his neighbor in a matter of deposit or security, or through robbery, or if he has oppressed his neighbor or has found what was lost and lied about it, swearing falsely—in any or all of the things which men do and sin therein, when one has sinned and become guilty, he shall restore what he took by

robbery, or what he got by oppression, or the deposit which was committed to him, or the lost thing which he found, or anything about which he has sworn falsely; he shall restore it in full and shall add a fifth to it, and give it to him to whom it belongs, on the day of his guilt offering.[2]

The origins of reparative justice are not only found in ancient Judaism, and these origins are in no way dependent upon Judaic theology. Reparative justice is inchoately present in the context of the phrase "an eye for an eye" in the Code of Hammurabi some fifteen hundred years prior to Moses, and then it was expressed independently of that kind of context some seven centuries after Moses in classical antiquity in the writings of both Plato and Aristotle.[3] In the discussion about the purpose of punishment in *The Laws*, Plato had his spokesperson, the Athenian, say,

> The lawgiver...must keep his eye on these two things, injustice and injury. He must use the law to exact damages for damages done, as far as he can; he must restore losses, and if anyone has knocked something down, put it back upright again; in place of something killed or wounded, he must substitute something in a sound condition. And when atonement has been made by compensation, he must try by his laws to make the criminal and the victim, in each separate case of injury, friends instead of enemies.[4]

Although compensation is a form of reparation discussed frequently in *The Laws*, Plato clearly understood reparative justice more

---

[2] *Leviticus* 6:2-7

[3] G.R. Driver and John C. Miles, *Legal Commentary*, Volume I of *The Babylonian Laws* (London: Oxford University Press, 1952), pp. 500f. The strong evidence of Moses' indebtedness to Hammurabi regarding specific statutes should not obscure the fact that the ethical context in which the textual Moses speaks appears to be unprecedented by Hammurabi's Code.

[4] Plato, *The Laws*, tr. Trevor Saunders (Middlesex: Penguin Books, 1975), 862. The presence of reparative justice in criminal law is perhaps clearer in a later passage that begins, "When one man harms another by theft or violence and the damage is extensive, the indemnity he pays to the injured party should be large, but smaller if the damage is comparatively trivial." 933.

broadly. In the case of culpable offense, he wanted to restore friendship, i.e., the moral equilibrium between criminal and victim. The point of the compensation was to effect a reconciliation, i.e., reparative justice.

Aristotle's use of the concept was restricted to civil law.[5] He had referred to criminal injustice in the relations between people, but then seems to have slighted reparative justice in favor of a greater concern for distributive justice.[6] Ross translated his Greek word as "rectificatory justice," and once as "corrective justice." Other translations (Apostle, Chase) use the latter. Ross's choice best denotes the idea of righting a previous wrong, but the word is almost unpronounceable. When Del Vecchio traced it to Aristotle, he indicated the latter's correct concern for restoring justice between people, but was concerned like Moses to implement it in respect to criminal law when he said, "There follows from the idea of justice the power of the State to demand as far as possible reparation be made for harm willfully or culpably caused to the society which it represents (*reparative* or *penal* justice)."[7]

The idea of reparative justice is simply that someone is morally obligated to repair any damage or injury that occurs when he or she violates just law. The obligation is a distinctly moral duty if the law is just, i.e., necessary to establish equal freedom, and if the injury or damage is the result of one's action contrary to law. A responsible moral agent, moreover, wants to make reparations for his own errors even without a legal determination. It is the principle that obliges one to apologize after stepping on someone's toes or jostling him or her in a crowd.

Reparative justice becomes part of law when the criminal offender is legally obligated to repair such damages as may be caused by an infraction of law. This may occur instead of punishment as in civil law, or with the addition of punishment in the painful sense when it, too, becomes a necessary part of corrective justice.

---

[5] Aristotle, *Ethica Nicomachea*, tr. W.D. Ross (London: Oxford University Press, 1942), 1131a to 1132a.

[6] Ibid., 1131a.

[7] Del Vecchio, *Justice*, p. 121.

III. Reparative Justice as a Human Right

It seems Del Vecchio was correct to say that elemental justice requires that the violator of a just rule or law "undo" any harm done by repairing the damage or injury in an effort to restore the situation as it was to the extent possible. When it is not possible, punishment in the painful sense may be warranted by the need to repair the damage to the moral equilibrium of the community. This means that punishment in the painful sense can be justified on reparative grounds, i.e., that reparative justice is a human right.

An example in which the damage cannot be repaired in any direct way will show how punishment can establish reparative justice and furnish the basis for saying it is a human right. Suppose that after a freely given confession and duly obtained conviction a rapist who had terrorized the victim for ten hours of repeated acts of humiliation was sentenced to thirty days in jail.

The victim would feel that society was unjust and did not adequately protect her. Friends and relatives would be morally outraged and perhaps enter into collusion to give the rapist the rest of his punishment on the thirty-first day. The local feminist group would put the name of the sentencing judge on their black list. All the women in the community would become alarmed. The victim, friends and relatives, supportive interest groups, and potential victims would agree that the rapist is "getting off scot-free," to use their term, that he would probably repeat the crime, and that he deserves greater punishment. If an appeal by the prosecutor secured a change in the sentence to five to ten years, most of these feelings of vengeance would subside.

The retributive feelings cannot be dismissed. On the one hand, the victim and sympathizers cannot determine the punishment of the criminal. That has to be set by law to insure the impartiality of justice. On the other hand, the injury is very real and the moral indignation over the rape of the wife, mother, daughter, friend, and fellow human being is a genuine moral sentiment. The retributive feelings are in themselves good, and feelings of forgiveness would be morally blameworthy. The criminal has done more than victimize one woman. He has indicated to all these others that he will ignore their interests and concerns in the pursuit of his own activities. He has disturbed innumerable moral equilibriums, including that of the community in general. He is obligated to repair them. Should he have a change of heart and want to make amends to the victim and to society, all he can do is penance. He can ask the victim how long an imprisonment, or what kind of punishment, she thought he deserved. He could not ask her forgiveness, and a contrite heart can do no less than want the punishment the victim thinks is deserved. This can make things right with her to the extent possible.

Two of the disturbed equilibriums seem to be much more important than the others. These do not include the relation between the criminal and victim because there is no way the damage can be repaired or undone. The criminal ought to try to repair it by begging forgiveness, but the victim cannot forgive him without loss of essential dignity. It differs from a physical assault, which can be forgiven as the body heals. The equilibriums that can be restored are those between the victim and society and between the criminal and society. The sentence of five to ten years, or whatever has come to be deemed appropriate in a given, historical context, convinces friends, relatives, associates, and potential victims that justice has been done, which enables them to retain their respect for the law. This is why justice must be seen to be done. The proverbial debt to society that the criminal is obliged to pay restores the respect for the law that is essential to the existence of the law as law.

The relationship of the victim to society ought also to be restored by the criminal. The victim is entitled to regain a belief that the legal system will in fact protect the dignity of her person. She has no reason to feel protected by the law unless the punishment is at least "an eye for an eye," that is, somehow comparable in pain and suffering to that which was inflicted on herself. If she knows promptly that the rapist will be in prison for as long as it will take her to overcome the trauma, she can feel justice is on her side. Her desire for justice in this sense is her human right. The desire for retribution is understandable, but the desire for reparation is her human right. Thus reparative justice is a human right.

There have been recent efforts to award monetary compensation to victims of violent crimes, such as physical assaults, maiming, and even murder (to next of kin), especially when these involve permanent disability. It is not clear that there can be such a thing for rape, but this is only an illustration of the principle that the criminal ought to be legally required to repair whatever damage has been done in violating a law to whatever extent possible. This includes undergoing punishment to restore the general moral equilibrium if the disturbance can be pacified in no other way. This is a reparative justification of punishment in the narrower, painful sense. In Del Vecchio's words, "The intrinsic justification of punishment lies precisely in its function of making reparation for and re-integrating the right offended against: therein also lies its rational limit."[8]

This idea of its rational limit is quite important. Reparative justice can often be obtained without the use of punishment in the sense of the infliction of suffering. Then even if one does authorize his own punishment when he violates a law, such requital is morally legitimate but not always necessary or obligatory.[9] To say that a person deserves punishment in Stammler's sense is to indicate a necessary condition for punishment in the painful sense. The sufficient condition is that reparation can be effected in no other way.

This conclusion probably could serve as a criterion to reject much of the current practice of penal systems on moral grounds. It differs from the rejections of retributive justice that would reform and rehabilitate the criminal instead of punishing him, for these involve a mistaken compassion for the criminal that neglects the very real damage done to the victim. Law has to side with the victim to be on the side of justice.

Punishment is deserved and ought to be meted out unless reparations can be made without it. Otherwise society becomes an accessory after the fact, guilt remains, and justice disappears. To claim that reparation is a human right merely maintains the right of the victim against the criminal. Efforts to replace punishment with reformation and rehabilitation, however, are aimed in the right direction when channelled through efforts to let the offender repair the damage done, i.e., to let him replace a bad deed with a good one, as Del Vecchio put it. This can enable him to sense the rightness of the specific law

---

[8] Ibid., p. 183.

[9] Ibid., p. 181.

violated, to come to respect it, and to establish the moral equilibrium between himself and the law shared by all moral agents. Because it enables a return to the community of moral agents, reparative justice is also the criminal's human right.

A violation of law can disturb four or five distinct moral equilibriums. If one violates one's own conscience, the guilt feelings are genuine and have to be absolved by voluntarily making amends to restore the harmony with the offended person as a condition of establishing one's own peace of mind. The third equilibrium, between the criminal and friends and relatives of the injured parties, is quite distinct from that between the criminal and society. It can be restored only through a return to the general moral equilibrium that existed prior to the crime. Justice requires the restoration of those equilibriums that were actually disturbed, to the extent possible, according to the exigencies of the particular case, by the offender himself.

Reparative justice can be implemented without punitiveness or authoritarianism. It does not involve the intentional infliction of pain or suffering. It is true, as Del Vecchio said, that every crime carries its own punishment, for if the criminal suffers during mandatory reparation, this suffering is not inflicted by such coercion.[10] To the contrary, compulsory reparation creates the opportunity to rejoice. The most reasonable feeling to have while setting things right again is joy.

The dignity of the criminal offender is therefore enhanced by the replacement of punishment by other means of reparation whenever possible. Reparative justice is therefore in accordance with the value and dignity of a human being.

The pursuit of other juridical possibilities prior to punishment was not expressed in, but is in accordance with, the principles originally formulated by Beccaria and then concisely stated in the 1789 Declaration of the Rights of Man:

> In order for punishment not to be, in every instance, an act of violence of one or many against a private citizen, it must be essentially public, prompt, necessary, the least possible in the circumstances, proportionate to the crime, dictated by the laws.[11]

---

[10] Ibid., p. 183.

[11] Quoted in the *Encyclopedia of Philosophy* (New York: Macmillan, 1967), Volume 1, p. 267.

IV. Reparation in Education

The question of discipline and dignity in education can be re-phrased within the parameters of reparative justice by applying to classrooms and schools Del Vecchio's way of phrasing the question of punishment, "How can we justify the infliction of suffering upon the wrongdoer *in addition* to the reparation of damage?"[12] Because it does not inflict suffering and creates general expectations that it is good to repair things one has harmed and thereby recover one's responsibility as a moral agent, reparation is more compatible with human dignity than punishment. It should therefore replace it in education wherever it can sufficiently enforce school rules. Punishment has remained in schools because there have been no satisfactory substitutes. The theorists who have sensed something wrong with it often make recommendations for its elimination that seem to deny the necessity for rules, their enforcement, and the maintenance of discipline as such. Their progressive ideologies merely result in polemics with traditionalists willing to argue for the retention of punishment. The "pendulum" swings back and forth, without resting in the middle. This ideological warfare can be transcended by granting rules of behavior to the traditionalists and the rejection of punishment to the progressivists. Perhaps there can be both discipline and dignity. The question of discipline, then, is whether classroom and school rules can be adequately enforced by inducing their violators to make reparations when normal routines, passing reminders, and requests prove insufficient. It is whether reparative justice will work. Can the methodological practice of requiring students to make amends cope with problems of discipline in classrooms and schools? Is punishment also needed? Under what circumstances?

If the rules are established to create the moral equilibrium necessary to maximize learning under the conditions of equal freedom, i.e., to create the community of scholars under law, then any rule violation is the disturbance of one or more equilibriums. To administer punishment directly takes the misbehavior out of context, as if breaking the rule as such were wrong. Instead, it should be asked what the pupil harmed by violating a rule in addition to violating it. That

---

[12] *Justice*, p. 211. Emphasis his.

damage should be repaired as quickly and effectively as possible so that the enforcement of the rule restores the conditions of learning without additional interference. Such effectiveness is exemplified in the brief reminders like, "No hitting," or, "Shhhh," for these obtain "instant equilibrium." To be educative, the repair should be discussed, when necessary, in such a way that the offender and onlookers understand the obligation to set things right again soon after one has erred, not to set an example but to restore more fully the moral equilibrium of the learning situation when the bystanders have already become disturbed. In the case of a rule violation that requires disciplinary action, then, one should ask three questions:

Which moral equilibriums, if any, have been disturbed?
What damage, if any, requires repair?
How can it be done effectively, ethically, and educatively?

These principles will be considered in the context of some examples, beginning outside the classroom. Suppose a teacher happens upon two boys, about fifteen or sixteen years old, fighting on the grounds of a high school. In one school the teacher might be afraid to intervene because the only way to restore the equilibrium is to call the police as quickly as possible. In another school it could be most effective to chat with the boys to find out what it is all about. Stopping the fighting already restores the physical equilibrium between the boys, and the inquiry finds out what else was disturbed. If it was a bully picking on someone smaller, this can be readily ascertained and the bully sent off for punishment. This is necessary to restore the moral equilibrium, for otherwise the smaller boy would feel unjustly treated, like the rape victim whose assailant got off "scot-free." If it is the common situation where one thing led to another and neither started it because both accelerated things in turn, it may very well suffice to talk it through until both agree they should have resolved their differences by talking. They can then apologize to each other, shake hands, and be friends again. In a school with very little fighting, the sight of the teacher talking to them and the handshake is enough to restore the general moral equilibrium. A warning about the penalty for fighting would probably be more effective as a general deterrent than the punishment itself because it would elicit respect for the rule as such and establish the equilibrium on a positive basis. Where fighting is a frequent occurrence, however, the moral equilibrium is tenuous and the pre-specified punishment may be necessary for its maintenance. The public reconciliation should still be sought, but then the boys should be sent to the office to receive their five detentions. Whatever it is should be specified immediately and within earshot of all witnesses to the fight. This makes it public, gives maximum deterrent effect, is most productive educationally, insures everyone of the integrity of the school's justice, and restores the general equilibrium at once. Because the punishment is then served routinely, the immediate "sentencing" brings closure to the incident at once.

In other words, where there is little fighting, the equilibriums disturbed are within the boys, in the violation of their consciences, and between the boys, in the disruption of their friendship. Their repair does not require punishment. Where there is a good bit of fighting, these equilibriums may not exist. Even if they do, the greater damage to the school's equilibrium requires punishment for its repair. Where fighting is frequent, punishment for it is taken lightly and can be considered a routine matter after reconciliation is effected.

Repair of the damage can be undertaken literally when a high school student breaks a window, or some other thing, at school. The person is obliged to repair the window, pay for its repair, or work at school to earn money to pay for the window's repair. There is no reason for additional punishment. The graffiti artist similarly can be asked to wash down the walls to remove graffiti, perhaps somewhat more than he personally was responsible for as a small penalty. Accidental breakage and normal wear and tear should be exempted, but willful damage to school property and breakage that normal care would prevent should be repaired or replaced by students as they get older. When this is not feasible, punishment is even less so. This reparation enables the student to take care of property for the right reasons, i.e., it is valuable, and someone has to pay for it. The moral equilibrium between the individual and the object's owner is repaired by the object's repair, and that between onlookers and offender is rectified when they know he paid for it.

Fighting at school is analogous to criminal law; damaging school property, civil law. That punishment may be needed in one case and not the other is the way it works in the adult world. When punishment for fighting is mentioned but forgone "this time," it is like the suspended sentence. The analogy does not hold for stealing school property, however, for simple restitution will suffice when it is tantamount to neglecting to return a borrowed item.

It is a different matter when students take things belonging to each other. They should be learning about not using each other's things from the first year of school. In the early years simple restitution with a mild rebuke restores the equilibrium with the owner of the article. With older children, restitution is not enough to rectify the relation with the victim, who may have had to go without lunch, walk home, or miss a homework assignment, and also suffer mental distress because of these discomfitures. If punishment is meted out in the context of restoring the relationship with the owner of the stolen things, however, it can also have a deterrent effect. In a school where stealing is rampant, everyone has to learn not to leave things accessible to theft. It is a hard lesson, but it maintains the moral equilibrium.

Suppose a teacher has begun a presentation and a student comes late to class. What equilibrium is disturbed? If the student enters quietly and joins in, none. The conscientious student will correct himself. If he or she is late again, and if this encourages others, or makes it difficult to have a necessary, routinized beginning, and if it is without excuse, then there is a disturbance to the equilibrium established by having the class start at a set time. More attention to the latecomer than a full two-second hard stare, however, might not be worth the additional disruption of the rest of the class, although a very brief reminder or rebuke might save a larger disturbance later on. Then, too, there is the situation in the shop, or laboratory, or theatre or dance rehearsal, or excursion, in which no one can begin until everyone is present. When the latecomer makes everyone else wait, the disturbance is so great that it is proper to start without him, even if it means dropping him from the class, team, crew, choir, cast, etc. In this case no additional punishment is justified. A middle course is for the teacher to wait until the class is over and then ask the person who was late to stay a moment after the others leave. A simple question like, "Do you think you can get here on time next time?" asked in private should make things right again without creating more disruption, for the teacher can count on the other students feeling rewarded, indirectly, for their promptness.

The persistent offender of ongoing classroom processes may require special attention. Someone who does not respond to reminders, requests, warnings, etc., given in response to minor disruptions can often be asked to step out into the hall and wait for the teacher. This restores the classroom equilibrium immediately. When the teacher asks the student in the hall if he is ready to come back in, the expectation of good behavior goes without saying. If it is quite beyond expectation, one can try a "heart to heart" talk. Some teachers might be able to give just the right amount of scolding for the particular case, but others would not find this necessary because of their dialogical ability in personal discussion. The teacher could even talk about some topic unrelated to the disruption in the classroom, letting the student "off the hook" but establishing rapport, getting the student "on side," and restoring the equilibrium that way. Returning to the classroom together, smiling, lets everyone know things have been worked out, thereby completely repairing the disturbance. This kind of closure is important when onlookers are waiting to see if there is more to see, for their disturbance should be tranquilized, too.

The classroom equilibrium is more greatly disturbed if one pupil hurts another physically. Suppose most students in an upper primary or middle school class see a boy jab a girl in the posterior with a compass point. In addition to disturbing her, he has disturbed the equilibrium of the whole class. Everyone wonders what will happen next. Will he poke someone else? Will he torment her more? Will someone else poke someone? Will the girl retaliate? The teacher has to act to settle the uncertainty at once to enable onlookers to return to their lesson. Some teachers could demand an instant apology, get it, and thereby do all that was needed to repair the damage because all the equilibriums would be restored. An immediate exclusion from the class, followed by a private discussion and/or scolding, would visibly let everyone know that the violation of unspoken rules would also be corrected. A great deal depends upon whether the boy intended to flirt or hurt, whether he was careful not to hurt her or whether she virtually requires medical attention. If the girl rather enjoyed the harmless attention, it would suffice for the teacher to walk over to that side of the room for a few minutes, relying on her sheer presence to be intimidating, but if there is physical pain the advocate of corporal punishment might very well make the most sense. At least it would convince the girl that justice was on her side. It could also reinforce the boy's belief that physical force is all right if one has enough of it. On the other hand, if he is at Kohlbergian stage one, physical force is the language he would not fail to understand. A great deal depends upon the general stability of the classroom. The girl is not exactly in the same situation as the rape victim. It is possible that the relation with the tormentor could be repaired if he were made to sit on the other side of the room from then on, thus assuring her, and all others, that the sanctity of her person will be protected against a recurrence of the misdemeanor. This could occur more quickly than the apology and could achieve reparative justice without other talk or additional punishment.

Insolence and willful, persistent disobedience disturb the relation between the pupil and teacher. It is very difficult to see how the pedagogic relation can be restored if the teacher also contributes to its breakdown by the use of punishment. The situation, however, is similar to fighting in some respects. If the acts seriously undermine the authority of the teacher, the primary duty is to maximize the learning of the entire class by rectifying the general moral equilibrium even if it makes it difficult to re-establish the relationship with the insolent or disobedient pupil. If he is acting as a catalyst for generally disruptive behavior, it is a different situation from when most of the class is "on side" and feels contempt for the unruly pupil. If the student is merely being rude to the teacher, he can be ignored for the moment, and efforts to develop a pedagogic relationship with him can be initiated at some other time. An altercation in front of the class may occasionally be worth the time, but unless the teacher wins it by being perceived as right the damage to the equilibrium may be aggravated. A temporary exclusion from the class might solve the problem, for it would provide the private conversation in which a mutual understanding is achieved. An endearing pleasantry might be more effective. If the teacher's authority in the social office is seriously affected, however, then punishment according to a schedule might repair the damage in the way that imprisonment repairs the damage caused by the crime of rape. It can insure the injured party of justice, which is not so important for the teacher, but which must be seen to be done to facilitate further learning. It can restore respect for the teacher even if it makes the rehabilitation of the offender impossible. It may be necessary to establish what is right.

On the one hand, insolence and disobedience are among the most serious misbehaviors a student can commit, considering that any other misdemeanors can be remedied as long as minimal respect and compliance remain, but that when this is gone, everything is lost.

On the other hand, these are the least serious of misdemeanors, for the student is hurting no one but himself. The teacher with an unshakeable belief in the value and dignity of each student will find such things not worthy of attention. They "go with the territory," and the pupil will forget it and be different tomorrow. When a teacher finds the insolent and/or disobedient conduct emanating from a pupil he or she also finds genuinely unlikeable, then maintaining one's good-natured humor in the effort to establish a pedagogic relation with the "little imp" manifests the true dignity of teaching. To maintain one's own dignity by remaining aware of the others' dignity even when they have temporarily forgotten it helps them to regain their dignity.

The completion of learning tasks, such as seat work, board work, homework, lab work, and shop work, is a different kind of problem because the teacher's primary obligation is to generate enthusiasm for such learning through the attraction of the content and the pride and joy in the quality of one's work, plus gold stars, allowance for some negligence here and there, and the use of instructional resources that do in fact procure an engagement in learning. Perhaps the homework situation can serve as an example. When most of the students in a class do not do their homework, there is no equilibrium present to be disrupted or repaired. One then gives daily grades for homework, uses class time to supervise its completion, or devises methods of instruction that do not rely on it. If only a few students do not do their homework, it can be discussed with them individually. Occasional lapses can be ignored, or treated with a "tsk, tsk." The failure to complete important homework should show in normal assessment procedures without further ado. A note can be sent to parents, for their signature, to request their supervision of homework, but the rest is their responsibility. Their obligation is not to the school, but to their own children. If they do not support the school, there is nothing for the teacher to do. If no one else's learning is interrupted, there is no damage to repair. No rule has been broken, and no penalty is due. There are no grounds for punishment because the parents are responsible.

It therefore seems improper for the teacher to punish students for the incompletion of learning tasks. If it does not show in normal assessment procedures, it is relatively unimportant. When they are creating a disturbance that interferes with others' learning, it is a question of equal freedom, just rules, and their enforcement, but the incompletion of learning tasks is not a discipline problem. It is not a problem of maintaining the discipline of learning in the classroom. It is, rather, a problem of pedagogy and curriculum.

Perhaps these examples allow for the extraction of a few principles for institutionalizing the practice of rectifying wrongs done in school as an alternative to punishment. When students hurt each other physically by fighting, punching, hitting, pranks, or accident, reparative justice is achieved when they are friends again. When a pupil damages property belonging to another pupil or to the school, reparative justice is obtained when the property is repaired, replaced, or paid for. Restitution will frequently secure reparation when something has been taken that belongs to another student, for the embarrassment functions as an additional penalty. When a pupil verbally abuses a teacher, reparative justice is achieved when rapport with the teacher is restored. When a pupil intentionally disrupts learning processes, reparative justice is achieved when she or he pursues learning tasks again. Each principle involves a goal: restoral of friendship, repair, restitution, rapport, and return to learning. The five "R's". The attainment of the goal is in each case a matter of degree, i.e., a certain amount of cordial feeling, whatever repair is reasonable, as much restitution as possible, whatever rapport is feasible, and the kind of attention to learning the pupil can give after an emotional disturbance. It is seldom necessary to make things right again in any literal sense. What is required is a genuine attempt to make amends based upon a recognition of what is right and renewed respect for the violated rule. Children have short memories and will soon forget all about it.

The list of five "R's" is not exhaustive, but pupils can nowhere be allowed to destroy school property, hurt each other, expropriate things, or frustrate the teacher's efforts to establish a community of learning. Perhaps it suffices to show how to resolve the problems of discipline in a context of reparative justice that transcends retributive justice and psychological manipulation by letting pupils correct their own mistakes through obliging them to set things right again when they have erred.

If the rules of the classroom and school are just rules, i.e., those required to establish equal freedom to learn, they are moral rules. Their violation is a moral offense. The reparation of the damage or injury resulting from such a violation is also a moral act. The chance to make things right again therefore enables the pupil to regain moral responsibility and moral agency in a general restoration of human dignity.

V. Punishment in Education

Whether the practice of reparation can suffice to maintain school discipline, or whether punishment in the painful sense is also justified, is a question that has been partly answered. It depends upon the school, neighborhood, and contingent factors. Perhaps the systematic use of reparation from kindergarten onward would result in the formation of a general disposition or attitude toward wanting to undo damage, etc. incurred through one's mistakes. At least it is unlikely for the latter to develop without the opportunity to learn that reparations are possible. Perhaps wherever schools find it necessary to maintain a system of punishments to maintain discipline, it would be worth the time for everyone in the school to spend a few days talking together about what the school is for, what rules are needed to provide equal freedom to learn, and what reparations are due when someone disturbs the educational atmosphere.

Some of the factors that make a school's discipline precarious, however, are not within the school's control. Where there is a great deal of fighting in the neighborhood (or home), for example, a failure to punish fighting in school is perceived as weakness and condoning it. If one considers the school where an electronic search of students coming into school resulted in the confiscation of more than twenty knives and guns on one day, where students complained about the search as a violation rather than as a protection of their rights, one realizes that the ideology of discipline suited for that school will require the concept of punishment, even if it might be dispensed with in another school. Factors beyond the school's control might require the practice of punishment to establish the "monopoly of power" essential to maintain a general truce.

Be that as it may, teachers and principals have been unimaginative about the forms of punishment used in schools. The dunce cap has disappeared, but hitting children with the hand, strap, or cane has not. Such standbys as writing out lines, doing extra homework, and detentions are as prevalent as ever. Corporal punishment has been eliminated from adult penal systems in the Western world and should be eliminated from schools as a cruel and unusual punishment. It may be "usual" at home, but not on other people's children, and there is no reason for the school to emulate lower-class mores. Writing out lines is not suitable because the insight should be acquired before writing the sentence the first time, and copying it over and over merely dulls the insight. Composing a paragraph about reasons for the rule broken requires a conversation to establish the insight that apparently was lacking, and then the paragraph is superfluous. If extra homework is assigned as punishment, then innocent children ought not do any homework. Policing the school grounds is reparative for those caught littering, but otherwise it repairs damage done by someone else in a perversion of justice. Doing work for the school except voluntarily and according to a publicized wage scale is exploitative and leads to victimization.

When the damage cannot be repaired without a penalty to let it be seen that justice has been done, detentions serve the function that imprisonment fulfills on the adult level. The violation of rules necessary to establish equal freedom is an abuse of one's own freedom. The least inappropriate punishment for their enforcement is therefore a curtailment of one's freedom. For an abuse of freedom, one owes a curtailment of one's freedom, i.e., detention. Detentions might be inappropriate at the primary school level because they require that the offender understands that if he abuses his freedom, it will be curtailed in order to establish equal freedom for others. This assumes the student can be responsible for his freedom, i.e., liable to punishment, to an extent possible only for older children and youth.

Detentions are the most reasonable punishment because they are a curtailment of liberty, but they should be pedagogically supervised. The time should be used on learning tasks in a rehabilitative effort to reintegrate the pupil into the life of the school, i.e., to repair this major disequilibrium. If the number of thirty-minute detentions that serve as penalties attached to specific rules is proportionate and publicized, their award can be in accord with Beccaria's ethic as stated in the Rights of Man. Pronouncing the "sentence" can be immediate, inevitable, and irrevocable. One can say, "Three detentions," with a smile and without personal, emotional involvement. Cordial relations can be instantly restored. There need be no hard feelings between the culprit and the supervisor of the detentions, who did not award them. There need be no intentional infliction of suffering, nor any suffering undergone while serving the detentions, if the person is enabled to take advantage of the time to study something. Everything can be handled with the impartiality and dignity required of justice.

There ought to be an option attached to all detentions. Older youth ought to be able to choose to devote an equal time on weekends working on some project in the community outside of school. For instance, the student could assist elderly, handicapped, or housebound people in household chores, or run errands for them, or assist patients in mental or geriatric hospitals, or help run a weekend project for a youth club (not his own), or clear and landscape derelict sites and public grounds, or repair toys or furniture, and so on. This kind of community service is not the punishment, or the penalty paid for the rule violation. The detentions are. The student should be given the option, after detentions are awarded, to serve an equal time working in the community in the same way that adult first offenders are beginning to receive this option in courts of law. Rather than working against the development of altruistic feelings, adult first offenders sometimes continue the community service after the required period. The rehabilitative effect of the grounding in the real, adult life in the community suggests that it may be worth the necessary supervision to enable youth to establish, if not restore, a "moral equilibrium" between themselves and society through a community service alternative to punishment in school.

Ordinary school punishments such as writing out lines, doing extra homework, groundswork, or corporal punishment all involve an artificially contrived imposition of pain or unpleasantness that has to be calculated to be appropriate to the offense. Whether it is justified by reformative or deterrent reasons, and whether it is pre-specified or not, it places the teacher into a position of deciding which kind of unpleasantness is most suitable in the specific case. This calculus of displeasure involves a frame of reference that is technological and contrary to human dignity and the requirements of justice.

Because the unpleasantness of detentions is of a very unique origin, i.e., the deprivation of liberty, it is not directly inflicted. Not even the detentions are inflicted. They can be announced, as a judge pronounces the sentence, irrespective of any subjective intentions or consequences, merely in accordance with requirements of law as corrective justice pertaining to the external regulation of conduct. This neutrality can facilitate the acceptance of the penalty as one's debt to the society of the school and bring the retribution into the explicit framework of reparative justice.

Detentions are modelled on the practice of punishment of adult society. Adults are fined, incarcerated, given community service, or executed. The first and last are not appropriate to people who are not financially independent or guilty of murder. If school punishment is restricted to detentions for older children and youth, it retains liability for punishment in proportion to responsibility in a manner as nearly like adult life as possible, which is most appropriate for older youth. Five detentions for illicit borrowing in school is like five months for shoplifting, or five years for grand larceny, later. The hypothetical reformative effects of school punishments cannot be overlooked when deciding upon the forms which they should take, and the detentions might save someone from a prison term later. Forms of school punishment other than detentions bear no resemblance to adult life. If they cannot be replaced by detentions, perhaps they can be replaced by reparations.

In other words, because youth are in the process of accepting more and more responsibility for themselves, the deprivation of liberty for short, fixed, prescribed, intermittently scheduled durations seems to be the "eye for an eye" due to the community of learning for disturbances to its morale caused by an excessive use of freedom when the morale cannot be otherwise restored. This deprivation of liberty, furthermore, seems to be owed to the offender as his or her human right. It is an essential part of an education to freedom.

Conclusion

Because the maintenance of discipline occurs in the midst of ongoing processes of teaching and learning, it is frequently most effective if the teacher, not the student, repairs the damage to the moral equilibrium of the classroom caused by a rule violation. To avoid wasting valuable time for other students and accentuating the disturbance, the teacher can establish routines and say things in passing to remind students why they are in school and thus restore the equilibrium personally.

When the occasional discipline problem arises with an individual student, however, the teacher ought to be concerned with more than the immediate, effective, external regulation of conduct. To handle these problems with maximum dignity, reparation should replace retribution. The teacher as a teacher is properly concerned with the inner being, morale, and moral growth of the misbehaving student. Reparation is not retributive, for although it is the violator of the rule who is obliged to repair any damage, this is not something given to him as reward or punishment. It is required of him. The matter should be discussed individually with the student until he wants to repair the damage out of a desire to make things right again.

The emergence of this compassionate desire indicates that reparation enhances human dignity. To attain the joyous state of replacing the bad deed with a good one, the pupil has to understand the damage or injury he has done, empathize with the victim or victims, experience a lowering of morale with the realization of what he has done, recognize the rightness of the rule prohibiting the act, accept responsibility for having acted against a rule he now respects, figure out a way to "undo" what he now believes he should not have done, perform the good deed that repairs the damage, and then begin afresh.

This develops human dignity because it becomes a mini-lesson in moral education that enables the student to exercise moral responsibility and become more of a moral agent. It enables the teacher to "teach" the violated rule instead of merely enforcing it. The "enforcement" occurs through the promotion of the learning essential to the desired outcome, i.e., the preferably voluntary reparation. If the teacher assumes, even if it is not true, that the pupil did not know the rule, or forgot it, or was unaware of the consequences to others if he or she violated it, then the expectation that the pupil will want to rectify the error is created. This expectation shows that the teacher believes in the student, who can then believe in himself or herself and perhaps find the honesty to admit the rightness of the rule and the courage to make the reparation as publicly as the violation.

In the final analysis, however, the enforcement of the rules that maintain the classroom as a community under law devoted to learning is justified by the need to repair the damage done to its moral equilibrium by their violation, i.e., by the need to maintain discipline. When punishment in the painful sense is also necessary, it, too, is justified by the requirements of reparative justice. To say that the person deserves it simply because she or he violated the rule in retributive justice is correct, except that then the particular rule has to be justified, and its justification is its necessity to establish the conditions of the equal freedom to learn. When punishment is justified, then, it is because of the need to maintain the general discipline of learning.

To learn to respect the rules of equal freedom is essential to become a human being. It is a human right, because respecting them is a necessary condition of moral agency, the most basic human right. Reparation is more compatible with human dignity than retribution. Punishment in the painful sense is always extrinsic to the rule, but reparation requires understanding the right reasons for the rule and respecting it for its intrinsic value in expressing a moral duty.

Chapter Nine

DEMOCRACY IN EDUCATION

> If human dignity can today be fully recognized without our necessarily falling into the old groove of abstract rationalism, it is on condition that we place ourselves in the perspective of fraternity and not equalitarianism.
>
> Marcel[1]

The effort to turn classrooms into cooperative communities in the actual practice of democracy in schools has been an application of the third democratic ideal, fraternity. Unfortunately, it was mixed with a pseudo-egalitarianism. This blunder has made it virtually impossible to recognize (a) "democratic leadership" does not necessarily promote brotherly and sisterly love between students, and (b) brotherly and sisterly love between students can be fostered in classrooms without practicing democracy. To maintain the distinction and lay the foundation for the subsequent investigation of the question of fraternity, or brotherly and sisterly love, in education, it is necessary to begin with the question of democracy in education.

I. The Question of Democracy in Education

This question is unlike the question of freedom or equality because

---

[1] Gabriel Marcel, *The Existential Background of Human Dignity* (Cambridge: Harvard University Press, 1963), p. 130.

democracy, like authority, is not a moral principle. More importantly, it was not originally a student's question. It was first raised by Dewey to develop a model of the classroom that emphasized its social aspects to restore the sense of community allegedly lost through urbanization. His model purported to be the way democracy should be practiced in education, but its involvement of group planning of the curriculum depended upon an idiosyncratic definition of democracy as a mode of associated living in which numerous and varied interests are widely shared that lost the salient characteristics of the word and actually defined democracy away.

The question was also raised by the educational psychologists who objected to so-called authoritarian teaching styles and preferred allegedly democratic forms of leadership. Sometimes they simply objected to teacher-controlled didactic instruction and asked whether other forms of social interaction were possible in the classroom. Whereas Dewey advocated a form of participatory democracy, these psychologists implied that participation was democracy because they equated the percentage of student-initiated verbal exchanges with the degree of democracy present. They were perhaps less concerned with creating a community in the classroom and more with respecting the student as a person. They mostly rejected petty, abrasive, dominating teacher behaviors that violated the student's dignity when they expressed their anti-authoritarianism in terms of political ideology and in favor of a more democratic role for the teacher.

Students themselves finally raised the question at the university level in the worldwide student movement of the 1960's. They often confused concepts, too, however, for though they were often explicitly concerned with the question of democracy in education, some thought the university was undemocratic unless they had more freedom, whereas others desired greater equality with their teachers. In other words, they were really raising the questions of freedom and equality in education and employed the word "democracy" rhetorically, not insincerely but in a genuine intellectual error as large as Dewey's. Less confused students raised the question of democracy in the governance of higher education when they sought student representation on all major university decision-making bodies. This, however, is democracy in the school (university), not in the classroom. Many of these students expressed agreement with Neill's Summerhill, without recognizing that the democracy practiced there occurred only on Saturday mornings when all forty-five students assembled to discuss common problems.

There was also a raising of the question in the reform movement known as open education. The ideas here, however, were indigenous to schools and quite removed from their origin in Dewey, his disciples, and educational psychology. The concept of democracy was largely replaced by the more powerful insight of opening things up in the classroom, which achieved a very similar humanistic goal.

The question is an extremely important one. It can be simply stated as asking whether classrooms in liberal democracies should be run differently from schools in other kinds of societies to reflect the democratic cultural ideology. It is the question of whether the people in a democracy should be schooled for citizenship by being educated in institutions characteristically different because they are preparing people to live in a democratic society rather than in a monarchy, aristocracy, or totalitarian society. Should classroom practice influence the kind of citizens students become? Should they practice democracy in classrooms to learn how to practice it in society later on? If so, how? What would it mean to run a classroom democratically?

These questions are logically independent of the questions of freedom and equality in the classroom. It can be argued that whatever freedom a classroom will have depends upon the teacher's decision, which changes the quality of freedom to such an extent it no longer deserves the name. It can also be argued that the teacher's duty regarding equal consideration requires the recognition of each and every pupil in his or her full, concrete individuality as the precise person he or she is, and that this equivalent treatment no longer deserves the name of equality. Even in liberated, perfectly fair classrooms, one can ask whether their governance should be a microcosm of the macrocosm.

The questions are also logically independent of the question of discipline. Because a classroom or school is run democratically, it does not necessarily entail that the students themselves enforce the rules. Whether they formulate them or not, their enforcement can be a function reserved for teachers in the way the judiciary is separated from legislative and executive functions in some political democracies.

The question of democracy in education is also logically distinct from the question of the promotion of fraternity, i.e., communal feelings and brotherly and sisterly love, in education. The latter were unknown to Athenian democracy, which is sometimes praised as the paradigm of political democracy. The question of social democracy, i.e., the question of brotherhood and sisterhood, of community, will therefore be discussed after the question of political democracy in education is investigated.

II. The Meaning of the Word "Democracy"

The word "democracy" can be used in the social sense to refer to the interrelations between people in their egalitarian aspects, as contrasted to relatively stable patterns of social stratification embodying prestige, status, and economic differences. It can also be used in an economic sense to refer to a desired state of affairs in which the disparity between the haves and the have-nots is eliminated in order to secure social justice through a more equitable distribution of economic goods. In either case the point is an egalitarian one, for it is social equality or economic equality that is desired.

When the word is used in the strictly political sense, it also has this egalitarian intent, for to say that everyone is entitled to one vote and to run for public office is to oppose an elitist ruling class. That political democracy appears to be ineffective in preventing government by a ruling class is clearly related to the fact that political democracy does not require social or economic democracy. Existing liberal democracies are in fact democracies in the political sense but not in the social or economic senses of the word. Measures such as the graduated income tax and welfare legislation are efforts in the direction of social and economic egalitarianism that by their very existence indicate there is no basic acceptance of any principle that denies that people can become wealthier, more powerful, or more prestigious than others. Social, economic elitism is quite compatible with political democracy. This is proved by the existence of political parties on either side of the issue in liberal democracies. The concept of democracy itself does not, therefore, entail the kind of egalitarianism that is associated with it when it is used in the social or economic senses, or when all three senses are lumped together.

The applications of democracy to the classroom have not always distinguished these senses. The word has been used mostly in the social sense to emphasize egalitarianism and an anti-elitism that is better expressed in terms of the human right to equal consideration. That the point is well-taken does not justify the use of the word "democracy" to make it.

It is quite unfortunate that the area of human relations in the classroom has been considered with the concept of democracy rather than with the principle of fraternity, or brotherly and sisterly love. What is of concern is a matter of feelings, the realm of emotional and attitudinal perspectives toward other people. The vague, ephemeral atmospheric conditions of the classroom are much more appropriately expressed in terms of the teacher's love for students and the students' love for each other than in the language of politics, for in politics there is more room for honesty than affection.

To make the matter tangible, the way Dewey applied the concept of democracy to the classroom will be considered. His view will be rejected, but to retain the genuine, partial truth in his view, the main point of his concern for social democracy in the classroom will be supported in the next chapter. This will allow for the isolation of the concept of democracy in the political sense and some very specific educational applications in this chapter. The facility with which Dewey equated the socialized with the democratized classroom appears in his last educational writing.

> The most widespread and marked success of the progressive education movement...is a greater awareness of the needs of the growing human being, and the personal relations between teachers and students have been to a noticeable extent humanized and democratized....

> Of course, the conditions still too largely prevailing in the school... make it difficult to carry on the educative process in any genuine cooperative, democratic way. These conditions, however, are not the sole causes for the failures in educational democracy....[2]

---

[2] John Dewey, "Introduction," *The Uses of Resources in Education*, in *Dewey on Education*, ed. Martin S. Dworkin (New York: Teachers College Press, 1959), pp. 129, 130.

These judgments make sense only because he accepts his own earlier definition of democracy as "more than a form of government; it is primarily a mode of associated living, of conjoint, communicated experience,"[3] and the idea that "democracy stands in principle for free interchange, for social continuity."[4]

The word "democracy," however, means government by the people. Whatever more it is than this is an extra-political accretion, i.e., social democracy, or equality and fraternity in society, i.e., "a mode of associated living." It is Dewey, not democracy, that stands for free interchange. The right to the secret ballot is the right to have private political opinions, and to be protected from all persecution for having them, without being obliged to defend them publicly. If societies where there are free interchanges of ideas are better societies, it does not make them better democracies. Nor does it mean that societies without them are not democratic on that account unless the people are prevented from the free expression of ideas they choose to make public.

Literally understood, democracy in education means that the students should elect one of their peers to be their teacher, even if the class comprises seven-year-old children. They could also choose their teacher from among themselves by lot. Democracy assumes everyone is equally qualified to run for office, so one seven-year-old child can teach as well as another. Because short terms of office make leaders more responsive to their constituencies, they could even choose a different teacher every day.

This reduction to absurdity clears the air. It makes sense to ask Dewey what he meant by democracy in education, and why he also had to point out the importance of the teacher to educators who took his words too literally.[5] When anyone says a classroom should be run democratically, one can query him critically and question his competence and sincerity and ask if he means the students should select one of themselves to be the teacher, and if not, why he calls his proposal "democratic." In the lower grades the children are quite obviously too

---

[3] *Democracy and Education*, p. 87.

[4] Ibid., p. 344.

[5] In *Experience and Education* (New York: Macmillan, 1938), passim.

young to teach each other, and in the high school the sophistication of the subject matter also forbids it except on the odd occasion. It is not true that an innovative practice is good simply because it is democratic. Its value depends upon its characteristics other than its democratic nature. Dewey's suggestions, for example, are valuable largely because they increase the sociality of the classroom, not because one can say they are democratic after one distorts the concept of democracy to make it true. Teachers are selected for children, and it is neither democratic nor undemocratic that they cannot elect their teacher. It is simply a category mistake to construe educational phenomena in political terms. This does not criticize allegedly democratic innovations any more than one criticizes a potato by insisting it is not a fruit. It is simply an intellectual mistake to call an innovation democratic if the pupils do not elect their teacher.

It may, however, be an oversimplification to define the word "democracy" in the political sense as government by the people, particularly in the advanced industrial societies that have representative government. It may be better to ask about the conditions that have to be present to ascribe democracy to the government of a complex society. This can insure that one is concerned with democracy in the political sense without expanding its meaning for ideological purposes, but still allow for a richer grasp of the concept. A good source of the necessary conditions of democracy is the last chapter of Peters' *Ethics and Education*, although his ideas will have to be recast into the style of a linguistic analysis by indicating that a society would not ordinarily be said to be governed democratically unless three conditions are satisfied:

a. There are well-defined procedures that compel the government to consult the people,
b. There is institutionalized protection of freedom of speech and assembly,
c. There are well-defined procedures for insuring the public accountability of government officials.[6]

---

[6] Peters, *Ethics and Education*, pp. 300f.

The first criterion for the use of the word is fulfilled by frequent, compulsory elections, referendums, and effective lobbying, but not necessarily all three. These, of course, do not function properly unless there is freedom of speech to criticize the government before any audience one can assemble, including the use of the mass media to make one's views known. The point of either of these first two conditions is to enable public pressure to force the government to operate within ascertained, agreed parameters of accountability to the governed. Then if the people do not actually govern through their representatives, they nevertheless hold the ultimate power to refuse to re-elect them. In addition to the necessity to run for re-election, procedures for accountability include the recall, impeachment, limited terms of office, investigative committees, freedom of information procedures, votes of no confidence, the ombudsman, and so on. Peters seems right to state that the forms of consultation, criticism, and accountability can vary from society to society. The forms are accidental, or contingent, but the procedures themselves are essential to the existence of democratic governance. They are its necessary conditions.

This approach to the meaning of democracy in the political sense avoids the "glittering generalities" of political philosophy by reducing it to a quasi-operational definition. If a government wants to be democratic, it should consult with the people, listen to their advice, and remain accountable to their criticism. These are only some of the conditions of democracy, however, for the sufficient conditions also include brotherly and sisterly love. Before that is considered, however, it is necessary to discuss democracy as a human right and to indicate its necessary conditions in education.

III. Democracy as a Human Right

If government is the art of legislation, including the drafting, enactment, execution, and enforcement of laws, then a government is compatible with human rights if the laws it promulgates are just laws, i.e., if they are constitutive of equal freedom and compatible with human dignity. There is no prima facie reason why a monarch or aristocracy could not promulgate just laws, and democracies are liable to become majoritarian tyrannies that trample on the human rights of the minority. If a government of any form can be compatible with human rights, it is not only irrelevant but also immoral to pretend that some one form of government is a human right. That is to say that the attempt to show that democracy is itself a human right involves a demonstration that all other forms of government are necessarily incompatible with human rights, but this is probably not true.

An approach that will suffice for the present is to argue that the necessary conditions of democracy are human rights. This has been done already for the second condition. The principle of moral freedom includes whatever freedoms are necessary to act as a responsible, adult moral agent. This includes freedom of speech, thought, and action. These in turn include freedom of assembly, freedom of the press, freedom of religion, and even freedom to violate the law in acts of civil disobedience, providing one willingly accepts the statutory penalty. Because freedom is a human right, because a society can be said to be democratic if it institutionalizes the conditions of freedom (among other things), it can be said that to this extent democracy is a human right. This argument is that if A is B, and if C does A, then C is B, to that extent. This argument will not work, however, for although freedom may be a condition of democracy, that is not all it is. If it is a human right, it is a condition of any civilized society whatsoever. It is a universal obligation of every person toward every other person, regardless of the particular form of government under which they may happen to live.

This sort of claim about universal obligations between all mature adults of the human species, however, invokes Kant's "kingdom of ends." It is not drawn from a vision of what society ought to be, but it creates an understanding of a society of moral agents that education ought to be promoting, among other things. Education should be promoting the development of a society of reciprocally obligated human beings, i.e., a society of self-governing people, i.e., a democracy. If moral agency is a human right, and if reciprocating relations with other moral agents are part of that human right, then the form of government most compatible with a society of moral agents, i.e., democracy, is a human right.

A similar argument can be developed from the human right to

equal consideration. A society wherein people give each other equal consideration is not necessarily egalitarian, but inequalities of wealth or power are not allowed to influence one's regard for another's dignity as a human being. In this context the governors would want to consult with the governed about decisions affecting them, and reciprocally, the people would look upon their politicians as doing a job for the community without investing charisma in them. This, too, would mean that if equality is a human right, the form of government most compatible with equality of consideration, i.e., one in which the people felt their governors were merely employed by them to do a specific job, i.e., a democracy, is a human right.

A more convincing argument is that a society with a democratic government has more respect for human rights. Some evidence is the existence of national constitutions with bills of rights attached. The rights specified therein may not be sufficiently universal to be tantamount to human rights, but, nevertheless, the principle that its citizens do have rights against their government is thereby institutionalized in the critically important location. More than this, systematic elections operationalize moral agency, so to speak. Hardly ever do most people in most societies have anything at all to say about most of what happens in their society, but in the privacy of the voting booth they decide what they want their society to be like. There is not much power there, but this is only because the entire power of the society is at that moment equally divided, and everyone is equally confirmed in their belief that they count as much as anyone else. Even if the ballot is a delegation of that power, the chance to choose the delegate augments human dignity.

To argue that the consultative condition is a human right, however, would require one to maintain that human beings are the only animals that have laws, lawgivers, and legislative institutions; that it is necessary to participate in legislative functions to become a human being; and that one's stature as a mature moral agent is seriously jeopardized by the lack of participation in the kinds of consultative procedures characteristically found in democratic societies. All of this is true. Therefore, a government's obligation to consult with the citizens is their human right. It is their due because they are not robots to be controlled but human beings to be consulted. Being consulted, participating in whatever consultative procedures are institutionalized, is necessary to become a fully responsible, adult human being. It is a necessary condition of moral agency.

The attractiveness of the Kantian claim that the mature adult is autonomous, and that such autonomy includes the legislating of the laws that one will then freely obey, is due to its embodiment of the democratic idea. It is false to experience, however, for most people in modern democracies do not make laws, and no legislative assembly remakes all the laws on the books. Democracy cannot entail making one's own laws. Kant's notion of autonomy has to be rejected in any case because of its long association with rationalistic ethics, male chauvinism, and the technological consciousness. Its replacement with the concept of moral agency does not require that individuals make laws to attain moral maturity.

Moral agency is deepened through the expansion of personal responsibility that occurs while engaging in the consultative procedures characteristic of democracies, which are therefore a human right.

The case of accountability is analogous. The free flow of information to the people is necessary to manifest a genuine respect for their independent moral judgment. One might also argue that it is one's human right to live in a society wherein the governors are visibly responsible, moral agents. Thomas Jefferson did, in the Declaration of Independence. This, however, merely states in a different way that moral principles are universally valid. They apply to people in government as elsewhere. Insofar as moral principles such as truthtelling are human rights, the public accountability of the government in democracies is a human right.

Finally, it can be argued that insofar as the government in a monarchy, aristocracy, or mixed constitution manifests genuine concern for the human rights of the governed, and institutionalizes procedures for insuring their fulfillment, it is governing for the people and to that extent is democratic. Then insofar as it is necessary to insure it maintains this concern for the rights of the people by instituting some form of consultative procedures, to that extent it is democratic. To that extent it can be said that democracy is a human right.

Although "democracy" is not a moral principle because the word does not designate any universal obligation, the conditions that have to be present in a society for it to be called a democracy are themselves human rights. These conditions do not have to be present in an aristocracy or monarchy for it to be an aristocracy or monarchy, at least not when the words are used in the strictly political sense. This means that although democracy itself may not be a human right, it is the form of government most compatible with human rights. A number of human rights have to be observed for a democracy to be a democracy in the strictly political sense of the word. Democracy as the form of government most compatible with human rights is also that which, *ipso facto*, maximizes human dignity.

If so, the question of democracy in education is extremely important.

IV. Democracy in Education

The question of democracy in education in the strictly political sense concerns the procedures that ought to be used in classrooms for consultation, free speech and assembly, and accountability. Dewey's model of continuous student-teacher planning of the curriculum is only one way to implement the consultative condition of democratic governance. Other ways are undoubtedly more suitable in most circumstances. These include the use of actual parliamentary procedures, with a student presiding, to conduct some of the affairs of the class, or the use of the contract system in which the student individually "negotiates" a contract with a teacher, or in which he or she chooses a contract from several structured options. Older students who have already chosen an occupational goal involving a standardized curriculum with a highly structured content are probably adequately consulted if the choice to enter the program is informed and reasons for requirements manifest. This fulfills the consultative condition to the extent possible, which is all that can be expected without fanaticism. It accounts for a simple fact that any use of consultative procedures in education has to confront in an honest way. It is logically impossible for students to plan their own curriculum because they do not know what they do not know.

Although some procedure for consulting students is entailed by the concept of democracy the form it should take is extremely problematic. For example, if a primary school teacher decided unilaterally to tell a story, and asked a class which story they wanted to hear, she would be fulfilling the consultative condition. It would not be any more democratic to ask them first if they wanted to hear a story. When asked with the appropriate, endearing enthusiasm, no class will refuse. Even a unilateral decision to read or tell a particular story would not violate the consultative condition if prior attention were given to the interests of the children. Imagine this interchange:

"Hey. Who would like to hear a story?"

"Me." "Me." "I would." "I do." And so forth from each and every child.

"What about a story about...a fat pig?"

"Yeah!" "O Boy!" "Yah!" And similar exclamations from all children.

A strict interpretation would call this benevolent despotism, but it is merely good teaching. Children love to hear stories, especially ones they have not heard before. If they do not like one they have not chosen, the fault is not in the lack of consultation but in the presentation. It would be a bad story-teller, indeed, who found children unresponsive. To call the quoted episode an act of benevolent despotism is itself a despotism that lacks benevolence.

This kind of example should be analyzed at various age levels in various subject areas and with various learning activities to discover inductively, so to speak, exactly what the appropriate consultative procedures should be within each segment of the curriculum. The matter cannot be decided a priori without ideologically imposing a method of consultation on students that they themselves do not appreciate. That is to say that the students ought to be consulted about the consultation procedures. Prior to an analysis of specific situations, the only general principle that can be defended is that if the teacher consults with the students about the content of the curriculum to the extent possible within the circumstances, one of the conditions of democratic governance is fulfilled. If teachers cannot be trusted to conduct appropriate consultations in good faith—to the extent possible within the context—there is no reason to construct a more elaborate model of the classroom to insure they do occur.

The problem is partly that consultative procedures take time that ought to be used on learning tasks themselves, and it is partly that more intelligent students will point this fact out when Deweyan student-teacher planning occurs. It is also that the way students come to perceive classrooms when such procedures are employed is undesirable. They do not see them as places where they should learn things they do not already know, and they perceive the teacher as lacking the competence and enthusiasm to make decisions about their learning. It stifles the expression of the teachers' enthusiastic attitudes toward the knowledge and skills they are teaching because they value them highly, thereby eliminating the genuine source of motivation for learning, i.e., the perception of the teacher's love for the things the student is expected to study.

The point of the consultative condition of democracy is to protect the interests of the governed, i.e., the students, from arbitrary decisions by teachers and administrators. They have no value in and of themselves that can supersede the value of the skills and knowledge of the curriculum. To force an unwanted consultative procedure upon students is one of those arbitrary practices from which students need protection. The maximum amount of consultation is not necessarily the maximum democracy, nor the way to maximize learning.

Students ought to be consulted about what they believe to be the appropriate consultative procedure or else the second condition of democracy in education is not honored. Freedom of speech, thought, and assembly also mean that students must be free to express distaste for consultative procedures and to reject them. Their refusal cannot be refused without self-contradiction.

The general application of the second condition, however, is not so straightforward. It goes without saying that every classroom ought to be open for discussion and the critical analysis of the content of instruction, but students are often inhibited and always easily intimidated. Younger children should have a suggestion box in which to forward their complaints anonymously, and older children and youth ought to be encouraged to elect a class ombudsman the first week of school to serve the same function. The class ombudsman should be empowered to receive and investigate complaints, protect the anonymity of the plaintiff, make recommendations to the class or teacher, or take the matter up with the school ombudsman, who should be a responsible adult, preferably a parent. Complaints can be heard directly by a teacher of perceived integrity who has established an atmosphere of trust, candor, and dignity, but it is extremely difficult for a teacher to perceive when free speech is not honored. If it has to be safe-guarded against the teacher to prevent the voluntary self-censorship that results from the desire for approval, the principle of the ombudsman ought to be routinized in classrooms.

The third condition can be implemented through student evaluations of the course of study. Perhaps the evaluation of specific acts of teaching in the face-to-face situation would establish some account-ability, but the more important concern is the students' perceptions of the organized opportunities for learning provided by the teacher through the use of textbooks, other books, materials, assignments, assessment procedures, and whatever else is put together in the course of study. A teacher who wants to hold herself or himself accountable to students wants to know not merely what they think of her or his personality as it affects her or his teaching (to eliminate extraneous mannerisms, etc.). He or she will be especially concerned to discover which aspects of the pattern of learning activities provided are per-ceived as interesting, challenging, valuable, and negotiable, which are dull, too simple, too difficult, or trivial, and whether there are any complaints, suggestions, or recommendations in addition to state-ments about things that are satisfactory. One is accountable to stu-dents if the results of student evaluations are used to improve the course of study, for what a teacher can be accountable for is the provision of conditions of learning that enables most students to make reasonable progress toward the achievement of specified objec-tives. Their reports about this progress are the best source of data about the effectiveness of the course of study. No particular method of evaluation, however, seems necessary. The questionnaire can be designed and administered by the teacher, and the results can remain confidential to the teacher. If the "feedback" is earnestly sought and sincerely employed to improve the conditions of learning as perceived by students themselves, the teacher has fulfilled the accountability condition of democratic governance.

Such evaluations also supply the minimal procedure for consultation with students, for instead of offering an occasion to manipulate a majority opinion into doing what the teacher wants the class to do, the students are asked to submit a calm, independent, anonymous judgment of their educational provisions. It enables students to participate in student-teacher planning after they have mastered a course of study and know what they are talking about. When conducted anonymously, such evaluations are also the minimal procedure to insure the second condition of democracy, for the teacher herself intentionally assembles the students to let them formulate, express, and submit their collective, critical judgment of the matter of most importance to them as students.

These recommendations for the suggestion box, a class ombudsman, and student evaluation of courses of study avoid the rhetoric, sentimentality, psychological manipulation, and false generosity frequently found in exhortations to be democratic in classrooms. It can be claimed that unless their kind of routinized protection of the right to free speech and critical opinion is instituted, the rest of the talk about democracy in education is cant. Most such talk relieves the teacher from the responsibilities of teaching, but these recommendations provide the means whereby the teacher can acquire the information necessary to be able to assume full responsibility for the provision of the conditions of learning.

More important is their enlargement of the pupils' sense of involvement in the life of the school, the respect for them as persons that is felt when their opinions of the course of study are genuinely solicited, the assertiveness about their rights that is enhanced through a rectification of a legitimate grievance forwarded through the suggestion box or ombudsman, and the general growth of the self-conscious awareness of their responsibility that is promoted when their views about the conditions of learning are submitted in writing. More important is the enhancement of the students' sense of their own dignity.

Conclusion

The implication of the concept of democracy for pedagogy when stated as the practice of consulting students about the selection and organization of the curriculum to the extent possible within the circumstances, in order to receive their advice and to hold oneself accountable for providing the best conditions of learning, results from the basic restriction to the political sense of the word.

So much has been written about democracy in education it should be salutary to begin afresh with the simple claim that the minimum conditions under which one can ascribe "democracy" to the governance of a classroom are the use of the suggestion box, the ombudsman, and student evaluations of the course of study. Because these increase the respect for persons, they change authoritarian contexts to democratic atmospheres. They can democratize the classroom without destroying the heart of the pedagogic relation, which is necessarily a very undemocratic situation. The teacher is always responsible for the learning of every student in class, whereas each student is always responsible for only one person's learning. Even the most democratically governed class, functioning completely with cooperative curriculum planning, cannot absolve the teacher's responsibility for everyone's learning and cannot give any student the responsibility for anyone's learning but his or her own.

This conclusion is less surprising, and less conservative, when it is realized that innovations often recommended for education under the aegis of democracy are more properly classified under concepts such as freedom, equality, human dignity, and fraternity. If the implication of the concept of democracy is that these democratic ideals should be implemented in education, then a theory, or program, for their full operationalization leaves little for the application of the "umbrella word," democracy, itself.

A complete awareness of human rights in education, in other words, eliminates the necessity for the separate consideration of the question of democracy in education. This follows for anyone who believes that democracy is the form of government most compatible with human rights. In education as elsewhere, the practice of democracy can be justified only by its contribution to the realization of human rights.

Chapter Ten

FRATERNITY IN EDUCATION AS A HUMAN RIGHT

> Only those who know the presence of the You have the capacity for decision. Whoever makes a decision is free.
>
> Buber[1]

The practice of the appropriate consultative procedures allows the necessary conditions of democracy in the political sense to be taken for granted during the following investigation of its sufficient conditions. The question of democracy in education in the social sense is not about the involvement of the students in the governance of the classroom, for it is not the practice but the spirit of democracy that requires attention to community in the classroom and the principle of brotherhood.

I. The Question of Cooperation in Education

Democratic procedures are necessary but insufficient to produce democracy when they are used cunningly to promote the interests of a faction rather than the common good or when they are forced upon people undemocratically. The concern for democracy in education should extend to the question of its sufficient conditions, i.e., the

---

[1] Martin Buber, *I and Thou*, tr. Walter Kaufmann (New York: Scribners, 1970), p. 100.

social aspects of the classroom, communal feelings, and brotherly and sisterly love.

It would be digressive to demonstrate explicitly that the political and social senses of the word are conflated in discussions in education. What is usually wanted is not the political procedure but the spirit of democracy. The word is used ceremonially to lay a blessing upon general feelings of friendship, good will, and affectionate being together during cooperative learning. This is why the question concerns the extent to which the classroom should function as a community in which pupils want to participate because they like their classmates, their teachers, and being together.

Although the question was originally raised by Dewey, he himself strangely lacked concern for affection, love, and the moral principle of fraternity. He referred to "social sympathy," but this term was adapted to his Hegelian subsumption of the individual to the group through an emphasis upon behavioral socialization to the neglect of inner feelings toward each other. When, for example, he said, "True education comes through the stimulation of the child's powers by the demands of the social situations in which he finds himself,"[2] he overlooked a number of things, such as self-initiated curiosity, the influence of adults as such, and the stimulation of the world itself, which he could refer to only as the biological and physical environment. The environment is not the world. True education requires the acquisition of knowledge of things in the world. The statement is truer than Dewey's. The loss of the person in Dewey's view is especially clear in his next sentence, "Through these demands, he is stimulated to act as a member of a unity."[3] This overstates a half-truth because it glosses over the fact that the group is simply other people whom one can like, respect, and relate to individually on the basis of genuine affection for them.

Regardless of his particular distortion of the question, however, it is true that standard patterns of schooling involving common lessons and assessment can readily turn the conditions of equal opportunity

---

[2] John Dewey, "My Pedagogic Creed," in *Dewey on Education*, ed. Martin Dworkin (New York: Teachers College Press, 1959), p. 20.

[3] Idem.

into competition for grades and promote the pursuit of self-interest at the expense of bonds of affection with classmates. The genuine question is whether pupils can learn to work together in genuine cooperation with one another when they are encouraged to achieve higher degrees of excellence than each other.

The difficulty can be schematized in a continuum extending from competition to cooperation. It is on a different plane from the authority-freedom continuum, as can be realized as soon as the ideological intention of labelling everything good in education "democracy" is transcended. Totalitarian societies can be strongly united collectively, and a teacher with a strong, dominant personality can indeed maintain a cohesive, cooperative classroom informed with genuine feelings of solidarity and mutual respect. A *laissez-faire* classroom can also result in great cooperation, but not necessarily so. Similarly, the dictatorship, the democratic classroom, or the *laissez-faire* classroom can also function competitively. In other words, the democratic classroom is not the same thing as the cooperative one. This continuum can be shown in the following diagram:

All classrooms can be placed between the extremes of ruthless competition and cordial cooperation. Point B represents an ordinary classroom in which there is considerable cooperation but which is basically shaped by competitive striving for academic excellence and/or grades. Point C represents a classroom that involves some competition, but within an encompassing framework of cooperation. Most classrooms below the tertiary level would probably fall between points B and C. They are "traditional" if closer to B, but "progressive" or "open" if closer to C.

It is probably true that no classroom can be maintained without including some elements of competition and cooperation. The more competitiveness is enhanced through assessment procedures, the more students pursue only their own self-interest. Although this might occur at the expense of others, it can also result in self-satisfied clients, the aggregate of whom constitutes the common good. On the other hand, the more cooperation is encouraged, the more students acquire attitudes, habits, and skills of cooperation, and the more they are willing to work toward the achievement of the common good, from which each obtains his or her own satisfactions. Although Dewey and his disciples have claimed the cooperative classroom is the democratic one, this depends upon his interpretation of democracy. It may very well be that there is an inevitable conflict, or tension, between the goals of intellectual achievement and the development of the competencies required to work well with other people. When a choice between achievement and cooperation is necessary, moreover, the teacher may be obliged to choose cognitive achievement rather than affective development because the primary criterion has to be the long view and individual success in the economic world that individuals have to cope with throughout adult life.

The point is to become clear about the reality of the question of competition and cooperation in the classroom. If the classroom ought to be democratic in the social sense of the word, to what extent, and how, should it promote cooperation, social cohesiveness, a sense of belonging to the community of the classroom, and fellow-creaturely feelings, i.e., brotherly love?

The question is not whether the classroom should be cooperative in order to promote the development of a democratic society. That is another question, to be considered in the next chapter, about the use of the classroom to serve extrinsic goals. It is the question of education for democracy. The present question concerns democracy in education, i.e., the desirability of any classroom being democratic in the social sense of the word, and whether it is the student's human right to have fellow-creaturely feelings, fraternity, promoted in the classroom for values intrinsic to the classroom as a community under law devoted to learning.

To what extent should brotherly and sisterly bonds of affection be encouraged to develop between pupils? To what extent should bonds of affection be encouraged to develop between the teacher and students? To what extent does the presence of the requisite affectionateness constitute the spirit of democracy in education?

II. The Meaning of the Word "Fraternity"

It is not the word "fraternity" but the ideal of brotherhood that has to be understood before it can be said to be a universal obligation. The shift to brotherly and sisterly love to avoid sexism correctly emphasizes the affective focus of the ideal, but it loses the universality of the cosmopolitan ideal of the Eighteenth Century Enlightenment regarding the brotherhood of all mankind. If brotherly love is characteristically different from sisterly love, so be it. Even if they are appropriate manifestations of the one and same ideal, it is difficult to specify in these terms what it is to which everyone has the right. One can state the obligations clearly, for males can be said to owe brotherly love to all other people, male and female alike, and females, sisterly love, to each alike. On the other hand, it is not only awkward to say that one has a right to brotherly love from all adult males and a right to sisterly love from all adult females. It is sexist. Rights can be justified as human rights only if they apply without regard for gender. Although in the final analysis they convey its most satisfactory understanding, it begs the question to refer to the ideal expressed by the word "fraternity" as brotherly and sisterly love.

The eighteenth century ideal of the brotherhood of all humankind was not only cosmopolitan. It was humanitarian. Because all people were alleged to be children of God, they were said to be brothers. Considerable impetus was given to the understanding of people in other parts of the world, and a rationalization was supplied for the breakdown of hereditary social classes. The ideal thus expressed concern for the welfare of other people and the common good. Although the dominance of the ideal of liberty in classical liberalism supported *laissez-faire* government, the third ideal supports government action to promote the general welfare. It functions together with the ideal of equality to support legislation to provide food, shelter, and other economic necessities for the needy through such things as unemployment compensation, family support, and other subsidies that provide social security for the less fortunate. Whether these things ought to be done through legislation or through private charity is largely a technological question and a matter of whether one values liberty more highly than equality and fraternity. In either case the intent is clearly humanitarian. The basic meaning of the word "fraternity" as a democratic ideal is that when called upon, one is obliged to be his brother's keeper. Those who can afford it are morally obligated to be philanthropic.

The point can be clarified by noting that if one emphasizes liberty at the expense of the other two democratic ideals, it yields libertarianism and free-enterprise capitalism. To stress equality at the expense of the other two yields egalitarianism and welfare-state capitalism. If fraternity is emphasized at the expense of both liberty and equality, it yields right-wing totalitarianism, national socialism, and such things as the Ku Klux Klan, but if fraternity and equality are emphasized together at the expense of liberty, it yields left-wing totalitarianism, state capitalism, and such things as the Communist Party.

This suggests that the educational question could be understood as the question of socialism in the classroom except for the fact that the word has gathered such connotations its simple denotation is scarcely accessible. The phrasing "community in education" would falsely suggest the involvement of parents and other concerned citizens in schools. Whatever merit this has, it is something different from the development of communal feelings among students themselves. The effort to think of the whole school as a community in any literal sense would involve architectural and curriculum reform on a scale scarcely imaginable, and it would destroy the school as a community of scholars devoted to learning. The words "communism in education" would be totally misleading, although "communalism" or "communitarianism" might capture the sense of belonging that is central to the third ideal. The phrase "love in education" would overemphasize the correct concept and perhaps betray its origin in the Judeo-Christian doctrine of loving one's neighbor as oneself. The expression "fellowship in education" sounds denominational, whereas "comradeship" conveys a sense of partisanship. Any overemphasis on the group, the collective, or communal feelings and solidarity with others loses concern for the individual. It is the origin of totalitarianism and has been called "tribalism" in the emergence of the counterculture of the 1960s and 1970s. Its fanaticism becomes apparent whenever the feelings of brotherhood and sisterhood do not extend beyond the boundaries of the specific group toward "all humankind" to include those with whom one shares fundamental disagreement.

The problem is not only finding a non-sexist term. It is finding one that is descriptively adequate and politically non-partisan lest one person's party politics becomes another's "human right." There is something irreplaceable about the phrase, "the brotherhood of all mankind." What has to be retained is a sense of identification with the human species as such and an "instant rapport" with strange members of the species immediately upon encountering them. It is an affective layer of one's own being that is felt as a "positive regard" or a liking for other people simply because they are people, i.e., fellow human beings. This fellow creaturely feeling might be called "cousinly love," for it is not as close, intimate, or warm as one feels toward a brother who is actually a sibling, but it is closer than one would feel toward an alien being from another planet. The ideal of fraternity claims that one ought to feel something like cousinly love toward the stranger, for it is to the stranger that it becomes a moral obligation to extend the hand of friendship.

Perhaps the idea of friendship captures the essence of the ideal in a non-sexist way, except it seems to lose some of the moral texture that might be found in the expression "respect for persons." One can act in accordance with the principle of respect for persons even with people one does not like, however, for respecting someone does not require one to be fond of him. On the other hand, because one can be respectful without being sociable, and without feeling belongingness, the concept of friendship is more compatible with the ultimate worth and dignity of the individual, the reason one should feel kindly toward any human being.

Friendship is also most compatible with the educational question. Cooperation in classrooms helps students to remain friends, or to make new ones. The positive bonds of affection and mutual respect required by the principle of fraternity are clearly a form of love, the paradigm for which is friendship.

Friendship is the kind of love that must be added to the necessary conditions of democracy in the political sense to establish its sufficient conditions. To paraphrase Paul, if one has the necessary conditions of democracy in the political sense but has no friends, he is but a clanging cymbal. Love is the sufficient condition. Friendliness is the spirit of democracy.

If democracy is government by the people, there is no need to reify the word "government" and consider it as an entity in its own right. It can be considered as comprising those people to whom other people have temporarily delegated certain specific powers. The absence of a set of hereditary rulers makes a democracy essentially a society that governs itself cooperatively. One puts ordinary people, his friends, into public office, and calls them by affectionate nicknames such as Jack, Jimmie, and Ronnie. Such cooperation through the use of the technology of the polling booth, etc., can occur with or without getting into the spirit of the thing, i.e., with or without friendly feelings toward the other citizens with whom one is sharing the government of society.

The importance of friendship is manifested in the corollary of fraternity, i.e., the value and dignity of the individual person. The earlier claim was that all people are brothers because they are all alleged to be children of God, and this implied that each human being is of infinite worth in the eyes of God. That is for God to say. With or without cosmic support, brotherhood and individuality are major ideals, each of which assumes that the individual person should be the beneficiary of all value realization. Things should not be done for the sake of the state, church, aristocracy, institution, bureaucracy, or party. Whatever is done should benefit human beings, individuals like you and me. This is why it is essential for a legislative body to have the consent of the governed and why democratic government makes sense. It makes no sense apart from a belief that the individual person should be the center of all value realization, which depends upon the prior claim that each person has her or his own value and dignity.

In this way respect for persons and mutual affection have become part of the contextualized concept of democracy. Their absence from Athenian democracy is to be explained by noting that they are not part of the concept of democracy as a spaceless, timeless, disembodied, historical idea. This does not exist apart from someone's having it in mind in any case, but they are a part of what the concept entails in the twentieth century, and this is the context in which the concept has become involved in the educational question about the fundamental value of bonds of affection between individuals in classrooms, all of whom are of equal worth.

A political democracy can exist in a society in which no one has any respect for other people as individuals, each with their own value and dignity. Mutual respect and affection cannot be institutionalized any more than morality can be legislated. Nevertheless the principle of brotherhood, or reciprocated friendly feelings, respect for persons, and the sense of the worth of the individual has to inform the life of a society for it to be democratic. The sense in which the word "democratic" is used here is analogous to the ordinary distinction between following the letter of the laws and maintaining the spirit of the law. The first is legally correct, but the second fulfills the intent of law. The procedures of democracy can be followed legalistically, without enthusiasm or generosity of mind, to achieve the "letter" of democracy, but it requires a love of the other people in one's society to insure the presence of the spirit of democracy. One can behave democratically without it, but friendliness is necessary to be democratic.

That the sufficient condition of democracy can be expressed as the ideal of fraternity understood as simple friendliness is apparent when one realizes it suffices to believe in oneself and to believe in people. The spirit of democracy is present in a context of mutual trust and affection, for then people believe in each other.

III. Fraternity as a Human Right

There is no doubt that the child needs the love and acceptance of the parents to achieve normal, non-neurotic personality development, i.e., that parental love is the infant's human right. There is no doubt that social interactions with age cohorts in school are a form of secondary socialization and that the acquisition of the knowledge and skills in the curriculum can be understood as a kind of tertiary socialization. All knowledge is a social product, and so forth. There is no doubt that such socialization processes are necessary to become an adult human being, are distinctively human, and could be said to be a human right on these grounds. This approach, however, overemphasizes the socialization aspects of school learning and is a symptom of the fragmentation and loneliness of modern, industrialized societies. Such sociological "explanations" lose sight of individual persons and their perspectives on the cognitive aspects of the curriculum through which they become aware of things in the world.

It does not suffice to borrow constructed explanations from psychoanalysis or the social sciences to establish something as a human right, particularly in the study of education, or one begs the question. One can consider the logic of the use of the idea of the need for love and socialization in the child's development by progressive educators, who overstated their case with such enthusiasm it resulted in a generalized belief that children cannot learn from books and teachers. This is completely opposite to the common sense view of the matter, i.e., that children go to school precisely to learn from books and teachers.

One can argue that love and cooperation are indeed essential in education without engaging in the anti-intellectualism that results in an anti-book and anti-teacher ideology. To retain a proper sense of values, one might paraphrase Kant: Two things fill me with awe, learning from books and learning from older people. All of literate civilization rests upon these two kinds of learning because they are absolutely fundamental to the transmission of the human heritage, which is all that distinguishes civilized human beings from cave men. Learning from books and teachers, furthermore, is reducible to learning from teachers, for a book is merely a technological device to teach at a distance. The amazing thing is that one can learn from older people.

The child can and should explore the things in the world directly, without constant mediation by teachers or books, to be sure, but if human beings differ from animals it is because the exploration of these things in the world can become disciplined, mediated, and advanced through the use of the conceptual frameworks embodied in the symbolic culture that can be acquired through the help of teachers under conditions of formal learning.

That is to say that man is the educating animal.[4] He differs from other animals in that he educates his young. When human beings

---

[4] Martinus Langeveld, *Einfuhrung in die Theoretische Padagogik* (Stuttgart: Ernst Klett Verlag, 1969), ch. 8.

educate their young, they humanize them. Human beings are human beings insofar as they are educable and educated. The pedagogic relation is therefore necessary to personal humanization. Within the pedagogic relation, something happens that is essential to the humanization of the young: educating and being educated. To be educated within the pedagogic relationship is therefore a human right.

Because the teacher's love for students is a necessary condition of the pedagogic relation, pedagogic love is a human right. This does not justify all fellow-creaturely feelings called "fraternity" as a human right, but it does justify species-specific affection as one. The child deserves to be loved by its parents, teachers, and anyone else that assumes any kind of role involving sustained contact with him. The child deserves to be loved by all adults, except this love should be more avuncular than brotherly.

The human significance of pedagogic love may not be as apparent as it should be, for its advocates have not been its best representatives. They have seemed to suggest that love can replace a more satisfactory cognitive understanding of children, instead of forming the basis for such understanding. Neither love nor conceptual understanding is by itself sufficient. Sometimes the advocates of love in pedagogy appear to be unconcerned about the pupil's learning the knowledge and skills in the curriculum, which means they are in bad faith, and other times they have confused pedagogic love with other forms of affection.

Because the pedagogic relation grows out of the parental relation, pedagogic love is somewhat akin to parental love and might be confused with it. In their relations with their own children, parents frequently shift over into a teaching role to help their child learn to walk, talk, dress itself, etc. When the teacher takes over this teaching role, to which the child submits because he has learned how to learn from the parents, it is without the other parental interactions with the child. It is not possible for teachers to love other people's children as their own because of this lack of intimacy. Then, too, as the child grows older, he or she responds less emotionally to the teacher, and there are other children vying for attention.

Just as pedagogic love should not be confused with parental love, it should not be confused with brotherly love, sisterly love, filial love, romantic love, conjugal love, and other modes of love, each of which becomes structured by the objective characteristics of the kind of relation in which it develops. Just as the feelings of affection of males that are instances of brotherly love differ from the feelings of females that are instances of sisterly love, so does love assume different forms when the feelings of affection emerge from relations to one's children or one's parents. Similarly, romantic love occurs as part of the courtship of a mate, whereas conjugal love is different because it grows out of years of wedded bliss on the basis of the earlier romantic love.

The kind of affectionate fondness found within the pedagogic relation when the teacher simply likes children flows from the teacher to the pupil to constitute the pedagogic relation. Children often speak of liking their teacher, perhaps less often as they become older and more reserved, but it is appropriate to consider things largely from the teacher's side to concentrate the focus upon the necessity of pedagogic love as the affective consequence of the teacher's valuing each student for his or her own value and dignity. It is also the affective basis for respect for the pupil as a person.

It is unlikely that someone who was both a parent and a teacher would confuse parental and pedagogic love, and it is undesirable for someone who is a teacher but not a parent to lavish parental love on children as if they were surrogates for one's own offspring. It might help to compare pedagogic love to the affectionateness that doctors and nurses feel toward their patients, i.e., to the bedside manner. Within this the nurse's love can be clearly distinguished from the doctor's. Both are different from the love the clergy extend to their congregations, from the warmth social workers feel toward their clients, and from the quality of affection relative to the psychotherapeutic relation. The main point is that just as the hospital nurse opens warmly toward each patient in the ward regardless of the condition of his or her health, so, too, can the teacher extend affection toward each and every pupil, regardless of his or her learning ability. To say that the teacher ought to love students because it is their human right is to say they deserve it simply because they are students.

Educational psychologists claim that the good teacher is warm and outgoing. That is how pedagogic love appears to the external observer. The teacher who looks that way, however, is merely affectionate towards pupils in the way medical personnel are drawn out to their clients in the caring relation of medicine. The similarity is due to the caring for the well-being of the client at the heart of the professional relation. Pedagogic love is more like that shown in medical practice than it is like parental love, at least with older children. On the other hand, it is more like parental love than is the medical relation. Finally, although parental and medical relations, like the social worker and psychotherapeutic relations, can shift over into the pedagogic relation when there is something to teach the client, the pedagogic relation cannot slip over into any of these other relations. The teacher lacks qualifications. This signifies that the pedagogic relation, when founded in mutual respect, has its own dignity.

The teacher's respect for the pupil as a person should be oriented to believing in the unique possibilities of the child or youth and who she or he might become. Believing in the students enhances their forward orientation toward the responsible existence of the adult moral agent. Because it is unlikely that youth will believe in themselves unless the adults in their world believe in them, pedagogic love is their human right.

Then, too, the presence of a trusted, beloved adult is necessary to make the world accessible to the child. It is heuristically convenient to speak of the child's explorations of the things in the world as if this occurred before their disciplined study in schools, but it is probably more correct to see the child's consciousness as going out to the trusted adult within mutual feelings of affection as the more primordial relation, as Buber would have it. Out of the latter the child goes to the world, i.e., he or she explores the world within the horizons of the presence of the trusted, beloved adult. If so, then both parental and pedagogic love are necessary conditions of acquiring knowledge of the world, which is itself a necessary condition of becoming human, which makes pedagogic love a human right.

Pedagogic love does not require continuous smiling affection, not any more than parental love requires it. Believing in students involves believing in their desire to learn what one has to teach them, and therefore in what one has to teach them, and in oneself. It requires a continuous, respectful, mutual struggle for truth in which the teacher recognizes the pupil as a member of the same species, i.e., a search for truth conducted with the dignity befitting human beings. It is therefore not only compatible with academic standards. It is the natural attitude of a genuine adherence to standards of excellence when one believes in one's subject, in the students, and in one's own capacity to bring the pupils into the common world established by the disciplined knowledge of it.

The common world, established by the disciplined study of things utilizing currently tenable conceptual schemata, furnishes the cognitive foundation for being together in the same world, i.e., for fraternity. The cognitive basis for brotherly and sisterly love was previously justified when it was claimed that access to this common world was a human right.

A justification of neighborly love as a general moral principle of the adult world outside of the parameters of the pedagogic relationship can rest on the rather simple observation that to recognize the value and dignity of a person is to like him or her. To be recognized as a person of dignity and value is to be valued, appreciated, i.e., liked by others. That is to say that one ought to extend friendliness, or fellow-creaturely feelings of positive affection, toward each and every human being, regardless of who it is, simply because the other person is a human being. Perception of the other person as a human being, and not as a thing, is owed to the other person simply because she or he is a human being. As feminists have correctly pointed out, it is degrading, i.e., contrary to human dignity, to be considered solely as an object. The affective basis that accompanies the perception of the other's dignity and value, or love, is therefore a human right.

It cannot be overemphasized, however, that the operative significance of fraternity as a moral principle is in the concept of being one's brother's keeper. The obligations to less fortunate human beings is the main disclosure of the ideal. It obligates one to promote the development of a society that cares for crippled, handicapped, aged, penurious, insane, criminal, and chronically ill people simply because they are human beings. The attraction of socialism and communism has been their concentrated effort to furnish the minimal standards of material existence to these less fortunate people. The motive that prompts them, the love of the people, need not employ socialist or communist economies to fulfill their needs. These kinds of economies are merely alternative technologies for the distribution of goods that are not necessarily the most efficient, technologically speaking, nor the only systems entailed by the human right to have fellow-creaturely love be manifested materially when one is in severe material need.

In any case, it is beyond doubt that the responsible, adult moral agent would feel obligated to succor the less fortunate. It is beyond doubt that expectations of such feelings of benevolence are the human right of the destitute. This only means that those who are down and out, unemployable, feeble-minded, mentally ill, severely handicapped, no longer able-bodied, etc. ought to be given the minimum shelter and sustenance by society simply because they are human beings. This goes without saying.

An argument is necessary, however, to claim that fraternal feelings are among the necessary conditions of moral agency. Buber's view, quoted at the chapter's head, is that only the person who experiences other people in their humanity, i.e., as You, is able to make decisions, by which he means moral choices. He seems to be correct. Dialogical relations with other people are a necessary condition of moral agency. If one adds that the experience of another person as a You necessarily results in feeling affection for the other, the claim is tantamount to saying that feelings of affection for others are necessary in order to feel morally obligated to them, and this feeling is a constituent of moral agency. Fellow-creaturely love is therefore a necessary condition of moral agency. Because moral agency is a human right, so is brotherly and sisterly love, or fraternity.

Further elaboration of fraternity as a human right is unnecessary in view of the vastly greater significance of pedagogic love for the educational question.

IV. Friendship in Education

The question of democracy in education in the social sense leads to the concern for the affectionate aspects of the teacher's attitude toward students and for the relations among students. It concerns the spirit of democracy as manifested in pedagogic love and friendliness between students.

The importance of pedagogic love is that the main purpose of trying to implement democracy in education is to insure that children receive treatment becoming to human beings in accordance with the loving understanding appropriate to each child. This is why previous efforts to apply the idea of democracy to the classroom make most sense when interpreted as seeking to implement the spirit of democracy through the ideal of cooperative living as it occurs when the teacher believes in the students and they believe in each other.

This is less "idealistic" than it may seem, for the teacher can learn to believe in students and to love them. Any conscientious teacher carries out some sort of continuous assessment of learning, if only through conversation and response to recitation questions, to diagnose the students' cognitive status and decide upon the next strategy. The kind of "feedback" obtained through such means as the ombudsman and course evaluation can prove very helpful in eliminating problems of management and materials. Although some teachers find the use of these diagnostic tools a bit worrisome at first, their use in good faith draws teachers and pupils closer together. They enable the teacher to come to trust and respect the pupils' collective wisdom about the conditions of learning, and the pupils can come to appreciate and value the integrity of the teacher's pedagogic intentions. As pupils learn that their opinions are sought, weighed, and utilized to create perceived, valuable changes, they come to feel much more a part of things, and the authoritarian context changes to a democratic atmosphere.

There is a paradox involved that should be illuminated. The necessary condition of democracy is the use of consultative procedures such as the student evaluation of courses, but a conscientious teacher wants its kind of "feedback" quite independently of its democratic aspects. Otherwise teaching is like painting pictures with one's eyes closed. Consultations with students about the viability of the curriculum are therefore not only a condition of democracy in education. They are a necessary condition of good teaching, democratic or otherwise. The best reason for using them, moreover, is not that they are democratic but that they are pedagogically invaluable. Adapted for purely pedagogic reasons, they promote the development of the democratic atmosphere. This paradox can be dissolved by recognizing that it is the democratic teacher for whom it adds nothing to call them the conditions of democracy in education. A democratic teacher is one who would seek out "feedback" in any case because of a basic, underlying attitude of respect for students as persons and a general awareness that each child and youth has her or his own value and dignity. Students cannot teach themselves what they do not know, and they cannot choose to learn what they do not know, but they are always right when they say they have difficulty learning something because the explanation is unclear, the materials are illegible, or unintelligible, the content too remote from their perceived world, and so forth. If they say it, it is true. If it is true, it is right to say it.

Thus a willingness to function through the necessary conditions of democracy in education can be generated from the teacher's valuing students, i.e., from recognition of their human dignity and pedagogic love. Conversely, pedagogic love can be generated through willing submission to the conditions of democracy in education. At any rate, pedagogic love is the sufficient condition of democracy in education because it will enable the teacher to do those things that create a democratic atmosphere. Love is the spirit of democracy in education because it enables the teacher to respect every single student as a person with his or her own dignity and value.

The application of the ideal of brotherhood to pedagogy through respect for individuals and general feelings of friendliness has some similarity to the implementation of freedom and equality. If the teacher is correct to allow the students the freedom for which they can be responsible, no more and no less, he or she must learn through experience the kinds of responsibilities the students in this grade and this subject from this neighborhood can undertake successfully. If the teacher is correct to give equal consideration to the educational development of each pupil, no more and no less, she or he must then in large classes lessen the concern given to each pupil, proportionately, without favoring or neglecting any students because of the greater complexity of the situation. In neither case can the universal right be applied in blanket fashion, simply giving students "absolute freedom" or "absolute equality." Similarly, fraternity as a human right does not require the teacher to give students "absolute love," or even parental love. It requires only the degree of affection that can be given to the variety and number of other people's children that grace one's classroom with their presence. It does not require that this affection manifest itself as being "warm and outgoing" to adult observers, for children are not so easily deceived and soon learn that certain "cross" or "gruff" teachers love them very dearly. On the other hand, it does require that the teacher ought to learn how to be affectionate toward strange children that he or she might not otherwise like, and it does require that such affection be strictly limited to the bounds of the pedagogic relation. It also requires the simultaneous implementation of freedom, equality, and fraternity, i.e., that the teacher's appreciative recognition of the worth of each pupil accompanies the equal consideration of all pupils in the construction of the conditions of responsible freedom.

It is pedagogic love, furthermore, that prompts the teacher to enforce the rules of equal freedom through obliging students to make reparations, for making things right again is the means for students to learn their obligations to other students, rather than to the teacher or school, and it can induce cooperative behavior, if not friendship.

That the teacher love and respect each pupil is exceedingly important. It manifests that the teacher values each student, which deeply affects all students' perceptions and evaluations of each other. It not only enables them to perceive each other as valued by the teacher, it lets them see each other as valuable and worthy of respect and friendship. For example, if a teacher forestalls a negative assessment of "slow learners" by taking time to insure their learning is up to standard, it teaches everyone that they count, too, and it encourages "fast learners" to help the slower ones, particularly if the teacher also arranges things to enable them to work together and insures that the "fast learners" come to appreciate the value of the reinforcement given to their own learning when they help teach their slower "brothers" and "sisters." In this and other ways the teacher's affection for each pupil sets a pattern by showing all pupils that every one of their classmates is worthy of friendship.

It is not necessary to practice cooperation behaviorally through the use of group projects, etc., to establish an embodied cooperativeness in the classroom, or to encourage cooperative attitudes. It is logically possible, furthermore, to practice behavioral cooperation through large, group projects while developing competitive attitudes. It depends on how they function. This means that such actual cooperation is only the "letter" of democracy, whereas genuine cooperativeness is its spirit. It is also the essence of friendship.

This does not mean that group projects large enough to involve all students in a common work cannot produce attitudes of cooperativeness and feelings of brotherly and sisterly love. To the contrary. Proposals such as Dewey's to reduce the curriculum to large-scale projects, however, require system-wide changes because their intention is not only to develop cooperative habits but also the cooperative society. In the student-teacher planning of the project, each student is supposed to modify his original desire of what he or she wanted to do in favor of an emerging consensus about what the class as a whole should do, thereby learning how to set goals cooperatively. Then collaborating on the project is supposed to require rich communication and mutual adaptation and accommodation. This model can work superbly to establish the feelings of solidarity required by the principle of fraternity in education. The problem is that most of the curriculum cannot be learned through group projects. Cooperativeness and fellow-creaturely feelings can also be developed with other models of the classroom that are not so fanatical as to eliminate knowledge for the sake of love.

For example, an ordinary class discussion can occur among a few competing individuals striving to outshine, or upstage, each other, but it can also take place among most of the people in class in a common search for truth. Some subjects allow for the introduction of panel discussions, forums, roundtable discussions, simulations, games, and small group work, and these can all develop a sense of participation and cooperativeness without blunting the central cognitive concern of the school. On the one hand, routines and rules can be imposed to regulate conduct externally, but on the other hand they can be discussed openly when necessary to facilitate an understanding of the common good defined as the maximization of learning. Taking turns at performing tasks for the rest of the class (as monitors) can generate cooperativeness in the most traditional setting.

A major problem regarding the promotion of cooperation in education is that competition may be essential to motivation for higher levels of achievement. Libertarians sometimes argue for the necessity for competitive individualism to provide incentive for all human accomplishment. This psychological claim about what motivates people is not being invoked, although it ought to be mentioned to maintain perspective. What is referred to is that schools are good schools in direct proportion to their elitism in the cognitive domain. This is not saying that the school should give unequal attention to high achievers to be a good school. Not at all. A good school is one wherein everyone achieves as highly in the cognitive domain as possible, and where, if possible, such achievements are above average. It means that universities such as Harvard, M.I.T., California Tech, Oxford, Cambridge, the Sorbonne, and their peers are prestigious schools in direct proportion to their academic excellence, or elitism. So are conservatories of music, schools of the dance, etc. Institutions of learning are excellent as institutions of learning in proportion to the high degree of accomplishment their faculty has attained and the knowledge and skills these attainments make possible. It may very well be that these kinds of superior achievement in any area of the curriculum are intrinsically motivated and therefore occur independently of competitive conditions. The fact of differential achievement in learning, however, places severe strain on any plans for cooperation in learning tasks, particularly because the teacher's expectations ought to be oriented toward the maximization of everyone's learning in obedience to the principle of equal opportunity to make the most use of one's developmental time.

Instead of trying to "level down" superior achievement in a pseudo-egalitarianism, it may be more appropriate to accompany the elitism inherent in the school system with the principle of fraternity defined as being one's brother's keeper. Not only can "fast learners" use their extra time to help "slow learners," there can be a general positive emphasis upon the value and dignity of everyone regardless of their level of achievement and upon the notion that greater achievement in one area or another does not make one a better person. Cognitive "elitism" can be balanced by moral egalitarianism through the experience that the more able undergo in sustained giving of help to the less able, practicing, drilling, tutoring, explaining, and so on, and in any other way that can foreshadow the desirability of future members of professional classes helping less fortunate friends.

Democracy in education in the social sense does not, in short, require any specific practices. It requires that each pupil be regarded as of equal worth regardless of learning ability or achievement. It does not entail egalitarianism, for what it means to be of equal worth is to be a unique person with one's own value and dignity, incomparable and irreplaceable, equally worthy of the teacher's affectionate glance, counting as much as anyone in the proceedings of the classroom. It is the function of brotherly and sisterly love to insure that no one feels less important than anyone else. When everyone feels she or he belongs in the classroom just as much as everyone else, there is not only the minimum solidarity, there is also the spirit of democracy.

It is also important to apply fraternity to the policy of the establishment of equal access to all programs and equal opportunity within them. This is primarily a matter of justice, rather than brotherly love, but equitable educational provision can be made for previously discriminated groups with hostility, neutrality, or gladness. The principle of neighborly love can make one ashamed that such groups have found it necessary to ask for their educational rights.

Conclusion

The treatment of democracy in education in this chapter supplements the way it was discussed indirectly in previous chapters. The questions of the student's freedom, the teacher's authority, the right to education, equal access to education, and equal opportunity within education arise only in democratic societies. They arise only when people feel they have a right to freedom and a right to equal treatment. Similarly, only when people already have fellow-creaturely feelings of compassion do they raise the question of punishment and wonder whether it is compatible with human dignity.

Someone who asked for the import of democracy for education, in other words, might not be asking about the practice or concept of democracy as such, for he could be asking about the educational relevance of the three major democratic ideals, liberty, equality, and fraternity. These are vastly more important, particularly the right to education and to equal access to educational resources. Injustice here makes it irrelevant to consider higher values. There is not much democracy in practicing democracy in schools in affluent, professional, upper-middle-class suburbs, in other words, when the reading scores, etc. are below average in disadvantaged areas. Until what it means to provide equal educational resources to all groups is settled, the sincerity of anyone wanting to practice democracy in education is open to question. The problems of equal access to schooling may have to be resolved even before the question of freedom in education can be asked in good faith. Similarly, only after the question of human dignity during discipline and punishment in education is settled can one moot the question of fraternity and respect for persons in education.

In other words, the preceding chapters are quite pertinent to the question of how schools can be more democratic. They can be more democratic by developing responsible freedom, by eliminating authoritarianism, by making it possible for students freely to ascribe authority to the teacher, by obliging students to obey the rules of equal freedom and the canons of inquiry, through greater efforts to establish educational justice, through systematic efforts to minimize or eliminate the need for punishment, through a greater presence of pedagogic love, and through a permeation of the student body with friendliness.

Regardless of what the concept means, most people in most democratic societies do not make laws. They do not govern themselves in this sense. There is another sense, however, in which they do govern themselves, and this is when they try to become moral agents and responsible citizens by living in a community under law. One of the characteristics of a liberal democracy, in fact, is that it is not a government by men but a government under law. Because the social reality is that existing democracies are communities under law, it is most straightforward to claim that the correct application of the principles of democratic governance to education is through the model of the classroom as a community of scholars under law devoted to the maximization of learning.

This view is neither conservative nor progressive. There is nothing in the concept of the community under law which makes it inherently conservative, repressive, progressive, or liberating. What is imporant is that the laws are just, i.e., in accordance with the conditions of equal freedom, that they maximize the achievement of human rights, and that they be administered with the highest regard for human dignity.

This means that the spirit of democracy prevails in a school when there is a pervading sense of freedom, fairness, and fondness, which can be christened the three "F's" to suggest that human rights are as basic as the three "R's."

Chapter Eleven

EDUCATION FOR DEMOCRACY

Liberty is the cry of the bond, equality is the cry of the victim of discrimination, fraternity the cry of the outcast, progress and humanity are the cry of those whom their fellows use as means instead of respecting as ends....

Barnes[1]

The objectives of schooling include citizenship in one's own country. In representative democracies, this involves an education for democratic government, i.e., learning to obey laws, to participate in political parties, and to feel deep respect for one's native land. If Jefferson was right when he said a populace cannot be both ignorant and free, then participation in democratic institutions such as elections requires familiarity with the issues. An education for democracy is a necessary condition of responsible moral agency in a democracy.

I. The Question of Education for Democracy

Schools should teach students to obey laws, participate in politics, and feel patriotic. This can be taken for granted. The question is whether democracy can be taken for granted or has to be perpetually achieved anew each generation and whether the school ought to help society progress by increasing its democratization.

---

[1] Leonard J. Barnes, *Human Rights: Comments and Interpretations*, ed. UNESCO (New York: Columbia University Press, 1949), p. 242.

Its logic may make it seem to be a partisan question, but it is not. It can be conceded that schools should promote the further democratization of society, but then it can be claimed the schools should devote their major efforts to this task or that they should complete their proper tasks instead. The answers to the question can range across the entire political spectrum from the far left to the far right.

This indicates that the question concerns the appropriate relation of schooling to social change. The desire for the changes that lead to an increased democratization of society also wants the school to promote social change. This seems more radical than it is, for it may merely want society to practice its professed democratic ideals. The ideals of freedom, equality, and fraternity cannot resolve the matter, however, for they can be used in opposition to the use of the schools to promote social change, too. They can be arranged in a different constellation to substantiate the claims that society is already as democratic as circumstances permit, is too democratic already, that there are too many things in the school day as it is, or that the school should promote social stability rather than social change.

The question is logically distinct from those previously considered because its intent is macrocosmic. It is true that education for democracy will occur when the classroom protects the responsible freedom necessary for the development of moral agency, when individuals are enabled to make the most of their developmental time, and when students compete and cooperate amicably, disciplined by the morality of reparative justice, but these are "microcosmic" matters that fall within the jurisdiction of individual teachers independently of the total impact of the school on society. The "macrocosmic" question of education for democracy, on the other hand, concerns what the schools in general ought to be doing about maintaining or changing society. It is less concerned with human rights in education than with education for human rights in society.

The macrocosmic question is whether the schools can adopt a large-scale program to conduct a frontal attack on problems of social and economic injustice with the intent of establishing society on a reconstructed basis within a generation or two. It is the question to raise if one believes in the possibility of salvation through changing the economic system and that education can overcome the nihilism of the technological consciousness.

This kind of question is too large to think about. It is impossible to obtain a view of the whole of society that encompasses all of the material and normative conditions at the same time in order to discover how the schools could educate people to produce the kind of changes that would indeed further democratize society and guarantee progress. By the time one has gathered data from which to formulate such a view, and then formulates it, the reality has changed. The application to schools is behind the times, although it has to be ahead of the times to affect society progressively.

It is nevertheless the fundamental issue behind much public debate about educational policy. The back-to-basics movement of the late 1970s and 1980s arose like the movement in basic education of the late Thirties, i.e., because preceding "reforms" in education were designed to produce social changes that had come to seem undesirable to some people. For example, the debate between the so-called secular humanists and the advocates of "creation science" and prayer in schools manifests most clearly that the issue is not simply prayer and the first ten chapters of *Genesis*. It concerns the changes in society that have resulted in the secularization of the schools and all knowledge. It was first raised by those who advocated the use of the schools to further the democratization of society, then it was raised again by those who reacted against that use. The controversy occurred between those who would facilitate or reverse "progress." The question is the relation of education to social change.

II. The Meaning of "Education for Social Change"

Because the macrocosmic question attempts to consider the whole school system in the context of the whole society, neither of which can be borne in mind, all responses to it are necessarily ideological in the sense of being free-floating talk about some aspects of the whole that are mistaken for the whole. It may help to distinguish sharply between facts and values as, for example, in the following sentences:

A. The schools do reflect existing society.
B. The schools should reflect existing society.
C. The schools do affect the future society.
D. The schools should affect the future society.

Ideologues are so busily propagandizing for B or D that it is seldom recognized that all four of these sentences are true. The first two refer to the conservative functions of schooling. Whereas A claims it is a fact that schools perpetuate existing society, B claims that they ought to do this, perhaps more effectively than at present. The second two sentences about the innovative functions of schooling differ in the same way. Whereas C claims they do affect the future nature of society, D claims they ought to, perhaps more adequately than at present. One ought to accept both A and C because they are both true. It is not so clear that one ought to accept B and D as equally valid normative claims, for they seem to be logically contradictory. This appearance results only from an ideological, over-distancing from the schools, which are very richly textured, complicated institutions that do a great many things, some of which are designed to perpetuate aspects of society, and others of which are aimed to promote a better society.

These distinctions are frequently blurred. The only way to avoid A is through having no curriculum at all, and C is unavoidable because the school never teaches all the knowledge, beliefs, and values of a given society. It necessarily projects only a selection of the existing society into the future. The contentious points arise only with the advocacy of the use of most of the school's program to perpetuate the existing society and its traditions or to usher in the new era. The question, then, is not whether the schools should do A, B, C, or D, nor whether they should do B or D. They will do all of these. The significant question is whether the schools should promote the development of the new society at the expense of perpetuating the present, i.e., do D at the expense of B. It is not whether B should be done at the expense of D, for this is a reaction to, and therefore a part of, the question of reconstructionism.

Dewey's classical advocacy of D in an article characteristic of the Thirties occurred in the context in which, after he admitted that A and C occurred, he said there were only three positions the school could take:

> Educators may act so as to perpetuate the present confusion and possibly increase it. That will be the result of drift, and under the present conditions to drift is in the end to make a choice. Or they

may select the newer, scientific, technological, and cultural forces that are producing change in the old order; may estimate the direction in which they are moving and their outcome if they are given free play, and see what can be done to make the schools their ally. Or, educators may become intelligently conservative and strive to make the schools a force in maintaining the old order intact against the impact of new forces.[2]

Although he subsequently said there was not much to say for the first view, he admitted there was much to be said for an intelligent conservatism, which must differ from the stupid kind as intelligent drifting differs from stupidly perpetuating "confusion."

His recommendation that the schools "select the newer scientific, technological, and cultural forces that are producing changes" refers to changes going on in society and therefore remains within the perspective of reflecting existing society, i.e., statement B. It seems "progressive" because it aligns schools with "progressive" elements in society in an "intelligent" reconstructionism that would bring "lagging" elements into better adjustment with the *avant garde* of corporate capitalism. Dewey referred to long, slow changes in the fabric of Western civilization occurring in and after the industrial and political revolutions of the seventeenth and eighteenth centuries, i.e., the development of science, its application to industry through technology, and the democratization of society. Because he thought they had not also affected social institutions and the way values are formed, he said it was the task of the school to restore the equilibrium to society by educating people to reconstruct its institutions in harmony with each other. To agree with Dewey would require one to assume he had correctly identified the major social changes, that those changes are good, that their continued support is good, and that the achievement of a societal equilibrium in which the "lagging" institutions adjust themselves to the "newer" forces is good regardless of the details of that adjustment. Because none of these things is obviously true, it would require one to believe Dewey was the messiah who was to usher in the kingdom.

---

[2] John Dewey, "Education and Social Change," *The Social Frontier*, 3 (1937): 235-238.

He wanted people to have flexible values and tentative beliefs to enable them to change institutions and resolve social problems, but there is no reason to doubt that a firm set of stable values helps one to cope with instability, uncertainty, and anomie. Nor is there reason to doubt that the possession of a solid body of stable knowledge about society helps one to cope with social change. The necessity to use rhetorical propaganda about the alleged confusion of society, furthermore, shows Dewey does not believe in the integrity of his cause. The form of his argument is demagogic and elitist. He was correct to look for large-scale, major historical changes if he was to interpret the phrase "education for social change" in a meaningful way, but important historians such as Toynbee and Spengler have found decay and degeneration where Dewey found progress, and Marxists find the changes mentioned by Dewey to be the work of the rising middle class in their expropriation of the fruit of the labor of working classes, hardly the thing to be given "freer play." In the final analysis, it says nothing to claim that schools should be aligned with "the newer... forces that are producing change in the old order." These "forces" are not facts but ideological reifications, and there is no way to prove which "forces" are producing valuable change except through a value judgment independent of these reifications of "forces" and "the old order."

The alternatives have more merit than acknowledged by Dewey, especially "drifting," for "muddling through" avoids precipitous, partisan haste. If most teachers were to give some thought to the relation between what they are teaching and social change, its significance would not impress them. If the unintended consequence of most teachers merely doing their job well is a general school outcome of "drift," the metaphor should be "unpacked." One can drift with the current without paddling or steering and still reach one's destination downstream in due course. The Kon Tiki crossed the mighty Pacific by drifting. Life and education can be quite productive when one flows with the currents, especially when one has no doubt there are currents.

An "intelligent conservatism" on the part of the teacher, furthermore, would not necessitate "maintaining the old order intact against the impact of newer forces." It would suffice to teach one's subject well. Even if this did result in the school's drifting, one would not have to accept the "guilt trip" Dewey would lay on one. It can be regarded as the kind of pluralism that is the necessary outcome of the pedagogic encounter of individual teachers with individual students. If this is the heart of educational reality, there is no fault in a pluralistic outcome.

It is ethically questionable, moreover, to look at the schools in general and desire some sort of uniform outcome, for it is totalitarian. To ask the question of the role that education should take in respect to social change is to ask a totalitarian question, unless one accepts A, B, C, and D. Just as the ordinary medical doctor has no time to be concerned with promoting the existence of a healthy society in general, nor with educating his patients to reconstruct social institutions in order to raise the general state of health, because his basic art lies in the healing of particular people with particular illnesses, so, too, is the teacher ethically unable to use students as political pawns even when the school does adopt a uniform policy regarding social change because the art of teaching is concerned with educating unique people with unique destinies in some knowledge or skill in which one has the special competency to teach.

The totalitarianism inherent in the question becomes manifest when it is recalled that teachers have the same rights as other citizens. The various political orientations found in a pluralistic society are found among teachers, too. If they are not distributed on the political continuum in a manner that somewhat approximates the distribution of the general population, furthermore, it indicates political discrimination in employment that is contrary to human dignity. To recommend any one view of the relation of education to social change as the view the schools should adopt would therefore violate the political integrity of most teachers. It would recommend to them that they should work publicly for political goals with which they privately disagree. This cannot be justified in a liberal democracy that adheres to political freedom and multipartisan politics, no matter which view is favored by some temporary coalition of teachers or politicians. The evil is not left-wing totalitarianism nor right-wing totalitarianism, but simply totalitarianism of any kind.

III. Education for Human Rights as a Human Right

This does not mean that conservatism and reconstructionism

should be rejected. To the contrary, the case of the intelligent conservative should be accepted, de-ideologized, and combined with the de-ideologized case of the intelligent reconstructionist. This can enable schools to combine A, B, C, and D in balanced perspective as well as defend the right of the student to be protected from becoming a means to someone else's political goals.

It is conservative in an intelligent way to submit existing knowledge, skills, beliefs, values, and traditions to a hard examination with a view toward selecting those things that ought to be preserved at all costs. These would then become the core of the school curriculum, to which most of the time and effort of the school is devoted. This content should coincide with, or greatly overlap, the knowledge needed for the student's general education and the maintenance of the economic system. An intelligent conservative would also want to preserve the progressive traditions at the heart of liberal democracies, such as safeguards for the civil liberties of a free press, free speech, free assembly, and other political, economic, and social rights. These progressive traditions include their correlates in the moral domain that in earlier centuries were referred to by various names such as divine law, natural law, natural rights, and the rights of man. They are now most defensibly understood as the universally binding morality of human rights.

Similarly, an individual teacher who wanted to be intelligently conservative would think carefully about the learning he or she was promoting, pare it down to the essentials, then insure mastery in these areas.

An intelligent conservative orientation in education would not select curriculum content to support a conservative political ideology, to defend the so-called status quo, to change schools back to the way one imagines they were when one was a child, to deny the existence of social changes, or simply to effect a return to the "three R's" or to "basics" unless this resulted from a careful, open-minded survey of existing knowledge, skills, and social practice. It would be most intelligent to be neutral when selecting what is to be conserved, but then absolutely adamant about conserving those things that the impartial consideration indicated should be preserved at all cost. The point would not be to maintain "the old order intact," as Dewey maligned things, but to do what was within the power of the school to do as a school to insure that the best of existing society was maintained regardless of processes of social change.

The intelligent reconstructionist would want the same thing. Dewey, for example, wanted the schools to preserve the best knowledge in society, given the parameters of his ideology of knowledge. The quarrel is not over preserving the best knowledge. A reconstructionist who does not also want to preserve the core of existing society in schools lacks the wit to recognize that society has been going on for some time now and has always been graced with the presence of people trying to improve the human condition with the knowledge, values, skills and means at their disposal. To use the schools to help society reconstruct itself by aligning them with ongoing historical changes presupposes that students study these very changes and preserve and strengthen their continuity if in their opinion their evaluation of their goodness after their objective study indicates that their continuation is warranted.

This signifies that reconstructionism requires a kind of neutrality Dewey did not allow. At the end of the *Social Frontier* article, he employed the emotionally laden words, "I wish to recur to the utopian nature of the idea that the schools can be completely neutral. This idea sets up an end incapable of accomplishment." This is an appeal to prejudice, for no one likes utopian ideas that cannot be accomplished. Perhaps this is why no one argues that schools should be "completely" neutral, except for Dewey in order to refute the straw man through ridicule. He said the effect of trying to be neutral would have the effect of perpetuating confusion and blind conflict in a reactionary way, but this is not what most people think results when society is studied in an impartial, objective manner and when historically significant changes are studied carefully and in a disinterested manner. Nor would this kind of study keep "the oncoming generation ignorant of the conditions in which they live." It seems an intelligent reconstructionist should insist that any other than an objective, neutral, critical study of society would keep the "oncoming generation" ignorant of the conditions in which they live.

It would be reconstructionistic in an intelligent way to be intelligently conservative, as specified, but with an additional emphasis upon human rights in the context of the study of contemporary society in order to disclose the discrepancies between living realities and moral obligations. These discrepancies between the human condition and human rights, between the real and the ideal, between practice and professed values, are referred to as social problems by reconstructionists. They want them studied in order to promulgate their own solutions, or perhaps one should say "pseudo-solutions." Any such solutions, however, are merely the technological means to fulfill the basic moral obligations. As such, it is unintelligent to become committed to any particular means, or to advocate particular solutions supported only by an ideological rationale that entails partisan politics. It is heuristically better to conceptualize the "problems" as controversial issues to which various partisan solutions are offered, inasmuch as these various "solutions" are simply alternative means to fulfill human rights.

That is to say that it is more important for the student to study human rights in the given historical context than it is for the school to promulgate either conservative or reconstructive resolutions to the discrepancy between these rights and reality. The rights are universal, essential, and unexceptional, but the solutions to social problems are contingent, accidental, and provisional. It is valid to claim that students ought to learn about conservative and reconstructive solutions to social problems, but only if they learn about both of them in conjunction with human rights and duties in the historical context.

Learning about human rights is itself a human right. It is one of the cognitive conditions for the realization of the basic right to become as responsible a moral agent as possible. It is a necessary component of moral education. It is unnecessary to dispute the question of whether human rights, i.e., moral rights and obligations, are more effectively learned through the "hidden curriculum" of how classrooms and schools are run or through explicit study within the intellectual curriculum, or whether the school can be effective in moral education in either or both ways. Regardless of these matters, moral education requires their explicit study in the contemporary historical context. The right to access to an education that enables development to mature moral agency in one's own society therefore includes the right to study human rights as intellectual principles that should guide personal conduct and social life.

Human rights are traditional values with a radical edge. They are deeply rooted in the Hellenic, Judeo-Christian heritage, and the Universal Declaration of Human Rights adopted by the United Nations in 1948 was a response to the rapid social changes and totalitarianism of the first half of the century. The limitations of this finite statement of human rights are offset by the way in which it has pre-empted the field and by the subsequent international covenants promulgated by the UN that further specify human rights in particular areas and that are gradually being adopted by all nations for monitoring of their legislation by internal human rights commissions. Unless the UN Declaration is revised by the UN, or satisfactorily superseded by some other formulation, neither of which is probable, it is one of those things that the schools ought to preserve at all costs, i.e., through direct instruction to all students in conjunction with the contexts that make it meaningful. There is no better source by which to fulfill the student's right to an education for human rights.

The abstract nature of their statement in documents such as the 1948 Declaration makes it necessary to consider briefly the pedagogy of learning human rights conceptually.

The foundation needed for an adequate conceptualization of the sense of rightness is a perceptual consciousness of the positive qualities of friendship, keeping one's word, speaking truthfully, fair play, equal consideration, and human dignity. Any education in values should therefore be founded on a developed moral sensibility, i.e., on the perceptual moral consciousness developed in classrooms organized as communities under law. These classrooms are not the only place to acquire moral sensibility, but they are within the control of the school. Approaches to the study of values through verbal means such as values clarification and the discussion of moral dilemmas are invaluable, but only as the first phase of evoking the student's perceptual awareness of the moral domain. New concepts have to be introduced here as elsewhere, i.e., to insure that the phenomena in the lived world receive a moral interpretation and become understood in terms of obligations, rights, and duties. The educative reason for raising the inchoate meanings into consciousness is to submit them to a conceptualized schema that disciplines the consciousness of what was experientially perceived. Such disciplining of perceptual awareness of moral phenomena with conceptual schemata should occur at the level of conceptual processes that Kohlberg would classify as stage four or six. This squeezes it through a deontological sieve, so to speak, so that the language of obligations, duties, and rights is learned. It does not matter if the students are at the immediately preceding stage or if Kohlberg's theory is all wrong. What matters is that in values clarification or the discussion of dilemmas or in the study of social problems the teacher introduces the moral principles embodied in the language of human rights. These should be introduced at the sixth stage level, regardless of the student's readiness, for the student who is conceptually unprepared to deal with them as principles will convert them into "stage four" rules, and those not ready to reason with them as moral rules will memorize them and follow them for reasons that are understood, such as social approval, self-gratification, or threat of punishment. The stage theory is irrelevant to the pedagogy, for what is needed is an appreciation of the student's right to learn the language of human rights and a realization that the one thing worse than memorizing something is not learning it at all. What is memorized can one day receive a burst of insight. The rest of one's life is spent in developing a deeper understanding of moral phenomena in any case. To insure that this is possible, teachers should introduce the language of human rights into all discussions of value in schools. Even the most abstract of moral concepts, that of human dignity, can be learned by mildly mentally handicapped children who have teachers who take the time to explain to them what is nice and what is not nice. Given a teacher capable of sixth-stage reasoning, as it were, and able to communicate with students, human rights can be taught in an intellectually responsible manner to any child or youth in school.

IV. Education for Democracy

That education for human rights is itself a human right partly determines the school's role regarding social change. The knowledge of human rights should be conserved among the most precious elements of the heritage wrought throughout the ages, and it serves as the criterion for valuable social change because it is simply the account of people's obligations to each other. It is a moral rather than political criterion. It can therefore indicate when a greater democratization of society is ethically justifiable, i.e., when it promotes a greater realization of human rights. The question is whether an education for democracy founded in the context of human rights can transcend the political continuum through a concerted attempt to be neutral.

Ideological responses to the question of education for democracy representing the entire political continuum will be examined from left to right to furnish a basis for a synthesis of the partial truth in each, and then the question of neutrality will be considered in its own right in the next chapter. The original formulator of reconstructionism, Theodore Brameld, recommended that the primary school be devoted to preparing children for the study of social problems and that from the seventh through twelfth grades half of every day should be devoted to their study in a collective search for their most democratic solutions.[3] The other half day should be used for vocational and university preparation.

Brameld's seems the strongest reconstructionism the school can undertake. He justified it on a science-based Utopian view established through the use of cultural anthropology to determine universal human needs and claimed that social problems should be studied with a view toward reconstructing institutions to allow for the maximal fulfillment of most people's basic needs. He held that teachers should be committed to reconstructing social, economic, and political systems on the national and international level to fulfill the basic needs of the majority of the people of the world. In other words, he wanted teachers to be committed socialists. His main point, however, is not in the details of the reconstructed political and economic systems but in the alleged need for economic planning by governmental agencies and in the education of the people to elect leaders who would plan the economy for the people.

Although Brameld wanted social problems studied in a fair, objec-

---

[3] Theodore Brameld, *Education as Power* (New York: Holt, Rinehart and Winston, 1967), *Education for the Emerging Age* (New York: Harper & Row, 1965), *The Climactic Decades* (New York: Praeger, 1970), *Philosophies of Education in Cultural Perspective* (New York: Holt, Rinehart and Winston, 1955), and *Toward a Reconstructed Philosophy of Education* (New York: Dryden Press, 1956).

tive manner, with great pains taken to insure that students had access to all points of view to enable them to make up their own minds after critical investigation, he also claimed that teachers should be openly committed to the reconstruction of institutions to fulfill people's basic needs, i.e., that students should be aware of the teacher's commitment to socialism. He called this "defensible partiality"[4] and apparently believed teachers could be committed socialists and still promote the objective study of social problems. Part of his defense is that schools have always adopted policies supporting some interest groups and not others and now they should support the interests of the majority of the people.

Whereas Brameld wanted to use the schools to promote rapid social change to achieve the socialist blueprint for the good society, and therefore should be understood as an extremist on the far left, Dewey represents the near left because he merely wanted to educate people to have the flexible habits to enable them to reconstruct institutions and thereby cope with social change rather than initiate it. His acceptance of gradual change represents welfare-state liberalism. Whereas Brameld's view concerns the secondary school level because it requires the intellectual study of social problems of considerable magnitude and complexity, Dewey's is stronger in the primary school where the relative absence of departmentalization enables children to work cooperatively on group projects for at least half a day (using the other half on "basics"). A given school system could implement both of these programs of education for democracy.

The moderate view of Harry Broudy could also be combined with Brameld's. Broudy's idea of the proper relation of schools to social change is implicit in his belief that each social institution has a primary function and that the primary function of the school is to promote habits of acquiring, enjoying, and using knowledge.[5] In times of rapid social change, the schools should make a concerted effort to establish the best knowledge and teach that well to insure

---

[4] *Education for the Emerging Age*, pp. 88, 154.

[5] Harry S. Broudy, *Building a Philosophy of Education* (Englewood Cliffs: Prentice-Hall, 1961), ch. 4, and *Democracy and Excellence in American Secondary Education*, with B.O. Smith and J.R. Burnett (Chicago: Rand McNally, 1964).

that changes will occur in the light of the best knowledge to the extent possible. All students should study the evolution of institutions in their own society, conceptually, to develop cognitive awareness of the economic, political, and social systems. Only after they have acquired the best knowledge about their society are students ready to practice using it by applying it to social problems studied in the last year of high school. The goal is not, for Broudy, to turn society into a collectivity of cooperative problem-solvers, for advanced industrial societies are run by managerial and technological elites. The aim, rather, is to educate the populace to control the elites. This requires an understanding of the world of a complexity sufficient to realize who talks sense about social problems and to avoid victimization by charlatans, rogues, and demagogues. The emphasis upon the development of critical intelligence is liberal, but not necessarily modern liberalism, for it involves liberty and freedom of thought more than equality, as did classical liberalism. Broudy did not oppose social justice so much as argue for a more secure value, i.e., the knowledge basis for any worthwhile social change.

A more conservative view would omit the study of social problems and provide little room for the study of controversial issues. Very few people recommend their complete elimination. Quite a few people with unimpeachable conservative credentials recognize the importance of learning the best knowledge about drugs, alcohol, and reproductive functions, and virtually everyone concedes the necessity to study controversial issues in tertiary schools. It is not as conservative as it is "non-reconstructionistic" to claim that controversial issues should be studied in schools in an objective, neutral manner when students are mature enough to make up their own minds on the basis of evidence. This conserves the best knowledge about these issues, but not any particular social practice unless the knowledge recommends its value.

A clearly conservative view expressed by Austin Fagothy begins with the claim that it is the right and responsibility of parents to rear their children to adulthood.[6] He claims this is a human right, and

---

[6] Austin Fagothy, "Education," *Right and Reason* (St. Louis: Mosby, 1967), reprinted in J.P. Strain, *Modern Philosophies of Education* (New York: Random House, 1971), pp. 447-455.

categorizing it should not diminish its truth value. He held that the conditions of the modern world required that most parents delegate their right to educate their young to schools, but not necessarily to state schools. It is the right of the state to require minimum educational standards of all citizens, and to require school attendance to achieve them when parents are unable or unwilling to educate their own children, but this right does not extend to compulsory attendance in a public school. These principles are in fact accepted in liberal democracies where there are independent and religious schools.

Fagothy was explicitly anti-reconstructionistic when he claimed that the attempt to use the schools to change society places the educationists who advocate this into the role of the legislator. They are entitled to work toward the reconstruction of society in their roles as free, responsible citizens, but this occurs in the adult world with other citizens. The use of the schools to promote such partisan goals simply tries to accomplish through the schools what should be accomplished through legislative assemblies, usurping the role of legislator. If Fagothy is correct, and he seems to be, then the desire to use the schools to make society more democratic is inherently undemocratic and elitist.

Fagothy's view is about as far right as Dewey's is left. A more standard conservative view is to look at contemporary social changes with concern and recommend that schools should try to preserve existing institutions and values. The signs of "progress" are read as signs of decay and disintegration. The conservative mood occurs to ordinary people when they become aware of rising crime rates, drug rates, divorce rates, and so forth, which seem to indicate moral disintegration, and then turn to the schools to ask for a stronger emphasis upon the inculcation of enduring values. The desire for renewed emphasis upon traditional values is most valid when community or national traditions are the source of values. National traditions are a better source the older the nation, i.e., England is richer in tradition than the United States, which has a richer tradition than Australia, etc. National traditions are not limited to the specific nation—e.g., Canada, the United States, Australia, and New Zealand share in certain aspects of the British tradition, such as the Magna Carta, and various ethnic traditions within these newer nations extend their heritage to Europe and origins in classical antiquity and ancient Israel. The concern for enduring values thus turns to the Judeo-Christian heritage.

The view becomes reactionary only when it is deliberately developed in opposition to social change or reconstructionistic ideology. The most important ultra-conservative view seems to be related to biblical Christianity, which will be represented by the work of Opal Moore.[7] Moore attacked all use of inquiry methods in school, the study of social problems, the open-ended discussion of social or moral problems, the use of psychological techniques that have emerged from clinical practice, the study of group dynamics, or the psychology of learning, and almost all innovations in pedagogy developed in the twentieth century, particularly those trying to humanize the classroom. To reduce distractions from learning, she wants all desks facing the front, a teacher-directed classroom, and teacher-led discussions, with everyone's attention focused on the knowledge or skill to be learned. She rejects all changes in attitudes, beliefs, and values, and all efforts to create open-minded, flexible outlooks toward things, and she claims that the use of inquiry and psychological methods has turned classrooms away from the pursuit of truth. In short, Moore claims that "Johnny cannot learn" because he is not taught the truth.

When she claims that parents have the right and duty to teach their own children Christianity, and the right to send their children to public schools without having their children's moral values disturbed or challenged, she is correct. One need not be a Christian to agree with her, for religious liberty is entailed by freedom as a human right, and such liberty includes the right to supervise the education of one's own children. No one denies this, or that political liberty includes the same right to inculcate one's values in one's own children. Moore asks schools to do two things. They should avoid all practices that build attitudes, beliefs, habits, and values that might encourage children to question the moral values their parents have taught them, and they should use the time in school most productively for the maximum acquisition of the truth.

---

[7] Opal Moore, *Why Johnny Can't Learn* (Milford, Mississippi: Mott Media, 1975).

She claims that many educational writings are enclosed within an ideology that tries to be non-religious, or even anti-Christian, and it is true that Dewey and his reconstructionist disciples such as Brameld conducted extensive attacks on absolute values motivated by the desire to vanquish orthodox religions to reconstruct social institutions allegedly based in these absolute values. She sees the use of psychological techniques to change attitudes as non-rational and essentially mis-educative, believes that the use of the classroom as a social group is contrary to the acquisition of a firm set of moral values in the home, and wants to replace social studies with geography and history taught as factual subjects because it, like these other innovations, is the outcome of an encompassing orientation that functions as an ersatz religion, i.e., "secular humanism." Because the innovations are not designed to encourage or facilitate the pursuit of truth, and because they are generally advocated by people with an emotional commitment as intense as that of a new convert to some religion, Moore claims,

> The war is, in the final analysis, a religious war. Those of the humanist persuasions of John Dewey, whose philosophy has so long dominated public education, cannot be expected to turn loose easily or quickly. Such changes sometimes take years. In the meantime, a generation of Christian children must be saved from indoctrination in socialist and humanist beliefs.[8]

Moore's point should be put into "secular" terms to be fully appreciated. It concerns the development of character and citizenship. She does not want her own set of values, or Christian values, to be imposed on all children and youth in public schools. She merely wants the schools to stop undermining the formation of human personality by supporting relativism and/or skepticism in values. Her desire is for a deontological ethics such as that found at Kohlberg's stage four, and her view can therefore be considered as a valid interpretation of the meaning of education for democracy. It holds that society is already more democratized than desirable when consid-

---

[8] Ibid., p. 149.

ered in terms of the development of character and citizenship in a society that honors religious liberty.

If it is essential to go through a stage of deontological ethics in order to become a mature moral agent, as it seems to be, then Moore's attack on schooling practices that encourage relativism ought to be defended in terms of human rights.

Conclusion

None of the views of education for democracy is satisfactory, but each is illuminating. Brameld is correct to call attention to the need for developing awareness of things in society in the context of basic needs. This reification of "needs," however, is unnecessarily material-istic. It should be replaced by human rights, which ought to be studied in conjunction with the academic subjects of history, con-temporary history (or current events), anthropology, sociology, biol-ogy, and contemporary literature, for example, rather than with social problems carefully selected and arranged to promote socialism.

Dewey is correct to indicate that cooperation has to be learned, although his justification involves "overkill." Broudy is correct to encourage the disciplined study of things in society before confront-ing controversial matters, although he reifies knowledge and habits of acquiring, enjoying, and using "it." Fagothy is correct to claim that teachers should not use their position to win adherents to a partisan cause, not even if they are on the side of the angels, although this is merely a statement of ordinary professional ethics. Moore is correct to question the integrity of an education for democracy that does not respect the parents' right to inculcate their own values in their own children. She is correct to argue that the criterion for judging the value of a pedagogic innovation is its capacity to encourage the pursuit of truth, although she errs to find truth in someone with messianic delusions.

The main problem with the macrocosmic view is the absence of longitudinal studies that demonstrate what actually happens when the schools practice one program of education for democracy for the thirty or forty years necessary to have a significant impact on the adult population of a society. It might not in fact enable the people or the society to be more democratic. It is not known if studying social problems in high school the way Brameld suggests correlates with any particular kind of adult values or behavior. Nor is it known if raising children in Christian fundamentalist homes with adequate school support results in adult Christian conduct, attitudes, or behavior.

What is known is that the "religious war" between the "secular humanists" and the "Christian fundamentalists" ought to be studied, not waged, in academic situations. This requires some sort of cognitive neutrality and personal honesty in the search for the truth of the matter.

What is known is that education for democracy requires that students study human rights, controversial issues, and the various partisan viewpoints on those issues in an atmosphere of neutrality in which all the partisans are considered to be equally worthy of respect because they each have their own value and dignity. It is also known that truth is no respecter of persons, and that any of the canons of inquiry in any of the disciplines requires everyone to follow the evidence and argument, wherever they may lead.

Efforts to use the school to change society by increasing or decreasing the extent of its democratization ought first to acquire the support of state and national legislatures and of the people who elected them. When they have that support, it is not the schools that are changing society, however, for it is society using the schools to change itself. When they do not have that support, it is that legislature's prerogative to return the school's program to the parameters desired by the people. That is what legislatures in liberal democracies are for. They rightfully have the sovereign power, i.e., the authority to determine the social functions of all other institutions. That is what government is all about.

Because the normal channels of political activity are open to the reconstructionists, it is particularly undemocratic for them to turn to the schools for partisan political purposes. It not only usurps normal political functions, it assumes that some particular kind of education is a necessary condition for eligibility for voting. On the other hand, it is of the essence of the concept of democracy that any mature adult is as qualified to vote as any other mature adult, regardless of tested intelligence, educational qualifications, and moral character (except for felonious conduct legally ascertained). Literacy tests to determine voting eligibility, for example, are an affront to human dignity. Thus an education for democracy in the reconstructionist sense is inherently undemocratic.

This is not true of education for democracy in the sense of learning to obey laws, to be patriotic, and to participate in party politics and elections, for when the latter is taught, it goes without saying that there will be neutrality, or "equal time" for major parties, or the very point of the lesson is lost.

This leaves the question open as to whether an education for democracy considered as an education to human rights can transcend the political continuum through a concerted effort to be neutral. The response exemplified in the discussion of the representative views should now be stated explicitly in the phraseology of whether controversial issues can be studied without violating essential neutrality.

Chapter Twelve

NEUTRALITY IN EDUCATION AS A HUMAN RIGHT

> The policy of political neutrality is defensible only as being the best way to take a stand.
>
> McClellan[1]

An education for living in a democracy should include the study of the most important controversial issues the young will encounter as adults while they are still in school and can learn about them in disciplined ways. Because these issues are interwoven with deeply held values, however, the more important they are, the more emotional are their contexts. It is not obvious that they can be studied in a rational, epistemically valid, neutral manner that does not unduly favor a particular stand toward the issue.

I. The Question of Neutrality in Education

The question is not about the neutrality of education but about neutrality in education. It is not a macrocosmic question related to schooling for democracy and whether schools can be neutral but about neutrality in the study of controversial issues as part of an

---

[1] James E. McClellan, "The Politicizing of Educational Theory: A Re-evaluation," *Philosophy of Education 1968* (Edwardsville: Studies in Philosophy and Education, 1968), p. 103.

education for life as a free and responsible moral agent within a democracy. It is whether the pedagogy employed in the classroom in the study of controversial things should be neutral.

It has been generally accepted that the classroom should be neutral toward partisan controversies since Horace Mann's crusade for the common school in the first half of the nineteenth century. He maintained that religious and political matters should be excluded from the school, for they were certain to involve sectarianism, factionalism, and strife that was ill-becoming the temples of learning. This neutrality was severely questioned by the reconstructionists' notion of "defensible partiality," although it should not be forgotten that Brameld's own defense of the teacher's open commitment to reconstructionism was not supposed to interfere with the students' objective and supposedly neutral study of social problems. Brameld was perfectly convinced that their objective study would lead everyone to accept the necessity for the reconstructionist's solution. If this is not inevitable, the teacher's commitment to reconstructionism is not justified; and if it is, it is unnecessary.

The pedagogic question is more critical than Brameld's conflation of schooling and pedagogy allowed. The school can be said to be neutral if there are an equal number of reconstructive and conservative teachers of social problems in a school and if all teachers let their personal views show, or if they are all neutral in their classrooms. It is difficult to visualize conservative teachers being openly committed to Utopian reconstructionism, however, or to imagine reconstructionists abandoning their "secular humanism." On the other hand, one can imagine both reconstructionists and conservatives adopting a neutral position within the classroom during the study of controversial issues.

The question is not whether a teacher should be neutral toward everything or in all circumstances. For example, the teacher's preferences for correct spelling, the acquisition of proficiency in the symbolic skills, and the successful learning of factual and/or objective knowledge are not the kinds of things toward which the teacher can be neutral. Nor can the teacher remain neutral when a bully starts hurting another child, or when a student openly advocates violation of criminal law. There is no legitimate controversy in these areas, but the question of neutrality arises significantly only concerning matters (a) about which there is considerable controversy in society, and (b) in which the controversy is quite legitimate. The question is then not whether a teacher can be neutral, but how he or she would go about trying to be neutral if it is "the best way to take a stand."

All controversies, furthermore, are not legitimate. Only the issues about which there is significant difference of opinion among adults in a society, and about which there seems to be no way to settle the matter because of the values involved, are legitimately controversial, and only these are the focus of the question of neutrality in their disciplined study in schools.

The question is not one of expediency. It does not concern the public relations aspects of curriculum content, or whether neutrality should be adopted to placate various interest groups to insure the continuation of the study of controversial issues in schools. That would be a question of the politics and economics of school keeping. The pedagogic question concerns educational and/or moral reasons not for the neutrality of the classroom but for neutrality in the classroom.

It is not a psychological question. It is not about whether teachers are emotionally capable of adopting a neutral stance, or whether teaching is more effective if they do. Instead of being concerned with neutrality in the political, moral, or psychological senses, it is about neutrality in the cognitive sense of the word. It concerns the cognitive aspects of the issues themselves as they intersect with the student's gradual assumption of moral agency.

II. The Meaning of "Neutrality"

Instead of further distinguishing the cognitive from the psychological, political, and moral senses, a number of pedagogic approaches to neutrality will be cited to exemplify the use of the word in the cognitive sense. It seems that neutrality in the cognitive sense can be ascribed to each of the following situations, listed in order of increasing complexity.

At the first level, the classroom can be said to be cognitively neutral when all controversy is simply excluded and all the knowledge in the curriculum is objective and non-controversial.

Neutrality in the cognitive sense can also be ascribed to the classroom when the study of controversial issues includes only those aspects that can be dealt with objectively. This occurs, for example, when students learn knowledge about drugs, sex, or religion, but do not examine relevant questions of value. The teacher's talk is neutral because silent toward those values as a result of a conscious choice to restrict the study to information.

At the third level, "both sides" of the issue are also presented in an objective manner "without comment" to enable students to learn about the several views that are taken toward the issue. Neutrality might not be ascribed if the teacher is grossly unfair to one or another view, but the unqualified intent to present the issue and views fairly suffices to warrant the ascription regardless of complete success if it enables the student to learn about the various points of view with detachment.

On the fourth level, the teacher adds an evaluation of the various views by pointing out the advantages and disadvantages of each. This can still be said to be neutral if the intent is to help students make their own evaluation, if there is no attempt to present any of the views in a better or worse light than warranted, and if the evaluation of each view occurs within the tolerance for error that any fair-minded person would grant to any other fair-minded person in a similar situation. That the approach might be open to abuse indicates its proper use can be said to be cognitively neutral toward the issue itself.

A higher level of neutrality is attained when, instead of citing advantages and disadvantages, the teacher attempts to make an internal criticism of each view to extract its partial truth. An internal criticism is made within the parameters of the assumptions and frame of reference of the particular perspective such that adherents of the orientation are obliged to take cognizance of it and reduce their claims accordingly. Perhaps a greater margin for error is required at this level, but a sincere effort to show what is of permanent value in the various views to allow each student to appreciate the merit of each can be said to be neutral if the teacher has a visible, genuine, sympathetic understanding of the positions of the various parties to the controversy.

A sixth level of neutrality is attained when the teacher is able to enter into the spirit of each view in turn and convincingly persuade some students to adopt it for reasons similar to those of its adult partisans. At this level the teacher is more like an actor, playing the role of the spokesperson for each view as a legitimate expression of a human being with his or her own dignity. Neutrality can be ascribed if a basic sympathy for each and every view is evident throughout the teacher's role-playing.

At the first two levels, neutrality is achieved by avoidance of the issue. It can be called "negative neutrality." The third level might also involve an avoidance technique, depending upon the situation, but the fourth, fifth, and sixth levels require the teacher's conscious decision to take a neutral stand. This could be called "defensible neutrality" to counterpose it to "defensible partiality," but it seems more descriptively accurate to call it "positive neutrality" and emphasize the teacher's mental orientation toward fair-mindedness to all views. The more these levels involve the teacher in the conscious assumption of taking a neutral stand, the more they encourage fair-mindedness toward the various partisan views. In them the teacher is definitely not neutral toward fair-minded neutrality, but hangs on to it for dear life out of respect for the dignity of the adult partisans to the issue, the dignity of the students, and the dignity of studying these most important things with one's students.

In the third to the sixth levels the teacher's own point of view is likely to be represented among the views studied. Although there would be no need to state it explicitly, it would be a good test of the neutrality of the whole presentation if the teacher were able to state a personal view quietly without affecting students' orientations. When there is no reason to state the teacher's view, there is no harm in doing so. In any case the expression of the teacher's personal view would not violate the neutrality of the school if its teachers were as heterogeneous as society.

Neutrality is violated at these levels if the teacher is incompetent or intentionally or inadvertently uses the position of teaching to influence unduly student opinion when things should be studied as objectively as possible because the issue is genuinely controversial.

The criterion for the use of the word is not whether the entire study of an issue is precisely balanced so that all views receive exactly equal consideration. That is the ideal to be striven for, but to use this as a criterion for the ascription of neutrality changes the use of the word from a normative principle to guide one's action into a criterion of moral judgement. It shifts concern to the question of whether teachers can be neutral. It helps to try, and someone who cannot be neutral at the fifth or sixth level of complexity might be able to be neutral at the third or fourth levels, and a certain margin of error can exist without violation of an orientation that for all intents and purposes can be said to be basically one of neutrality.

III. Neutrality in Education as a Human Right

It may seem that neutrality in education is not the kind of thing that can achieve status as a human right, but education, which is itself a human right, requires an atmosphere of neutrality for its fullest realization, and the disciplined study of controversial issues ought to be governed by the canons of inquiry appropriate to them as required by the principle of freedom of speech, thought, and conscience and the right to equality of consideration, which, too, are human rights. This will become clear through an examination of the epistemic characteristics of controversial issues.

Most of the knowledge from the arts, crafts, trades, sports, professions, and academic disciplines that belongs in the primary and secondary school curriculum is non-controversial and can be taught objectively, neutrally, and with the certainty relative to its domain-specific foundation in evidence. The knowledge in the disciplines, however, is more controversial the closer it is to the frontiers of knowledge. Even in the natural sciences the knowledge on the frontiers is frequently disputed among the experts. Teaching this knowledge as knowledge ought to reflect the varying epistemic characteristics due to the varying foundation in evidence. That is, the student should always learn the degree of acceptance a fact or theory enjoys within a discipline because this is tantamount to understanding how well it is based in the relevant evidence and the degree of certainty that can be attributed to it. Part of acquiring knowledge is becoming aware of the degree of confidence that can be placed in it. For example, the theory of biological evolution is only a theory, but it enjoys a basis in evidence so massive, virtually absolute confidence can be placed in it. On the other hand, the theory that human intelligence is only a function of the transaction between a biological organism and its environment is quite speculative and should be considered together with other speculative views of mind in the branch of metaphysics concerned with philosophy of mind, the mind-body problem, and the relation of human beings to the universe.

There is something amiss with educational processes when students either lack trust in perfectly sound knowledge or become dogmatic over the least tenable beliefs. They ought to have confidence in knowledge relative to its basis in evidence and its degree of certitude. This point is independent of any ideology of evidence, which can be as domain-specific as one likes.

The epistemologic fault with the second and third levels of neutrality is that they convert knowledge of the issues into knowledge about them, which creates an objective mode of knowing that does not resemble the way in which the parties to the controversy hold their beliefs about the issue. If they are militant and aggressive, they hold them assertively and with ideological fervor, but if they are quiet, unassuming, and dignified people, they hold them as firmly but with quiet dignity and resoluteness. In either case this moodlike context is lost when the issues are studied objectively. The objectivity facilitates the rationality required in the disciplined study of controversial issues, but when the sense of partisanship is lost, students fail to grasp the way in which the issues are related to strongly held values. Then they do not know why the issue is controversial, nor what is at issue. That is, they do not know the issue, regardless of the "objectivity" with which it was studied. The objective knowledge about the issue should be retained, but then after it is mastered it should be re-empassioned, so to speak, through encouraging students to become partisan. For example, they should study their country's various political parties in an academically viable, neutral, objective manner, but then become avid adherents to a party of their choice. This means they have to become aware of the positive value of each party in turn in order to want to join one in terms of its values, which requires the fourth, fifth, or sixth level of neutrality. It can be hypothesized that the higher the level of neutrality, the more likely is the teacher to elicit a kind of partisanship toward the issue that resembles that of adult parties to it. If students have a right to education, they have a right to become aware of the controverted matter in the way adults in their society are aware of it, and they therefore have a right to the fifth or sixth levels of neutrality as its necessary means. If they have a right to be educated in controversial issues, they have a right to study them in an atmosphere of neutrality. Neutrality in education is therefore a human right.

That means that teachers of controversial issues are morally obligated to holders of various partisan views to give them equal consideration, and that it is morally wrong for them to denigrate views with which they personally disagree. Such denigration is an infringement of their freedom of thought, speech and conscience, defamation of their character, and an affront to human dignity.

It would be fallacious to argue that teachers committed to any kind of "defensible partiality" can elicit the requisite partisanship. A teacher explicitly committed to socialism can hardly encourage students to become ardent advocates of free-enterprise capitalism, or the reverse, without extreme embarrassment in the classroom, unless the teacher practiced neutrality at the fifth or sixth level. This stance would be defensible, but it no longer contains any significant partiality. In any case, the deep understanding of the issue necessary to be able to teach it at the fifth or sixth level allows the teacher to see why it is genuinely controversial and would encourage the promotion of partisanship for all of the legitimate views, without favor and with equal consideration, according to the individual student's own value.

The greater the understanding of an issue of legitimate controversy, the less one knows about it. For example, no one knows what is the best form of economy, government, or society, or the best form for the good life, except that they ought to be compatible with human rights. Only because no one knows these things can the controversy over an issue be legitimate.

Issues are legitimately controversial when the knowledge about the matter is not sufficient to be decisive. When this is true on principle, the matter can then be interpreted several ways without making an intellectual mistake. Equally well-informed people can disagree about what should be done without either being in intellectual error. Once a teacher realizes these epistemic characteristics of the issue controverted, she or he will want students to examine impartially the major, standard interpretations of the issue with a view toward adopting the one that makes most personal sense, i.e., with a view to becoming partisan because that is how one knows about these kinds of issues. The teacher can be fair-minded at the fifth and sixth levels when it is realized that all of the major, standard interpretations are needed to see the issue "in the round."

The students' right to neutrality in the study of controversial issues is the right to become aware of the issue through the various views available without distortion in their pedagogy. If, for example, the teacher suggests one or two views are held by "good guys" and the others by "bad guys," it shows the teacher is unaware of the issue as an issue, of the reasons it is controversial, and is actually not qualified to teach it, for this denies the student the knowledge necessary to become aware of what is at issue. The knowledge of what is at issue, however, is the student's more basic right because it is a necessary means to moral agency, which is itself the fundamental human right.

To learn that there is a genuine issue at issue, moreover, also includes a growing awareness that there are equally intelligent, equally informed, and equally moral people who, after adequate communication, are obliged to agree to disagree. This is what an issue is, and the epistemic reason the controversy is legitimate. A genuinely cooperative classroom in which there is full communication about a controversial issue is therefore completely compatible with students disagreeing with each other as the evidence, facts, reasons, and moral principles suggest. This disagreement is the sign that the controversy is being studied as a controversy and is being replicated in its epistemic characteristics in the students' minds. An attempt to establish a consensus in the classroom that does not exist in society, on the other hand, not only changes the issue into a "problem" to be "solved." It changes the nature of the cognitive components of what is learned.

This change in its cognitive components is a form of lack of truthfulness that can easily lead children and teachers into believing they are solving problems that adults are not able to solve. This is a cognitive delusion and miseducative in an extremely serious way. In the study of legitimate controversy, clever and/or demagogic teachers can always get a majority on their side and call it a "consensus," but only at the expense of truth. To end legitimate differences by obliterating disagreements with the view toward which the teacher is partial through the use of the social processes of the classroom is totalitarian and contrary to human dignity.

If the classroom is to be a miniature society, a microcosm of the macrocosm, then it ought to be a multi-partisan classroom during the study of issues of legitimate controversy. It ought to reflect the kinds of partisanship found in adult society, particularly in an education for democracy. All existing democracies are replete with legitimate controversies. If the purpose of studying controversial issues in school is to prepare the young for the issues they will confront in society soon after graduation, then classrooms should be neutral toward the issues studied in the sense of embodying legitimate controversy in their own proceedings to enable youth to learn to talk gently and in good humor with people with whom they most profoundly disagree.

If students are neutral, the issue itself has become neutralized. If they become partisan, it remains controversial, as it ought if it is a legitimate issue to begin with. Students can become non-neutral in epistemically valid ways, however, only if the pedagogy is basically neutral.

The positive neutrality that results in the multi-partisan classroom would have a definite effect on society if it were universally practiced. It would affect the nature of its democracy and the way in which subsequent social change occurred. Although it should not be chosen for these effects, but because it is the student's right to become aware of what is at issue, it would lead toward a society in which disagreements are expressed openly, without repression or falsification, and where honest disagreements are prized because of the sublimity the social climate acquires when people maintain the dignity to voice their deepest convictions without letting their ideological components serve unacknowledged personal or social functions at the expense of truth.

A second outcome is that the class is likely to finish the study of an issue with a proportion holding each view similar to that of the adult society, providing that students learn values at home and that their own values determine their own conclusions. This means that in a predominantly conservative community, the students would tend to come out mostly conservative, in a liberal one, liberal, and so on. To let this happen lets the society perpetuate its own values through the schools and acknowledges the rightful authority of the society to maintain its continuity. It therefore seems right to contend that the study of social issues in a classroom context of positive neutrality would educate the young for democracy in the most democratic way possible.

IV. Controversial Issues in Education

What constitutes a public controversy important enough to require disciplined study in school will vary with the time and place. Some perennial issues are, perhaps, sex education, sexual morality, abortion, the status of women in society, religious matters, uses of nuclear energy, the arms race, euthanasia, pollution and the conservation of natural resources, including the continuing viability of the planet, and things related to social justice such as policy regarding world hunger. The knowledge from the great variety of disciplines that is relevant will not settle these matters because a law, policy, or institution is being questioned, reformed, invented, or enacted when they are discussed. The controversy over these things will be around for some time, regardless of any specific resolution, for whatever is done can be undone with a change in government. This is one reason why democracies change governments, and why any issue important enough for school study is likely to be linked to social change.

The fact that some interest group is pressing for a particular reform does not by itself mean the issue is a legitimate controversy. For example, neither the explosion of nuclear devices in the Pacific by a European nation nor the use of prayer in schools in the United States are issues of legitimate controversy. The first is a temporary focus of the much larger issue of the arms race, which indeed does seem to be a matter of legitimate controversy, and the second is clearly a misplaced focus of the larger issue of religious education in state schools. Similarly, any controversy that can be resolved by knowledge or research ought to be settled cognitively and is not an issue. For example, whether the earth is flat or round is not a matter of legitimate controversy: it is not now and was not in the fifteenth century either, for even then it was false to believe it was flat and irresponsible to speculate about it. Whether astrology is a science is not controversial, for there are no connections between what merely appear to be constellations from a geocentric perspective. Nor are all moral questions matters of legitimate controversy, for some have clear answers of the right or wrong variety, e.g., it is always wrong to hurt another person needlessly, and it is always correct to speak the truth.

In addition to being of a magnitude that it affects public policy, or a law or program involving many people, so that it is indeed a public issue, it has to be one about which intelligent people disagree and form interest groups to consolidate their political interest and attempt to magnify their influence. It virtually has to include a moral or value question of considerable complexity, for this insures that people who are equally moral but also equally finite will disagree. The controversy is then legitimate because even with the best of will people will disagree about what ought to be done. This is why students should become informed about the different views but maintain their good will toward each other and their own dignity as they agree to disagree.

The difficult question concerns the amount of time that should be devoted to the study of controversial issues. It is obviously wrong to argue for as much or as little time as possible, for these would reflect left-wing and right-wing partisan interests without concern for the total educational context. It is clear that at the upper levels of tertiary school there may be little left to study except controversial issues, depending upon the domain, and that at the lower levels of the primary school there is no room at all for studying anything controversial. In between, the matter is itself controversial. The best case for it is that everyone has the right to study in a disciplined way the most important problems of life. The best case against it is that school time is too precious for attention to such unsettled things, and that the years in which youth are most intellectually mature should be occupied in studying the most sophisticated, systematic knowledge about their society in history, economics, government, and geography.

Both of these views have so much to say for them it would be unsatisfactory to choose either. They can be combined dialectically. At the primary school level the child should be exploring the things in the safe social world, beyond the horizon of which there is some danger. He should therefore learn only the settled knowledge in the social studies area, but also become alert to the unsettledness beyond the horizon that will be explored later on. The youth at the secondary school level should still be exploring the safe world and not be exposed to so much of the unsettled and perilous aspects that he or she becomes discouraged from entering society as a responsible adult. On the other hand, the security of the home and school must be left, and preparation for leaving requires venturing into the unknown in intermittent, brief forays to explore the things that adults, too, find puzzling, challenging, anxiety-arousing, and controversial. Youth should become aware that adults do disagree about very important things, but in ways that do not necessarily end friendships. In other words, youth should acquire some of the most settled, secure, and significant knowledge about their own society in their last years of schooling, but this should be interlaced with the study of a few major questions of legitimate controversy in order to promote the use of the settled knowledge in life as well as intelligent partisanship toward fundamental issues.

As Brameld recommended, this should begin at least as early as the seventh grade and continue for all students throughout secondary education. As Broudy recommended, this should not let the study of controversial things usurp the place of established knowledge, which has to be the basis of any disciplined study of controversial things that is to have educative value. As Dewey recommended, the students should be trusted to find their own way out wherever partisanship is legitimate. As Fagothy said, there should be no attempt by teachers to use students as political pawns for their own causes. Like Moore, this recognizes that the main work of schooling is with the knowledge and skills of a non-controversial kind, and that debilitating relativism is to be avoided through the pursuit of truth in whatever is studied in school. A partial truth is still truth. As Brameld and Moore both advocated, these issues should be studied in the context of objective values. As Broudy and Fagothy wanted, their study in the context, language, and terms of human rights will involve the universal obligations of deontological ethics.

If the issues are taught at the sixth level of neutrality and in the context of human rights, it is also an education for democracy as the word would be understood by Brameld, Dewey, Broudy, Fagothy, and Moore, respectively, in proportion to values present in society as the evidence and argument supports each of them.

The suggestion for the study of controversial issues intermittently with non-controversial knowledge in the context of human rights according to the sixth level of neutrality is itself based on the human right to moral agency and its concomitant right to have and to express an honest opinion in those matters about which people are morally obliged to disagree. It is based upon the absolute value of people and their right, regardless of the apparent eccentricity of their views, to be treated with human dignity.

It is also based upon the rights to religious and political liberty, which entail the right to try to gain converts to one's cause, including the right to influence the education of the young, for this does not interfere with academic freedom when it occurs within the disciplined study of controversial issues under the conditions of positive neutrality on an "equal time" basis.

Its justification, finally, rests upon the fact that the most controversial issues are the most important questions of human life. Their disciplined study is conducive to the responsible exercise of moral agency and is therefore a human right.

That is to say that legitimate controversy is the natural intellectual carrier of moral education understood as an education in human rights.

Conclusion

On their own initiative, schools are unable to reform or preserve society. People turn to them for these things when they cannot be achieved elsewhere, then become disappointed when the schools fail to do what cannot be done in adult society. On the other hand, society can preserve and reform itself through the schools. With a prior social mandate, the schools can help society preserve and reconstruct itself through enabling the disciplined study of the issues that the human heritage has raised to the level of legitimate controversy.

Recognition of the significance of this point makes it possible to exercise neutrality in an education for democracy. The teacher ought to be loyal to the particular people in her present class and to their education as individuals who are becoming responsible adults. She should also be loyal to the knowledge or skill being taught and learned, for without a loyalty to one's subject and its canons of inquiry one cannot be loyal to students. An equal loyalty is due to the social arrangement that enables these other loyalties to originate and become effective, i.e., to the institution of learning and its embodiment of the dedication to the transmission of the human heritage. This is a displaced loyalty, however, if it is not at bottom a loyalty to the human heritage and to human possibility.

Loyalty to human possibility, manifested through the disclosure of the heritage in the humanization of the young, is much more fundamental than any partisan bias toward any political ideology, moral point of view, religious denomination, or social cause. It makes all of them possible insofar as they are true expressions of authentic human possibilities. It is because the school and teacher ought to be loyal to the entire range of human possibility that it is morally obligatory to adopt a stance of neutrality during the study of controversial issues.

Neutrality is also the best way to take a stand regarding the most fundamental issue of the relation of the school to the further democratization of society. There are ways for the school to promote social change besides the frontal attacks urged by the radical right and the radical left. When students are educated to freedom through having as much freedom in the classroom as they can be responsible for, their assumption of moral agency as adults progressively democratizes society even without studying social issues in school. If schools continue to make more equitable distributions of educational resources to increase the equality of access to the world by enabling more and more children to make maximal use of their developmental time, it will continue to progressively democratize society. If discipline and punishment are rationalized to secure reparative justice in schools, it will gradually reduce the aggregate of violence and this humanization will progressively democratize society. The use of the classroom and school ombudsman, student evaluation of teaching, and the study of controverted issues within an atmosphere of good will and human dignity can communalize societal conflicts, free things for open discussion, and progressively democratize society.

The question is characteristically asked backwards. It is not whether the schools should democratize society, but whether society should democratize the people's schools. Ought the principles of freedom, equality, brotherhood, and human dignity be implemented in classrooms? The question is not whether the schools should dare to change the social order but whether the schools should facilitate the realization of human rights within the very institution established for the deliberate humanization of the young.

Index